AWS
Certified Solutions Architect
Practice Tests

AWS
Certified Solutions Architect
Practice Tests

Brett McLaughlin

Senior Acquisitions Editor: Kenyon Brown
Development Editor: David Clark
Technical Editor: Sara Perrot
Senior Production Editor: Christine O'Connor
Copy Editor: Judy Flynn
Content Enablement and Operations Manager: Pete Gaughan
Production Manager: Kathleen Wisor
Executive Editor: Jim Minatel
Book Designers: Judy Fung and Bill Gibson
Proofreader: Nancy Carrasco
Indexer: Johnna VanHoose Dinse
Project Coordinator, Cover: Brent Savage
Cover Designer: Wiley
Cover Image: Getty Images, Inc. / Jeremy Woodhouse

To Andrew Pawloski, easily the best AWS engineer I know. One of these days he'll realize how good he is and will stop answering my random AWS questions over text. Until then, I'm immeasurably glad to have him on my side.

Acknowledgments

Writing books seems to require two things: solitude and a sort of rhythm (at least for me). For both of those, I owe my family a great debt. Many, many times I had to shoo away my daughter, Addie, or put off my wife, Leigh, because I was in that rhythm and needed to see a particular question or tricky answer through to its end. I've also yelled upstairs more than once to my sons, Dean and Robbie, because I was on a call discussing some arcane bit of AWS knowledge while they were screaming into their headsets about flanking someone (something?) in *Call of Duty* or laughing hysterically at subverting an intended mission in *Red Dead Redemption 2*.

In other words, lots of people had to bend so I could get this book completed. I'm grateful for that, especially since most of their reward is these few sentences in a book they'll likely never crack open! (Well, Robbie might... he's the budding engineer in the family.)

Another set of thanks goes to the numerous folks at and associated with Wiley who helped see this through: Ken Brown and Amy Sell, who got things started; David Clark, patient and forgiving; Sara Perrot, who was *amazing* as a technical editor; and several others on additional projects who waited while I finished this one (James Schultz and Adaobi Tulton come to mind).

I also have to thank my agent, Carole Jelen, who keeps me busy. She seems to have figured out that if she gives me just a bit more than I think I can handle at once, I'm actually quite happy. If you need an agent in the technical space, you should give her a call. She's the best.

Last but not least, I must thank my friends at and connected with NASA who I worked with prior to writing this book: Andrew Pawloski, John Cromartie, Nathan Clark, Peter Plofchan, Dana Shum, Mark McInerney, Andy Mitchell, and many others. I think we all learned—painfully, most of the time—that AWS is no cakewalk. Certification isn't a magical solution, but the contents of this book helped us all at various times.

Oh, and last-er still, but also not least-er, Dan Pilone and Tracey Pilone. You gave me opportunity when I needed it, and I'm still working on paying that back. Thanks guys. Have a Cherry Coke Zero on me, Tracey.

About the Author

My qualifications are informed by a lifetime of teaching, even when I didn't realize it. I started reading at four, and by the time I was in elementary school, I was "writing" instruction manuals. I still recall the carefully illustrated guide to solving the Rubik's Magic that I put together in fifth grade.

In high school, I taught myself to program. (Turbo Pascal was the first language beyond Basic I learned; anyone remember the book with the Porsche on the cover?) Shortly after, I began teaching the programming class to my peers. Before I graduated, I was teaching two different periods of computer classes—mostly because the actual teacher liked to drink at lunch and showed up loaded most afternoons!

Once I'd knocked out a bachelor of science degree in computer science, I worked in technology, primarily at telecoms. But I never could let go of what I loved most: I was not just a programmer and system administrator. I was the guy who could translate customer requirements into user stories. I was the guy who could *talk*... and I talked *all the time*. I also figured out you could talk through writing. I authored the bestselling technology book *Java and XML*, followed by a number of other books for O'Reilly Media, and eventually joined that company.

More recently, I returned to my developer roots and spent nearly eight years working with NASA's Earth Science group. Never have I spent more time teaching, translating, and explaining what one group's words meant to another, and ultimately telling the story of what NASA is doing through a flagship website and eventually a massive, organization-wide cloud platform. And no matter how much I learned about Amazon Web Services (AWS) or EC2 or Lambda, it was always the storytelling that was most interesting; even better, it was always the storytelling that seemed to interest most clients. I could speak to them, in a way that they understood, and that was a good thing (TM).

Now, I teach and tell stories full-time. I record AWS certification courses on video and write exam prep books in a way that's actually more helpful for passing exams than rote memorization. I build websites and applications, small and large, most often for clients who have their own story to tell to their users. I write books on what I've learned and on how to tell stories the way I do.

Contents at a Glance

Contents

Introduction

Congratulations on your purchase of *the AWS Certified Solutions Architect Practice Tests*. This book will serve as a preparation tool for the Amazon Web Services (AWS) Certified Solutions Architect (CSA) – Associate exam as well as help you in the development of your career as an AWS Solutions Architect.

The objective of this book is to prepare you for the AWS Certified Solutions Architect – Associate exam by explaining the terminology and technology that will be tested on the exam. The main focus of this book is to help you pass the exam. Because of this focus, there are times when not every aspect of a piece of AWS technology is covered and other times when particularly unusual edge cases or details are emphasized. These are an effort to prepare you for the exam, which at times is not always perfectly aligned with the practicality of a real-world cloud architect.

That said, learning these odd details and edge cases will still come in handy in your career. The exam is largely use-case based, and often the answer bank has lots of "good" answers and one "best" answer. Additionally, these answers commonly have invalid or made-up terms. Learning the odd details about AWS will help you weed through these inaccuracies and throw out invalid answers.

Certification Pays

AWS has become one of the most common requirements for job applicants. However, with many organizations moving to AWS for the first time or hiring their first AWS cloud engineers or solution architects, it's not easy to figure out to whom it's worth paying those large engineering salaries. A certification from AWS can often be the credential that helps your resume, application, and experience rise above competitors. This is particularly true when you are being interviewed and evaluated by management, where certification is an easy distinguisher.

Additionally, certification makes you more competitive and employable in general. Research has shown that people who study technology get hired. In the competition for entry-level jobs, applicants with high school diplomas or college degrees who included IT coursework in their academic load fared consistently better in job interviews and were hired in significantly higher numbers.

Steps to Getting Certified and Staying Certified

Review the candidate overview and exam goals. AWS provides a lot of detail on the exam, and in particular what qualifications a candidate for the exam should have:

https://aws.amazon.com/certification/certified-solutions-architect-associate/

Review the exam guide.   AWS provides an exam guide with the domains covered by the exam and the question breakdown:

```
https://d1.awsstatic.com/training-and-certification/docs-sa-assoc/
AWS_Certified_Solutions_Architect_Associate_Feb_2018_%20Exam_Guide_v1.5.2.pdf
```

 This URL changes at times. You can always visit the candidate overview (the URL is listed earlier) and find links to the latest exam guide.

Practice for the exam.   After you have studied for the certification, review and answer as many sample questions as you can to prepare for the exam.

Schedule your voucher.   When you're ready, you can schedule and pay for your exam:

```
https://www.aws.training/certification?src=arc-assoc
```

Take the exam!   You'll take your exam at a testing center in a controlled environment.

Get an instant result.   You'll receive notification of whether you pass or fail immediately after completing the exam. You'll only receive that level of detail, though: PASS or FAIL.

Wait for your official results.   Within a few days, you'll receive email confirmation of your results as well as a more detailed breakdown of your scores organized by domain. You will *not* receive details about which questions you missed, though.

Go get a job! (And stay certified too).   Once you've passed, you'll receive a certificate and digital badges and you can include your certification on your resume. You can also download certification transcripts from AWS. You'll need to take the exam again every two years, but that should leave you plenty of time to add significant practical experience to your certification.

Taking the Exam

Once you are fully prepared to take the exam, you can visit the AWS certification site to schedule and pay for your exam:

```
https://www.aws.training/certification?src=arc-assoc
```

AWS partners with PSI Exams (https://candidate.psiexams.com), so when you schedule your exam, you'll locate a testing center for taking the exam as well as a time block. Exams typically take two hours, so you'll need to plan accordingly.

On the day of the test, make sure you arrive 10 minutes early in case there are any hiccups or a long line of folks waiting to take the exam. You'll need two forms of identification too. Remember that you will not be able to take your notes, electronic devices (including smartphones and watches), or other materials in with you.

The testing center will provide you with some scratch paper, and most centers will supply headphones or earplugs if you find it helpful to block out the minimal noise of the testing center. The test itself is taken on a computer and is fairly straightforward.

Make sure you double-check that you complete the exam before leaving; as silly as it sounds, it's rather easy to get nervous or anxious and not click through all the prompts at the end of the exam.

How to Use This Book and the Interactive Online Learning Environment and Test Bank

This book includes 1,000 practice test questions, which will help you get ready to pass the CSA Associate exam. The interactive online learning environment that accompanies the CSA Associate practice tests provides a large and varied test bank to help you prepare for the certification exam and increase your chances of passing the first time. There's a tremendous value in taking practice questions as often as possible, even leading up to your actual test. Don't worry if you start to recognize questions from earlier practice runs... that just means you're learning the material and committing it to memory.

The test bank also includes a practice exam. Take the practice exams just as if you were taking the actual exam (without any reference material). As a general rule, you should be consistently making 85% or better before taking the exam.

 You can access the AWS CSA Interactive Online Test Bank at www.wiley.com/go/sybextestprep.

Exam Objectives

The AWS Certified Solutions Architect – Associate exam validates your technical expertise in two key areas:

- Taking customer requirements and defining an appropriate solution at the architecture level using AWS design principles
- Providing guidance on implementation based on best practices that go beyond initial design and cover troubleshooting, optimization, and cost considerations

While the exam guide suggests a year of AWS experience, you'll most benefit from working extensively with the AWS console and setting up new infrastructure, especially related to compute (EC2), storage (RDS, DynamoDB, and S3), and networking (VPCs).

The actual exam is organized into five different domains, each focusing on a specific objective, with each domain broken up further into subobjectives:

Chapter 1, Design Resilient Architectures (Domain 1)   Choose reliable and resilient storage; determine how to design decoupling mechanisms using AWS services; determine how to design a multi-tier architecture solution; determine how to design high availability and/or fault tolerant architectures.

Chapter 2, Define Performant Architectures (Domain 2)   Choose performance storage and databases; apply caching to improve performance; design solutions for elasticity and scalability.

Chapter 3, Specify Secure Applications and Architectures (Domain 3)   Determine how to secure application tiers; determine how to secure data; define the networking infrastructure for a single VPC application.

Chapter 4, Design Cost-Optimized Architectures (Domain 4)   Determine how to design cost-optimized storage; determine how to design cost-optimized compute.

Chapter 5, Define Operationally Excellent Architectures (Domain 5)   Choose design features in solutions that enable operational excellence.

Objective Map

The following table lists each of the five domains and how much of the exam each domain affects. The subdomains are also listed for each domain. Because each chapter of this book focuses on a specific domain, the mapping is easy: for Domain 1, refer to Chapter 1. For Domain 2, flip to Chapter 2, and so on.

Domain	Percentage of Exam	Chapter
Domain 1. Design Resilient Architectures	34%	1
1.1 Choose reliable/resilient storage.		
1.2 Determine how to design decoupling mechanisms using AWS services.		
1.3 Determine how to design a multi-tier architecture solution.		
1.4 Determine how to design high availability and/or fault tolerant architectures.		

Domain	Percentage of Exam	Chapter
Domain 2. Define Performant Architectures	24%	2
2.1 Choose performant storage and databases.		
2.2 Apply caching to improve performance.		
2.3 Design solutions for elasticity and scalability.		
Domain 3. Specify Secure Applications and Architectures	26%	3
3.1 Determine how to secure application tiers.		
3.2 Determine how to secure data.		
3.3 Define the networking infrastructure for a single VPC application.		
Domain 4. Design Cost-Optimized Architectures	10%	4
4.1 Determine how to design cost-optimized storage.		
4.2 Determine how to design cost-optimized compute.		
Domain 5. Define Operationally Excellent Architectures	6%	5
5.1 Choose design features in solutions that enable operational excellence.		

Chapter

1

Domain 1: Design Resilient Architectures

✓ **Subdomain: 1.1 Choose reliable/resilient storage.**

✓ **Subdomain: 1.2 Determine how to design decoupling mechanisms using AWS services.**

✓ **Subdomain: 1.3 Determine how to design a multi-tier architecture solution.**

✓ **Subdomain: 1.4 Determine how to design high availability and/or fault tolerant architectures.**

Review Questions

1. Which of the following statements regarding S3 storage classes is true?

   A. The availability of S3 and S3-IA is the same.

   B. The durability of S3 and S3-IA is the same.

   C. The latency of S3 and Glacier is the same.

   D. The latency of S3 is greater than that of Glacier.

2. A small business specializing in video processing wants to prototype cloud storage in order to lower its costs. However, management is wary of storing its client files in the cloud rather than on premises. They are focused on cost savings and experimenting with the cloud at this time. What is the best solution for their prototype?

   A. Install a VPN, set up an S3 bucket for their files created within the last month, and set up an additional S3-IA bucket for older files. Create a lifecycle policy in S3 to move files older than 30 days into the S3-IA bucket nightly.

   B. Install an AWS storage gateway using stored volumes.

   C. Set up a Direct Connect and back all local hard drives up to S3 over the Direct Connect nightly.

   D. Install an AWS storage gateway using cached volumes.

3. You have a group of web designers who frequently upload large zip files of images to S3, often in excess of 5 GB. Recently, team members have reported that they are receiving the error "Your proposed upload exceeds the maximum allowed object size." What action should you take to resolve the upload problems?

   A. Increase the maximum allowed object size in the target S3 bucket used by the web designers.

   B. Ensure that your web designers are using applications or clients that take advantage of the Multipart Upload API for all uploaded objects.

   C. Contact AWS and submit a ticket to have your default S3 bucket size raised; ensure that this is also applied to the target bucket for your web designers' uploads.

   D. Log in to the AWS console, select the S3 service, and locate your bucket. Edit the bucket properties and increase the maximum object size to 50 GB.

4. For which of the following HTTP methods does S3 have eventual consistency? (Choose two.)

   A. PUTs of new objects

   B. UPDATEs

   C. DELETEs

   D. PUTs that overwrite existing objects

5. What is the smallest file size that can be stored on standard class S3?

    A. 1 byte

    B. 1 MB

    C. 0 bytes

    D. 1 KB

6. You've just created a new S3 bucket named ytmProfilePictures in the US East 2 region. You need the URL of the bucket for some programmatic access. What is the correct bucket URL?

    A. `https://s3-us-east-2.amazonaws.com/ytmProfilePictures`

    B. `https://s3-east-2.amazonaws.com/ytmProfilePictures`

    C. `https://s3-us-east-2-ytmProfilePictures.amazonaws.com/`

    D. `https://amazonaws.s3-us-east-2.com/ytmProfilePictures`

7. You've just created a new S3 bucket named ytmProfilePictures in the US East 2 region and created a folder at the root level of the bucket called images/. You've turned on website hosting and asked your content team to upload images into the images/ folder. At what URL will these images be available through a web browser?

    A. `https://s3-us-east-2.amazonaws.com/ytmProfilePictures/images`

    B. `https://s3-website-us-east-2.amazonaws.com/ytmProfilePictures/images`

    C. `https://ytmProfilePictures.s3-website-us-east-2.amazonaws.com/images`

    D. `https://ytmProfilePictures.s3-website.us-east-2.amazonaws.com/images`

8. Which of the following statements is true?

    A. The durability of S3 and S3-IA is the same.

    B. The availability of S3 and S3-IA is the same.

    C. The durability of S3 is greater than that of Glacier.

    D. The durability of S3 is greater than that of S3-IA.

9. Which of the following statements is not true?

    A. Standard S3, S3-IA, and S3 One Zone-IA all are equally durable.

    B. The availability of S3-IA and S3 One Zone-IA are identical.

    C. Standard S3, S3-IA, and S3 One Zone-IA all have different availabilities.

    D. S3 One Zone-IA is as durable as standard S3.

10. Which of the following AWS services appear in the AWS console across all regions? (Choose two.)

    A. S3

    B. EC2

    C. IAM

    D. RDS

11. Amazon's EBS volumes are _____. (Choose two.)

    A. Block-based storage

    B. Object-based storage

    C. Based on magnetic disk by default

    D. Available in a variety of SSD and magnetic options

12. You have spent several days of your last DevOps sprint building an AMI upon which all instances of your development team's application should reside. The application will be deployed into multiple regions and interact with multiple S3 buckets, and you now need the new AMI in us-east-2 and us-west-2, in addition to us-east-1, where you created the AMI. How can you make the new AMI available in us-east-2 and us-west-2?

    A. Copy the AMI from us-east-1 to us-east-2 and us-west-2. Launch the new instances using the copied AMI.

    B. Ensure that all application instances share a security group. AMIs are available to all instances within a security group, regardless of the region in which the AMI was created.

    C. You can immediately launch the AMI, as all AMIs appear in all regions through the AWS console.

    D. Copy the AMI from us-east-1 to us-east-2 and us-west-2. Apply launch permissions and S3 bucket permissions and then launch new instances using the updated AMI.

13. You have an S3 bucket and are working on cost estimates for your customer. She has asked you about pricing of objects stored in S3. There are currently objects in the buckets ranging from 0 bytes to over 1 GB. In this situation, what is the smallest file size that S3-IA will charge you for?

    A. 1 byte

    B. 1 MB

    C. 0 bytes

    D. 128 KB

14. You have been tasked with ensuring that data stored in your organization's RDS instance exists in *a minimum* of two geographically distributed locations. Which of the following solutions are valid approaches? (Choose two.)

    A. Enable RDS in a Multi-AZ configuration.

    B. Enable RDS in a read replica configuration.

    C. Install a storage gateway with stored volumes.

    D. Enable RDS in a cross-region read replica configuration.

15. Which of the following items are included in an Auto Scaling Launch Configuration? (Choose two.)

    A. The AMI to use for creating new instances

    B. The EBS storage volume for the instances to create

    C. The polling time for monitoring network latency

    D. The IAM role to associate with created instances

16. Which of the following would you use for setting up AMIs from which new instances are created in an Auto Scaling policy?

    A. The Auto Scaling policy itself

    B. The security group for the Auto Scaling policy

    C. The Auto Scaling group used by the Auto Scaling policy

    D. The launch configuration used by the Auto Scaling policy

17. You terminate an EC2 instance and find that the EBS root volume that was attached to the instance was also deleted. How can you correct this?

    A. You can't. A root volume is always deleted when the EC2 instance attached to that volume is deleted.

    B. Take a snapshot of the EBS volume while the EC2 instance is running. Then, when the EC2 instance is terminated, you can restore the EBS volume from the snapshot.

    C. Remove termination protection from the EC2 instance.

    D. Use the AWS CLS to change the DeleteOnTermination attribute for the EBS volume to "false."

18. In what manner are EBS snapshots backed up to S3?

    A. Via full backup according to the backup policy set on the volume

    B. Incrementally

    C. Synchronously

    D. EBS volumes are not stored on S3.

19. Can you attach an EBS volume to more than one EC2 instance at the same time?

    A. Yes, as long as the volume is not the root volume.

    B. No, EBS volumes cannot be attached to more than one instance at the same time.

    C. Yes, as long as the volume is one of the SSD classes and not magnetic storage.

    D. Yes, as long as at least one of the instances uses the volume as its root volume.

20. How does AWS allow you to add metadata to your EC2 instances? (Choose two.)

    A. Certificates

    B. Tags

    C. Policies

    D. Labels

21. Which of the following are valid criteria for determining which region to choose for your S3 buckets? (Choose two.)

    A. The distance between the region and your user base

    B. The distance between the region and your on-premises operations

    C. The distance between the region and other regions in your AWS account

    D. The distance between the region and your development team

22. Where are individual EC2 instances provisioned?

    A. In a specific region

    B. In a specific availability zone

    C. In a random availability zone within a specified region

    D. It depends upon the region.

23. Which of the following can be deployed across availability zones?

    A. Cluster placement groups

    B. Placement groups

    C. Spread placement groups

    D. Cross-region placement groups

24. Which of the following services is used at an on-premises site to build a site-to-site VPN connection?

    A. Storage gateway

    B. Virtual private gateway

    C. Customer gateway

    D. Virtual private network

25. What is the anchor on the AWS side of a site-to-site VPN connection between an on-premises site and AWS?

    A. IPSec tunnel

    B. Virtual private gateway

    C. Customer gateway

    D. VPC

26. How many tunnels for network traffic are involved when a customer gateway connects to an AWS VPC via an AWS-managed VPN connection?

    A. One

    B. Two

    C. Three

    D. It depends on the settings in the AWS VPC.

27. Choose the correct order in which traffic flows from an on-premises site to a VPC within AWS when a VPN connection is used.

    A. Customer gateway to Amazon VPC to virtual private gateway

    B. Virtual private gateway to customer gateway to Amazon VPC

    C. Amazon VPC to customer gateway to virtual private gateway

    D. Customer gateway to virtual private gateway to Amazon VPC

28. You are setting up a site-to-site VPN from an on-premises network into an AWS VPC. Which of the following are steps you may need to perform? (Choose two.)

    A. Set up a public IP address for the customer gateway.

    B. Set up a public IP address for the AWS VPC.

    C. Set up a public IP address for the virtual private gateway.

    D. Set up a public IP address for the VPN tunnels.

29. Which of the following services is used at an on-premises site to connect to cloud-based storage?

    A. Storage gateway

    B. Virtual private gateway

    C. Customer gateway

    D. Virtual private network

30. Which of the following are valid options for storage gateways? (Choose two.)

    A. File gateway

    B. Volume gateway

    C. Cached gateway

    D. Virtual private gateway

31. You are tasked with recommending a storage solution for a large company with a capital investment in an NFS-based backup system. The company wants to investigate cloud-based storage but doesn't want to lose its software investment either. Which type of storage gateway would you recommend?

    A. File gateway

    B. Cached volume gateway

    C. Stored volume gateway

    D. Tape gateway

32. You are helping a medium-sized business migrate its large datasets to the cloud. However, the business has limited resources and has long used a tape backup system. It does not want to lose the investment in the software and systems that already have been configured to use this backup system. Which storage gateway would you recommend?

    A. File gateway

    B. Cached volume gateway

    C. Stored volume gateway

    D. Tape gateway

33. You are tasked with prototyping a cloud-based storage solution for a small business. The business's chief concern is low network latency, as its systems need near-instant access to all of its datasets. Which storage gateway would you recommend?

    A. File gateway

    B. Cached volume gateway

    C. Stored volume gateway

    D. Tape gateway

34. You are the solutions architect for a mapping division that has inherited a massive geospatial dataset from a recent acquisition. The data is all on local disk drives, and you want to transition the data to AWS. With datasets of over 10 TB, what is the best approach to getting this data into AWS?

    A. S3 with Transfer Acceleration

    B. Cached volume gateway

    C. Snowball

    D. Shipping the drives to AWS

35. Which of the following are not reasons to use a cached volumes storage gateway? (Choose two.)

    A. You want low-latency access to your entire dataset.

    B. You want to reduce the cost of on-site storage.

    C. You want to support iSCSI storage volumes.

    D. You want low-latency access to your most commonly accessed data.

36. Which of the following storage gateway options is best for traditional backup applications?

    A. File gateway

    B. Cached volume gateway

    C. Stored volume gateway

    D. Tape gateway

37. Which of the following storage gateway options is best for applications where latency of specific portions of your entire dataset is the priority?

    A. File gateway

    B. Cached volume gateway

    C. Stored volume gateway

    D. Tape gateway

38. Which of the following storage gateway options is best for applications where latency of your entire dataset is the priority?

    A. File gateway

    B. Cached volume gateway

    C. Stored volume gateway

    D. Tape gateway

39. Which of the following storage gateway options is best for reducing the costs associated with an off-site disaster recovery solution?

A. File gateway

B. Cached volume gateway

C. Stored volume gateway

D. Tape gateway

40. Which of the following storage classes is optimized for long-term data storage at the expense of retrieval time?

A. S3

B. S3-IA

C. S3 One Zone-IA

D. Glacier

41. Which of the following need to be considered across all regions in your account? (Choose two.)

A. Launch configurations

B. IAM users

C. EC2 instances

D. S3 bucket names

42. What HTTP code would you expect after a successful upload of an object to an S3 bucket?

A. HTTP 200

B. HTTP 307

C. HTTP 404

D. HTTP 501

43. What is the durability of S3 One Zone-IA?

A. 99.0%

B. 99.9%

C. 99.99%

D. 99.999999999%

44. What is the durability of S3-IA?

A. 99.0%

B. 99.9%

C. 99.99%

D. 99.999999999%

45. What is the durability of S3?

    A. 99.0%

    B. 99.9%

    C. 99.99%

    D. 99.999999999%

46. What is the availability of S3 One Zone-IA?

    A. 99.5%

    B. 99.9%

    C. 99.99%

    D. 99.999999999%

47. What is the availability of S3-IA?

    A. 99.5%

    B. 99.9%

    C. 99.99%

    D. 99.999999999%

48. What is the availability of S3?

    A. 99.5%

    B. 99.9%

    C. 99.99%

    D. 99.999999999%

49. Which S3 storage class supports SSL for data in transit?

    A. S3

    B. S3-IA

    C. S3 One Zone-IA

    D. All of the above

50. Which S3 storage class supports encryption for data at rest?

    A. S3

    B. S3-IA

    C. S3 One Zone-IA

    D. All of the above

51. For which of the following storage classes do you need to specify a region?

    A. S3

    B. S3-IA

    C. S3 One Zone-IA

    D. All of the above

52. For which of the following storage classes do you need to specify an availability zone?

    A. S3

    B. S3-IA

    C. S3 One Zone-IA

    D. None of the above

53. How does S3 store your objects?

    A. As key-value pairs

    B. As relational entries.

    C. Using a NoSQL interface

    D. As blocks in a block storage

54. In what ways can you access your data stored in S3 buckets? (Choose two.)

    A. Through FTP access to the bucket

    B. Through SFTP access to the bucket

    C. Through a REST-based web service interface

    D. Through the AWS console

55. Which of the following are true about S3 data access when traffic spikes (increases)? (Choose two.)

    A. S3 will scale to handle the load if you have Auto Scaling set up.

    B. S3 will scale automatically to ensure your service is not interrupted.

    C. Scale spreads evenly across AWS network to minimize the effect of a spike.

    D. A few instances are scaled up dramatically to minimize the effect of the spike.

56. You have been tasked with helping a company migrate its expensive off-premises storage to AWS. It will still primarily back up files from its on-premises location to a local NAS. These files then need to be stored off-site (in AWS rather than the original off-site location). The company is concerned with durability and cost and wants to retain quick access to its files. What should you recommend?

    A. Copying files from the NAS to an S3 standard class bucket

    B. Copying files from the NAS to an S3 One Zone-IA class bucket

    C. Copying the files from the NAS to EBS volumes with provisioned IOPS

    D. Copying the files from the NAS to Amazon Glacier

57. Which S3 storage class would you recommend if you were building out storage for an application that you anticipated growing in size exponentially over the next 12 months?

    A. Amazon Glacier

    B. S3 standard

    C. S3-IA

    D. There is not enough information to make a good decision.

58. How many S3 buckets can you create per AWS account, by default?

   A. 25

   B. 50

   C. 100

   D. There is not a default limit.

59. How are objects uploaded to S3 by default?

   A. In parts

   B. In a single operation

   C. You must configure this option for each S3 bucket explicitly.

   D. Via the REST API

60. When does AWS suggest you start uploading objects via the Multipart Upload API?

   A. When you're uploading a lot of files at once

   B. When you're uploading files of 10 GB or more

   C. When you have multiple applications uploading files to the same S3 bucket

   D. When you need the greatest network throughput for uploads

61. Which of the following are the ways you should consider using Multipart Upload?

   A. For uploading large objects over a stable high-bandwidth network to maximize bandwidth

   B. For uploading large objects to reduce the cost of ingress related to those objects

   C. For uploading any size files over a spotty network to increase resiliency

   D. For uploading files that must be appended to existing files

62. How is a presigned URL different from a normal URL? (Choose two.)

   A. A presigned URL has permissions associated with certain objects provided by the creator of the URL.

   B. A presigned URL has permissions associated with certain objects provided by the user of the URL.

   C. A presigned URL allows access to private S3 buckets without requiring AWS credentials.

   D. A presigned URL includes encrypted credentials as part of the URL.

63. Which of the following can be put behind a presigned URL?

   A. An S3 object store

   B. An EC2 instance with a web interface

   C. An AWS CloudFront distribution

   D. All of the above

64. How long is a presigned URL valid?

   A. 60 seconds

   B. 60 minutes

   C. 24 hours

   D. As long as it is configured to last

65. Which of the following HTTP methods with regard to S3 have eventual consistency? (Choose two.)

   A. UPDATEs

   B. DELETEs

   C. PUTs of new objects

   D. Overwrite PUTs

66. Which of the following behaviors is consistent with how S3 handles object operations on a bucket?

   A. A process writes a new object to Amazon S3 and immediately lists keys within its bucket. The new object does not appear in the list of keys.

   B. A process deletes an object, attempts to immediately read the deleted object, and S3 still returns the deleted data.

   C. A process deletes an object and immediately lists the keys in the bucket. S3 returns a list with the deleted object in the list.

   D. All of the above

67. In which regions does Amazon S3 offer eventual consistency for overwrite PUTs and DELETEs?

   A. All US regions

   B. All US and EU regions

   C. All regions

   D. No regions, eventual consistency is not the model for overwrite PUTs.

68. Which of the following storage media are object based? (Choose two.)

   A. S3-IA

   B. EBS

   C. EFS

   D. S3 standard

69. EBS stands for what?

   A. Elastic Based Storage

   B. Elastic Block Storage

   C. Extra Block Storage

   D. Ephemeral Block Storage

70. What is the consistency model in S3 for PUTs of new objects?

    A. Write after read consistency

    B. Read after write consistency

    C. Eventual consistency

    D. Synchronous consistency

71. How many PUTs per second does S3 support?

    A. 100

    B. 1500

    C. 3500

    D. 5000

72. You have been asked to create a new S3 bucket with the name prototypeBucket32 in the US West region. What would the URL for this bucket be?

    A. `https://s3-us-east-1.amazonaws.com/prototypeBucket32`

    B. `https://s3-us-west-1.amazonaws.com/prototypeBucket32`

    C. `https://s3.prototypeBucket32-us-east-1.amazonaws.com/`

    D. `https://s3-prototypeBucket32.us-east-1.amazonaws.com/`

73. What unique domain name do S3 buckets created in US East (N. Virginia) have, as compared to other regions?

    A. s3.amazonaws.com

    B. s3-us-east-1.amazonaws.com

    C. s3-us-east.amazonaws.com

    D. s3-amazonaws.com

74. Which of the following are valid domain names for S3 buckets? (Choose two.)

    A. s3.us-east-1.amazonaws.com

    B. s3-us-west-2.amazonaws.com

    C. s3.amazonaws.com

    D. s3-jp-west-2.amazonaws.com

75. What are the two styles of URLs that AWS supports for S3 bucket access? (Choose two.)

    A. Virtual-hosted-style URLs

    B. Domain-hosted-style URLs

    C. Apex zone record URLs

    D. Path-style URLs

76. Which of the following are valid URLs for accessing S3 buckets? (Choose two.)

   A. `https://s3-us-west-1-prototypeBucket32.amazonaws.com/`

   B. `https://s3-us-west-1.amazonaws.com/prototypeBucket32`

   C. `https://s3-mx-central-1.amazonaws.com/prototypeBucket32`

   D. `https://prototypeBucket32.s3-us-west-1.amazonaws.com`

77. What is an AWS storage gateway?

   A. A device to reside at a customer site that is part of a VPN connection between an on-premises site and AWS

   B. A device that enables an on-premises site to upload files to S3 faster than over the public Internet

   C. A device to facilitate large data migrations into S3

   D. A device that can be used to cache S3-stored objects at an on-premises site

78. Which of the following statements is not true about an AWS storage gateway?

   A. It is a virtual appliance.

   B. It is available as both a physical and virtual appliance.

   C. It caches data locally at a customer site.

   D. It interacts with S3 buckets.

79. Which of the following are not true about S3? (Choose two.)

   A. Buckets are created in specific regions.

   B. Bucket names exist in a per-region namespace.

   C. Buckets are object-based.

   D. Each S3 bucket stores up to 5 TB of object data.

80. Which of the following consistency models are supported by S3? (Choose two.)

   A. Read after write consistency

   B. Synchronous consistency

   C. Write after read consistency

   D. Eventual consistency

81. Every object in S3 has a _____. (Choose two.)

   A. Key

   B. Value

   C. Both A and B

   D. Version ID

82. Which of the following is the best approach to ensuring that objects in your S3 buckets are not accidentally deleted?

    A. Restrictive bucket permissions

    B. Enabling versioning on buckets

    C. Enabling MFA Delete on buckets

    D. All of these options are equally useful.

83. What HTTP request header is used by MFA Delete requests?

    A. x-delete

    B. x-amz-mfa

    C. x-aws-mfa

    D. x-amz-delete

84. Which of the following operations will take advantage of MFA Delete, if it is enabled? (Choose two.)

    A. Deleting an S3 bucket

    B. Changing the versioning state of a bucket

    C. Permanently deleting an object version

    D. Deleting an object's metadata

85. When using an MFA Delete–enabled bucket to delete an object, from where does the authentication code come?

    A. A hardware or virtual MFA device

    B. The token section of the AWS console

    C. The AWS REST API under delete-codes in a bucket's metadata

    D. None of these

86. Who can enable MFA Delete on an S3 bucket?

    A. All authorized IAM users of the bucket

    B. All authorized IAM users that can update the bucket

    C. The bucket owner

    D. The root account that owns the bucket

87. Who can enable versioning on an S3 bucket?

    A. All authorized IAM users of the bucket

    B. A, C, and D

    C. The bucket owner

    D. The root account that owns the bucket

88. Which of the following exist and are attached to an object stored in S3? (Choose two.)

    A. Metadata

    B. Data

    C. Authentication ID

    D. Version history

89. Which of the following is the AWS mechanism for adding object metadata using the AWS console?

    A. Labels

    B. Tags

    C. Metadata

    D. Object name

90. Which of the following is the exception to S3 storing all versions of an object?

    A. When an object is deleted via MFA Delete

    B. When all of the versions of an object are deleted

    C. When an object's current version is deleted

    D. There are no exceptions.

91. You have an S3 bucket with versioning enabled. How can you turn off versioning?

    A. Update the bucket properties in the AWS console and turn off versioning.

    B. Versioning can only be turned off through the AWS CLI or API. Use your application keys to change versioning to "off" on the bucket.

    C. Send a message to the S3 bucket using the HTML request header x-amz-versioning and the value of "off."

    D. You can't turn off versioning once it has been enabled.

92. CloudFront is a web service for distributing what type of content? (Choose two.)

    A. Object-based storage

    B. Static files

    C. Script-generated or programmatically generated dynamic content

    D. All of the above

93. What are the sources of information that CloudFront serves data from called?

    A. Service providers

    B. Source servers

    C. Static servers

    D. Origin servers

94. Which of the following are typical origin servers for a CloudFront distribution? (Choose two.)

    A. EC2 instances

    B. Amazon Glacier archives

    C. API Gateway

    D. S3 buckets

95. Which of the following are not origin servers for a CloudFront distribution? (Choose two.)

    A. Docker containers running on ECS

    B. MySQL ResultSet

    C. S3 buckets

    D. Redshift workloads

96. What is the location where content will be cached in a CloudFront distribution called?

    A. Availability zone

    B. Edge location

    C. Remote location

    D. Origin edge

97. Which of the following are not origin servers for a CloudFront distribution? (Choose two.)

    A. Elastic load balancer

    B. Route 53 recordsets

    C. SQS subscription endpoint

    D. SNS topic retrieval endpoint

98. What is a collection of edge locations called?

    A. Region

    B. Availability zone

    C. CloudFront

    D. Distribution

99. Rank the total number of regions, availability zones, and edge locations in order from the least number to the greatest number.

    A. Availability zones < regions < edge locations

    B. Regions < availability zones < edge locations

    C. Edge locations < regions < availability zones

    D. Edge locations < availability zones < regions

100. Which of the following statements are true? (Choose two.)

    A. There are more edge locations than availability zones.

    B. There are fewer regions than edge locations.

    C. There are fewer edge locations than availability zones.

    D. Each availability zone has a corresponding edge location.

101. Which of the following store content that is served to users in a CloudFront-enabled web application? (Choose two.)

    A. Availability zones

    B. Edge locations

    C. Route 53

    D. EC2 instances

102. Which of the following are true about edge locations? (Choose two.)

    A. Edge locations are readable.

    B. Edge locations are read-only.

    C. Edge locations are write-only.

    D. Edge locations are writable.

103. To which of the following can objects be written? (Choose two.)

    A. Edge locations

    B. EC2 instances

    C. S3 buckets

    D. Availability zones

104. What does TTL stand for?

    A. Time to Live

    B. Total Time to Live

    C. Total traffic life

    D. Traffic total life

105. You support a web application that uses a CloudFront distribution. A banner ad that was posted the previous night at midnight has an error in it, and you've been tasked with removing the ad so that users don't see the error. What steps should you take? (Choose two.)

    A. Delete the banner image from S3.

    B. Remove the ad from the website.

    C. Wait for 24 hours and the edge locations will automatically expire the ad from their caches.

    D. Clear the cached object manually.

106. By default, how long do edge locations cache objects?
   A. 12 hours
   B. 24 hours
   C. 48 hours
   D. 360 minutes

107. What is the default visibility of a newly created S3 bucket?
   A. Public
   B. Private
   C. Public to registered IAM users of your account
   D. None of the above

108. Which of the following are valid ways to set up access to your buckets? (Choose two.)
   A. NACLs
   B. ACLs
   C. Bucket policies
   D. JSON

109. Which of the following languages is used for writing bucket policies?
   A. XML
   B. YAML
   C. JSON
   D. AML

110. How are datasets utilized by stored volumes backed up to S3?
   A. Asynchronously
   B. Synchronously
   C. The backup method is specified by the user at configuration time.
   D. Synchronously unless the backup takes more than 2 seconds; then the backup switches to asynchronous

111. Which of the following is equivalent to a tape volume?
   A. VTL
   B. VPC
   C. NetBackup
   D. VPN

112. What is Amazon's petabyte-scale data transport solution?
   A. Snowball
   B. Glacier
   C. Transfer Acceleration
   D. Edge transport

113. What language(s) are supported by Snowball?

    A. Perl, PHP

    B. JSON, YAML

    C. CloudFormation

    D. None of these

114. When should you use AWS Direct Connect instead of Snowball?

    A. AWS Direct Connect is usually a better option than Snowball.

    B. AWS Direct Connect is almost never a better option than Snowball.

    C. If you have more than 50 TB of data to transfer, use Snowball.

    D. If you have less than 50 TB of data to transfer, use Snowball.

115. What is the difference between Snowball and Snowball Edge?

    A. Snowball is for data transfer; Snowball Edge provides local data processing prior to returning the data to AWS.

    B. Snowball Edge is for data transfer; Snowball provides local data processing prior to returning the data to AWS.

    C. Snowball and Snowball Edge are both for data transfer, but Snowball Edge offers caching when the data arrives at AWS.

    D. Snowball and Snowball Edge are both for data transfer, but Snowball Edge offers additional storage capacity.

116. Which of the following can Snowball do?

    A. Import data into S3 (but not export data)

    B. Export data from S3 (but not import data)

    C. Import data into S3 and export data from S3

    D. Snowball can import data into S3, but only Snowball Edge can export data from S3.

117. What is the main benefit of decoupling an application?

    A. To enforce different security models

    B. To enforce different network transport models

    C. To reduce interdependencies to isolate failures from an entire application

    D. To reduce network connections to improve performance

118. Which of the following AWS services provides analytic data warehouse provisioning and tooling?

    A. Aurora

    B. ElastiCache

    C. DynamoDB

    D. Redshift

119. Which of the following is a basic principle of fault tolerance in AWS?

    A. Launch instances in separate VPCs.

    B. Launch instances in separate regions.

    C. Launch instances in separate subnets.

    D. Launch instances in edge locations.

120. Which of the following services use AWS edge locations?

    A. CloudFront

    B. Customer gateway

    C. Storage gateway

    D. Snowball

121. Which of the following is a benefit of running an application in two availability zones?

    A. It is more secure than running an application in a single availability zone.

    B. It is more performant than running an application in a single availability zone.

    C. It increases the fault tolerance of running an application in a single availability zone.

    D. It decreases the network latency of running an application in a single availability zone.

122. Which of the following AWS services can be used to store files? (Choose two.)

    A. Amazon Athena

    B. S3

    C. MySQL

    D. EBS

123. Which of the following AWS services can be used to store large objects? (Choose two.)

    A. Redshift

    B. S3

    C. Oracle

    D. EC2

124. How would you speed up transfers of data to S3?

    A. Use Snowball to transfer large files more quickly.

    B. Enable S3 Transfer Acceleration.

    C. Configure AWS to use multiple network paths to your S3 bucket.

    D. Configure AWS to use an internet gateway for routing traffic to your S3 buckets.

125. What users would benefit most from S3 Transfer Acceleration?

    A. Users geographically closest to your S3 buckets

    B. Users geographically farthest from your S3 buckets

    C. Users taking advantage of HTTPS for uploads

    D. All users equally benefit.

126. Which of the following are good reasons to use S3 Transfer Acceleration? (Choose two.)

    A. You have customers that upload to your buckets from around the world.

    B. You have customers complaining about performance of your applications.

    C. You transfer gigabytes of data on a regular basis across continents.

    D. You are seeing network latency in uploads to your S3 buckets.

127. Which services can you use to host websites? (Choose two.)

    A. EC2

    B. Elastic Load Balancing

    C. S3

    D. Glacier

128. You have a bucket called newyorkhotdogs in US West 1. You have enabled static website hosting on this bucket and want to provide its URL to beta customers. What URL should you provide?

    A. `http://newyorkhotdogs.s3-website.us-west-1.amazonaws.com`

    B. `https://s3-us-west-1.amazonaws.com/newyorkhotdogs`

    C. `http://newyorkhotdogs.s3-website-us-west-1.amazonaws.com`

    D. `http://newyorkhotdogs.s3-website-us-east-1.amazonaws.com`

129. You have created a static website and posted an HTML page as home.html in the root level of your S3 bucket. The bucket is named californiaroll and is located in US West 2. At what URL can you access the HTML page?

    A. `http://californiaroll.s3-website.us-west-1.amazonaws.com/home.html`

    B. `http://s3-website-us-west-1.amazonaws.com/californiaroll/home.html`

    C. `http://californiaroll.s3-website-us-west-2.amazonaws.com/public_html/home.html`

    D. `http://californiaroll.s3-website-us-west-1.amazonaws.com/home.html`

130. You have a variety of images with names like `image-001.jpg` and `image-002.jpg` in an S3 bucket named phoneboothPhotos created in the EU West 1 region. You have enabled website hosting on this bucket. Which URL would allow access to the photos?

    A. `http://phoneboothPhotos.s3-website-eu-west-1.amazonaws.com/phoneboothPhotos/image-001.jpg`

    B. `http://phoneboothPhotos.s3-website-eu-west-1.amazonaws.com/phoneboothphotos/image-001.jpg`

    C. `http://phoneboothPhotos.s3-website-eu-west-1.amazonaws.com/public_html/phoneboothPhotos/image-001.jpg`

    D. `http://phoneboothPhotos.s3-website.eu-west-1.amazonaws.com/phoneboothPhotos/image-001.jpg`

131. You have your own custom domain and want to host a static website on that domain. You also want to minimize compute costs. Which of the following AWS services would you use to host your website on your custom domain? (Choose two.)

  A. S3

  B. EC2

  C. Lambda

  D. Route 53

132. You have your own custom domain and want to host a dynamic website on that domain. You also want to minimize compute costs. Which of the following AWS services would you use to host your website on your custom domain? (Choose two.)

  A. S3

  B. EC2

  C. Lambda

  D. Route 53

133. Which of the following provide capability for serverless websites? (Choose two.)

  A. S3

  B. EC2

  C. Lambda

  D. Route 53

134. Which of the following provide capability for dynamic websites? (Choose two.)

  A. S3

  B. EC2

  C. Lambda

  D. Route 53

135. Which of the following does Elastic Beanstalk provide? (Choose two.)

  A. Deployment of code

  B. Security

  C. Capacity provisioning

  D. Cost optimization

136. Which of the following does Elastic Beanstalk not provide? (Choose two.)

  A. Deployment of code

  B. Security hardening

  C. Application health monitoring

  D. Log inspection and backup

137. Which of the following does Elastic Beanstalk support? (Choose two.)

    A. Docker

    B. C++

    C. Scala

    D. Node.js

138. Which of the following application types does Elastic Beanstalk support?

    A. Node.js

    B. Java

    C. Python

    D. All of the above

139. Which of the following database technologies does Elastic Beanstalk support? (Choose two.)

    A. All AWS-supported RDS options

    B. DynamoDB

    C. Oracle running on EC2

    D. Redshift

140. How do you convert application code managed by Elastic Beanstalk from test to production?

    A. Update the codebase to use a production-driven CloudFormation file.

    B. Update the database connection string in your application code.

    C. Set the Elastic Beanstalk environment to use your production database in that particular environment's Elastic Beanstalk configuration.

    D. You cannot deploy to production using Elastic Beanstalk.

141. Which AWS service allows you to run code without provisioning any of the underlying resources required by that code?

    A. EC2

    B. ECS

    C. DynamoDB

    D. Lambda

142. Which of the following AWS services allow you to run code without worrying about provisioning specific resources for that code? (Choose two.)

    A. Elastic Beanstalk

    B. ECS

    C. DynamoDB

    D. Lambda

143. Do Lambda functions run on servers?

    A. Yes, they automatically spin up an EC2 instance as needed without user intervention.

    B. Yes, you must provide an existing EC2 instance to run on.

    C. No, Lambda code runs purely in the cloud without a server involved.

    D. No, Lambda code runs in a container.

144. Which of the following languages work on Lambda? (Choose two.)

    A. JavaScript

    B. Node.js

    C. Scala

    D. C++

145. Which of the following are reasons to use Lambda versus EC2? (Choose two.)

    A. You need to install Oracle and want to avoid compute costs.

    B. Your code primarily responds to events from other AWS services.

    C. Your primary concern is scaling.

    D. You want to deploy your own Docker containers.

146. What AWS service converts media files to formats suitable for different sized devices?

    A. Elastic Transcoder

    B. SWF

    C. Lightsail

    D. Elastic Beanstalk

147. What AWS service is ideal for gathering business intelligence from multiple data sources?

    A. Lightsail

    B. QuickSight

    C. CloudTrail

    D. RDS

148. What is AWS's system for sending out alerts and alarms based on specific events in an environment?

    A. SQS

    B. SNS

    C. SWF

    D. CloudTrail

149. Which service would you use to create a single-sign on system for a user base that already has credentials they want to use outside of AWS?

    A. Cognito

    B. Kinesis

    C. SWF

    D. IAM

150. What does an AWS region consist of?

A. A collection of virtual data centers spread across a continent

B. A collection of virtual data centers spread across a specific geographic area

C. A collection of virtual servers spread across a continent

D. A collection of virtual databases spread across a specific geographic area

151. What type of services are associated with an AWS VPC?

A. Storage services

B. Database services

C. Compute services

D. Networking services

152. What type of services are associated with ECS?

A. Storage services

B. Database services

C. Compute services

D. Networking services

153. What type of services are associated with RDS?

A. Storage services

B. Database services

C. Compute services

D. Networking services

154. What type of services are associated with Route 53?

A. Storage services

B. Database services

C. Compute services

D. Networking services

155. What type of services are associated with a customer gateway?

A. Storage services

B. Database services

C. Compute services

D. Networking services

156. What type of services are associated with S3 lifecycle management?

A. Storage services

B. Database services

C. Compute services

D. Networking services

157. What type of services are associated with Amazon Lightsail?

    A. Storage services

    B. Networking services

    C. Compute services

    D. All of the above

158. What type of services are associated with Elastic Beanstalk?

    A. Storage services

    B. Networking services

    C. Compute services

    D. All of the above

159. What type of services are associated with EFS?

    A. Storage services

    B. Networking services

    C. Compute services

    D. All of the above

160. What type of services are associated with Redshift?

    A. Storage services

    B. Networking services

    C. Database services

    D. All of the above

161. What type of services are associated with CloudFront?

    A. Storage services

    B. Networking services

    C. Compute services

    D. Both B and C

162. What type of services are associated with Amazon Athena?

    A. Storage services

    B. Networking services

    C. Compute services

    D. Analytic services

163. What type of services are associated with EMR?

    A. Storage services

    B. Analytic services

    C. Compute services

    D. Networking services

164. What type of services are associated with Cloud9?

   A. Storage services

   B. Analytic services

   C. Developer services

   D. Networking services

165. What type of services are associated with Direct Connect?

   A. Storage services

   B. Analytic services

   C. Developer services

   D. Networking services

166. What type of services are associated with Workspaces?

   A. Mobile services

   B. Analytic services

   C. Developer services

   D. Desktop services

167. What type of services are associated with Kinesis?

   A. Mobile services

   B. Analytic services

   C. Developer services

   D. Desktop services

168. What type of services are associated with Elastic Transcoder?

   A. Mobile services

   B. Analytic services

   C. Media services

   D. Desktop services

169. What type of services are associated with OpsWorks?

   A. Mobile services

   B. Analytic services

   C. Media services

   D. Management services

170. What type of services are associated with Lex?

   A. Machine learning services

   B. Analytic services

   C. Media services

   D. Management services

171. Which service is best suited for monitoring the performance of your compute instances?

　　A. CloudWatch

　　B. CloudTrail

　　C. OpsWorks

　　D. Config

172. What is an availability zone?

　　A. A virtual data center

　　B. A geographical area with redundancy within that area for compute, networking, and storage service

　　C. A distinct location within AWS designed to be isolated from failures

　　D. Both A and C

173. What is a region?

　　A. A virtual data center

　　B. A geographical area with redundancy within that area for compute, networking, and storage service

　　C. A distinct location within AWS designed to be isolated from failures

　　D. Both A and C

174. Which of the following statements do not describe a region? (Choose two.)

　　A. A region is an area with specific AWS managed services (compute, networking, storage, etc.).

　　B. A region is a virtual data center with built-in redundancy.

　　C. A region is a collection of availability zones for redundancy.

　　D. A region is a geographic area with at least two virtual data centers.

175. Which of the following statements do not describe an availability zone? (Choose two.)

　　A. An availability zone hosts your compute instances.

　　B. An availability zone provides redundancy for your applications.

　　C. An availability zone is isolated from other availability zones except with regard to networking.

　　D. An availability zone contains virtual data centers.

176. Which of the following statements are true about availability zones? (Choose two.)

　　A. An elastic IP is always tied to one specific availability zone.

　　B. A region always contains two availability zones.

　　C. An availability zone's name (for example, us-east-1a) may change across AWS accounts.

　　D. You can specify an availability zone in which to launch your instance when creating the instance.

177. Which of the following are actual region identifiers within AWS? (Choose two.)
   A. us-east-2
   B. jp-south-2
   C. ap-south-1
   D. uk-west-1

178. Which of the following are valid region identifiers within AWS? (Choose two.)
   A. US East 2
   B. eu-west-1
   C. ap-south-1a
   D. us-east-1

179. Which of the following is a valid availability zone identifier within AWS?
   A. us-east-2b
   B. eu-west-1
   C. us-west-az-1
   D. az-sa-east-1a

180. Which AWS service functions like a NAS in the cloud?
   A. EBS
   B. Tape gateway
   C. EFS
   D. DynamoDB

181. Which of the following is a caching engine?
   A. ElastiCache
   B. DynamoDB
   C. memcached
   D. IAM

182. Which of the following are caching engines used by ElastiCache? (Choose two.)
   A. Redis
   B. DynamoDB
   C. memcached
   D. CloudFront

183. Which of the following can you use reserved instances with?
   A. RDS
   B. EC2
   C. Both A and B
   D. None of the above

184. For which of the following can you use reserved instances?

    A. RDS Multi-AZ deployments.

    B. RDS standard deployments

    C. ElastiCache nodes

    D. All of the above

185. In which situations will an RDS instance with Multi-AZ configured fail over? (Choose two.)

    A. When you manually force a failover

    B. When the primary zone is unreachable

    C. When the secondary zone is unreachable

    D. When two successive database reads fail

186. Which of the following can you select when you create an RDS instance? (Choose two.)

    A. The type of database to use

    B. The number of network connections to allow before failing over

    C. The number of database processes to allow

    D. The availability zone to deploy the instance to

187. Which of the following may happen when you have a single-AZ RDS database and a backup begins? (Choose two.)

    A. Latency increases.

    B. Database responses may temporarily slow.

    C. The database goes offline temporarily.

    D. Network requests will fail for up to a minute.

188. Which of the following database engines are available for RDS? (Choose two.)

    A. Hyperion

    B. Cassandra

    C. Oracle

    D. SQL Server

189. Which of the following is true about RDS? (Choose two.)

    A. Reserved instances can be used for Multi-AZ deployments.

    B. Automated backups are turned off by default.

    C. Every database supported by RDS can also be installed directly on EC2 instances.

    D. All RDS databases support SQL as an interface.

190. What is the default port for MySQL via RDS?

    A. 80

    B. 443

    C. 22

    D. 3306

191. When AWS uses the term *OLAP*, what does that acronym stand for?

    A. Online analytics processing

    B. Offline analytic processing

    C. Online aggregation processing

    D. Offline activity and payment

192. When AWS uses the term OLTP, what does that acronym stand for?

    A. Offline training and practice

    B. Offline transaction processing

    C. Online traffic provisioning

    D. Online transaction processing

193. Which of the following is most suitable for OLAP?

    A. Redshift

    B. ElastiCache

    C. DynamoDB

    D. Aurora

194. Which of the following is most suitable for OLTP?

    A. Redshift

    B. ElastiCache

    C. DynamoDB

    D. Aurora

195. Which of the following are most suitable for OLTP? (Choose two.)

    A. memcached

    B. Oracle

    C. DynamoDB

    D. SQL Server

196. Which of the following is best suited for data warehousing?

    A. redis

    B. Oracle

    C. DynamoDB

    D. Redshift

197. Which of the following is best suited for big data processing?

    A. EMR

    B. QuickSight

    C. ElastiCache

    D. Athena

198. Which of the following is best suited for real-time analytics?

    A. EMR

    B. QuickSight

    C. Kinesis

    D. Athena

199. Which of the following is best suited for dashboards and visualizations?

    A. EMR

    B. QuickSight

    C. Kinesis

    D. Athena

200. Which of the following is best suited for interactive analytics?

    A. EMR

    B. QuickSight

    C. Kinesis

    D. Athena

201. What are the most common frameworks used with Amazon EMR? (Choose two.)

    A. Scala

    B. Hadoop

    C. Java

    D. Spark

202. How many copies of data does Aurora store by default?

    A. One

    B. Three

    C. Four

    D. Six

203. Across how many availability zones does Aurora store your data by default?

    A. One

    B. Three

    C. Four

    D. Two

204. In an RDS, managed service capacity, which of the following databases is generally fastest?

    A. PostgreSQL

    B. MySQL

    C. Aurora

    D. They are all equivalent.

205. In an RDS, managed service capacity, which of the following databases is most resistant to disaster by default?

    A. Aurora

    B. Oracle

    C. MySQL

    D. They are all equivalent.

206. Which of the following databases can Aurora interact with seamlessly? (Choose two.)

    A. DynamoDB

    B. PostgreSQL

    C. MySQL

    D. HyperionDB

207. Which of the following is allowed on your RDS instance? (Choose two.)

    A. SSH

    B. SQL queries

    C. RDP

    D. HTTP-accessible APIs

208. What is the maximum backup retention period allowed by RDS, in days?

    A. 15 days

    B. 30 days

    C. 35 days

    D. 45 days

209. If you install Oracle on an EC2 instance, what should you use for storage for that database?

    A. EBS

    B. S3

    C. EFS

    D. RDS

210. Which of the following are suitable for OLTP? (Choose two.)

    A. EBS

    B. Aurora

    C. DynamoDB

    D. MariaDB

211. Which of the following are not suitable for OLTP? (Choose two.)

    A. Kinesis

    B. PostgreSQL

    C. Redshift

    D. SQL Server

212. Which of the following does a Multi-AZ RDS setup address? (Choose two.)
- **A.** Disaster recovery
- **B.** Read performance
- **C.** Data redundancy
- **D.** Network latency

213. Which of the following does a read replica RDS setup address? (Choose two.)
- **A.** Disaster recovery
- **B.** Read performance
- **C.** Offline backup
- **D.** Network latency

214. Which of the following does a read replica support? (Choose two.)
- **A.** Reads from applications
- **B.** Writes to applications
- **C.** Writes from the primary instance
- **D.** Writes from applications using the RDS API

215. Which of the following does a Multi-AZ setup not provide?
- **A.** Disaster recovery
- **B.** Data redundancy
- **C.** Improved performance
- **D.** Access to all RDS databases

216. Which of the following does a Multi-AZ setup provide?
- **A.** Decreased network latency
- **B.** Synchronous replication
- **C.** Asynchronous replication
- **D.** Multiple read sources for applications

217. Which of the following does a read replica provide?
- **A.** Increased network latency
- **B.** Synchronous replication
- **C.** Disaster recovery
- **D.** Asynchronous replication

218. Which of the following is associated with read replicas?
- **A.** High scalability
- **B.** Primary and secondary instances
- **C.** High durability
- **D.** Automatic failover

219. Which of the following is associated with Multi-AZ RDS?

    A. Manual backup configuration

    B. Independent database upgrades

    C. High durability

    D. More than two database instances

220. How many read replicas are supported in a read replica setup?

    A. Three

    B. Five

    C. Seven

    D. Unlimited (although cost applies for each replica)

221. Which of the following databases do not support a read replica setup? (Choose two.)

    A. DynamoDB

    B. Redshift

    C. MySQL

    D. MariaDB

222. Which of the following statements about DynamoDB are true? (Choose two.)

    A. DynamoDB offers push-button scaling.

    B. DynamoDB supports read replicas.

    C. DynamoDB databases can scale up without needing a bigger underlying instance.

    D. DynamoDB instance sizes are selected at runtime.

223. Which of the following statements about DynamoDB are true? (Choose two.)

    A. DynamoDB is more difficult to scale than RDS.

    B. DynamoDB uses SSD storage.

    C. DynamoDB is spread across at least three regions.

    D. DynamoDB uses magnetic storage.

224. What is the default consistency model for DynamoDB?

    A. Eventually consistent reads

    B. Immediately consistent reads

    C. Eventually pristine reads

    D. Eventually consistent writes

225. Which of the following are supported consistency models for DynamoDB? (Choose two.)

    A. Eventually consistent reads

    B. Strongly consistent writes

    C. Immediately consistent reads

    D. Strongly consistent reads

226. You are a solutions architect for a data-driven company using DynamoDB. They want to ensure always-accurate responses, so they have enabled strongly consistent reads. However, API calls to read data sometimes do not immediately return, and sometimes fail. What possible causes could there be? (Choose two.)

    A. A recent write was made and is not yet complete. As a result, a read operation is delayed waiting on the write operation to complete.

    B. A recent write was made and is replicating to the secondary instance. Until that replication completes, the read operation will lag.

    C. A network outage has interrupted a recent read, and subsequent reads of that data are delayed as a result.

    D. A network outage has interrupted a recent write, and subsequent reads of that data are delayed as a result.

227. Which of the following is a valid VPC configuration?

    A. A single public subnet without any private subnets

    B. A single private subnet without any public subnets

    C. A single public subnet with two private subnets

    D. All of the above

228. Which of the following are assigned to an EC2 instance in a default VPC? (Choose two.)

    A. A private IP address

    B. An elastic IP address

    C. An internal AWS-only IP address

    D. A public IP address

229. Which of the following can an EC2 instance in a public VPC be assigned? (Choose two.)

    A. A private IP address

    B. An elastic IP address

    C. An IPv6 address

    D. Both A and B

230. Which of the following can you peer a VPC in your AWS account with? (Choose two.)

    A. Itself

    B. Another VPC in your account

    C. A VPC in another AWS account

    D. A public subnet in another AWS account

231. Which of the following offers the largest range of IP addresses?

    A. /16

    B. /20

    C. /24

    D. /28

232. What does the SWF in Amazon SWF stand for?

    A. Simple Workflow

    B. Simple Workflow Formation

    C. Simple Web Forms

    D. Simple Working Automation

233. What languages can you use with SWF?

    A. Java, Node.js, JavaScript, and Ruby

    B. Java, Node.js, and JavaScript

    C. Perl, PHP, Node.js, and JavaScript

    D. All of the above

234. How are requests and responses to SWF sent and received?

    A. Via the AWS-specific API using application keys

    B. Via HTTP request and response codes

    C. Via web-accessible language-specific endpoints

    D. All of the above

235. Which of the following is a good use case for SWF?

    A. Managing single-sign on

    B. Managing authentication and identification

    C. Managing logging and auditing of VPC interactions

    D. Managing tasks across multiple components

236. How does SWF communicate?

    A. Synchronously

    B. Asynchronously

    C. Both A and B

    D. Neither A nor B

237. What does SES stand for in Amazon SES?

    A. Simple Electronic Service

    B. Simple Email Service

    C. Scalable Elastic Service

    D. Sample Engagement Service

238. What service is queue-based and focused on messaging within your applications?

    A. SWF

    B. SNS

    C. SES

    D. SQS

239. Which of the following are true? (Choose two.)

   A. SNS and SQS are interchangeable at an API level.

   B. SNS is a pull-based system while SQS is a push-based system.

   C. SNS manages notifications and SQS manages messages.

   D. SNS is a push-based system while SQS is a pull-based system.

240. Which of the following terms are associated with SQS? (Choose two.)

   A. Tasks

   B. Messages

   C. Notifications

   D. Worker node

241. Which of the following terms are associated with SNS? (Choose two.)

   A. Tasks

   B. Notifications

   C. Push

   D. Pull

242. Which of the following terms are associated with SWF? (Choose two.)

   A. Single delivery

   B. Tasks

   C. Multi-delivery

   D. Messages

243. Which of the following terms are associated with SNS? (Choose two.)

   A. Subscription

   B. Topic

   C. Message

   D. Queue

244. How many times are tasks assigned in SWF?

   A. Once and only once

   B. Once in general, but a task can be reassigned if it fails

   C. Up to three times within the set polling period

   D. A and C are both valid, depending upon the workflow configuration.

245. How are topics represented in SNS?

   A. By a linked list

   B. By an Amazon Resource Name

   C. By an IAM role

   D. By a named message

246. How many times are messages delivered in SQS?

    A. Once and only once

    B. Up to a single time

    C. Up to three times within the set polling period

    D. At least once

247. What is a collection of related SWF workflows called?

    A. A group

    B. A policy

    C. A domain

    D. A cluster

248. How are messages arranged in an SQS queue by default?

    A. FIFO

    B. LIFO

    C. In reverse order, that is, the last message received is the first available, as much as is possible

    D. In the order in which they were received, as much as is possible

249. The company at which you have been hired as an architect is using Amazon SQS. The company's applications process orders out of the queue as they are received, ensuring that earlier orders get any limited items that may run out of stock over time. However, some early orders are skipped, and later orders actually get the limited items. How would you correct this problem?

    A. Move from SQS to SWF to ensure single delivery of messages.

    B. Configure the SQS queue as FIFO to guarantee the order of message delivery.

    C. Move from SQS to SNS and implement a queue in the application code.

    D. Turn on order locking in the SQS queue.

250. You have a hub-and-spoke network model, with VPC C at the center of the hub. There are six spokes, VPCs A, B, D, E, F, and G. Which VPCs can communicate with VPC C directly? (Choose two.)

    A. VPCs A and B

    B. VPCs D and E

    C. VPCs F and G

    D. Options A and B

251. You have a hub-and-spoke network model, with VPC C at the center of the hub. There are six spokes, VPCs A, B, D, E, F, and G. Which VPCs can communicate with VPC A directly? (Choose two.)

    A. VPCs A and B

    B. VPC C

    C. VPC A

    D. Any additional VPCs peered directly with VPC A

252. You have a hub-and-spoke network model, with VPC G at the center of the hub. There are six spokes, VPCs A, B, C, D, E, and F. Which of the following are true? (Choose two.)

  A. VPCs A and B can communicate with each other directly.

  B. VPCs G and B can communicate with each other directly.

  C. VPCs A and C cannot communicate with each other directly.

  D. VPCs G and D cannot communicate with each other directly.

253. You have a hub-and-spoke network model, with VPC B at the center of the hub. There are three spokes, VPCs A, C, and E. Which of the following are not true? (Choose two.)

  A. VPCs A and B can communicate with each other directly.

  B. VPCs C and B can communicate with each other directly.

  C. VPCs A and C can communicate with each other directly.

  D. VPCs C and E can communicate with each other directly.

254. Select the statement that is true.

  A. Security groups are stateless and NACLs are stateful.

  B. Security groups are stateful and NACLs are stateless.

  C. Both security groups and NACLs are stateless.

  D. Both security groups and NACLs are stateful.

255. Select the statement that is true.

  A. In a NACL, explicit rules must exist for both inbound and outbound traffic for a single request to get in and come back out.

  B. In a security group, explicit rules must exist for both inbound and outbound traffic for a single request to get in and come back out.

  C. In both NACLs and security groups, explicit rules must exist for both inbound and outbound traffic for a single request to get in and come back out.

  D. Neither NACLs nor security groups require both inbound and outbound explicit rules for the same piece of traffic.

256. Select the statement that is true.

  A. In a NACL, traffic that is allowed in is automatically allowed back out.

  B. In a security group, traffic that is allowed in is automatically allowed back out.

  C. In both NACLs and security groups, explicit rules must exist for both inbound and outbound traffic for a single request to get in and come back out.

  D. Neither NACLs nor security groups require both inbound and outbound explicit rules for the same piece of traffic.

257. Into how many subnets must an ALB be deployed (at a minimum)?

  A. One

  B. Two

  C. Three

  D. Five

258. Which of the following are created automatically when you create a new custom VPC? (Choose two.)

    A. Security group

    B. NAT gateway

    C. Subnet

    D. Route table

259. Which of the following are created automatically as part of the default VPC? (Choose two.)

    A. NAT instance

    B. NAT gateway

    C. Subnet

    D. Route table

260. Which of the following are created automatically as part of the default VPC? (Choose two.)

    A. Internet gateway

    B. NAT gateway

    C. NACL

    D. IAM role

261. What is the size of the default subnet in each availability zone within the default VPC?

    A. /20

    B. /16

    C. /28

    D. /24

262. What is the size of the CIDR block created in the default VPC?

    A. /20

    B. /16

    C. /28

    D. /24

263. What is the size of the CIDR block created in a custom VPC?

    A. /20

    B. /16

    C. /28

    D. You must select a size at VPC creation.

264. Which of the following offers the most available IP addresses?

    A. /20

    B. /16

    C. /28

    D. /18

265. Which of the following are not created as part of the default VPC? (Choose two.)

    A. Internet gateway

    B. Security group

    C. NAT gateway

    D. Bastion host

266. Is the default VPC created by AWS public?

    A. Only if you set it to be public at creation time

    B. Yes

    C. Only for traffic over port 80

    D. No

267. Which of the following statements are true? (Choose two.)

    A. The default VPC has an internet gateway attached by default.

    B. Custom VPCs do not have internet gateways attached by default.

    C. The default VPC does not have an internet gateway attached by default.

    D. Custom VPCs have internet gateways attached by default.

268. Which of the following statements are true? (Choose two.)

    A. The default VPC has a NACL created by default.

    B. All incoming traffic is allowed by the default security group on a VPC.

    C. All outgoing traffic is allowed by the default security group on a VPC.

    D. The default security group for the default VPC allows inbound HTTP traffic.

269. Which of the following statements are true about both the default VPC and custom VPCs? (Choose two.)

    A. They have NACLs automatically created.

    B. They have internet gateways automatically created.

    C. They have subnets automatically created.

    D. They have security groups automatically created.

270. Which of the following are created automatically for the default VPC but not for custom VPCs? (Choose two.)

    A. A route table

    B. A subnet

    C. A security group allowing outbound traffic

    D. An internet gateway

271. All EC2 instances in the default VPC have which of the following by default? (Choose two.)

   A. An elastic IP address

   B. A public IP address

   C. A private IP address

   D. HTTP access for incoming requests

272. You created a new instance in the default VPC. You want this instance to be publicly available and serve web content. What steps do you need to take? (Choose two.)

   A. Create an private IP for the instance.

   B. Create a public IP for the instance.

   C. Neither A nor B, these are done automatically.

   D. Update the security group to allow traffic over HTTP and HTTPS to the instance.

273. You created a new instance in a custom VPC. You want this instance to be publicly available and serve web content. What steps do you need to take? (Choose two.)

   A. Create an elastic IP for the instance.

   B. Create an internet gateway for the VPC.

   C. Update the security group to allow traffic over HTTP and HTTPS to the instance.

   D. Both A and B

274. Why would you use a VPC endpoint to connect your VPC to S3 storage? (Choose two.)

   A. To reduce the number of public IP addresses required by your VPC

   B. To avoid leaving the AWS network when traffic flows between the VPC and S3

   C. To increase security of the VPC-to-S3 traffic

   D. To increase the speed as compared to using a NAT instance

275. Which of the following does a VPC endpoint require?

   A. Internet gateway

   B. NAT instance

   C. VPN connection

   D. None of the above

276. Which of the following statements about a VPC endpoint are true? (Choose two.)

   A. It is a hardware device.

   B. It is a virtual device.

   C. It is automatically redundant.

   D. It scales vertically.

277. Which of the following statements about a VPC endpoint are true? (Choose two.)

    A. It requires a VPN connection.

    B. It can connect to DynamoDB.

    C. The VPC it is attached to must have an internet gateway.

    D. It never routes traffic over the public Internet.

278. Which of these are types of VPC endpoints? (Choose two.)

    A. Interface endpoint

    B. Peering endpoint

    C. Gateway endpoint

    D. Service endpoint

279. Which of the following can a VPC gateway endpoint connect to? (Choose two.)

    A. S3

    B. Route 53

    C. A Kinesis data stream

    D. DynamoDB

280. Which of the following can a VPC interface endpoint connect to? (Choose two.)

    A. An API gateway

    B. A VPN

    C. A Kinesis data stream

    D. DynamoDB

281. Which of the following is true about instances in a VPC using a VPC endpoint to connect to S3 storage? (Choose two.)

    A. They must have a public IP.

    B. They must route traffic through a NAT instance to get to the endpoint.

    C. They do not send their traffic over the public Internet to reach the VPC endpoint.

    D. They must have routes to the VPC endpoint in the VPC routing table.

282. At what level do security groups operate?

    A. The subnet level

    B. The VPC level

    C. The instance level

    D. All of the above

283. Which types of rules do security groups allow?

    A. Allow rules only

    B. Allow and deny rules

    C. Deny rules only

    D. Allow, deny, and permit rules

284. Security groups use which models for traffic? (Choose two.)

    A. Traffic is denied by default.

    B. Traffic is allowed by default.

    C. Traffic is only allowed if there are specific allow rules.

    D. Traffic is only denied if there are specific deny rules.

285. Which of the following is true about security groups?

    A. They evaluate all rules before deciding whether to allow traffic.

    B. They evaluate rules from top to bottom before deciding whether to allow traffic.

    C. They evaluate rules in numeric order before deciding whether to allow traffic.

    D. They evaluate orders from high to low before deciding whether to allow traffic.

286. In which order are rules evaluated when a security group decides if traffic is allowed?

    A. Top to bottom

    B. High to low numeric order

    C. Low to high numeric order

    D. All rules are evaluated before a decision is made.

287. How many VPCs can you create in a single AWS region by default?

    A. 3

    B. 5

    C. 10

    D. 20

288. Which of the following is true about a new subnet created in a custom VPC that was set up with the default configuration?

    A. It needs a custom route table created.

    B. It can communicate with other subnets across availability zones.

    C. It will not have a NACL.

    D. It will have an internet gateway attached.

289. Which of these allow you to SSH into an EC2 instance within a private subnet?

    A. A NAT gateway

    B. An internet gateway

    C. A NAT instance

    D. A bastion host

290. Which of the following allow a private instance to communicate with the Internet? (Choose two.)

    A. A NAT gateway

    B. An internet gateway

    C. A NAT instance

    D. A bastion host

291. How many internet gateways can each VPC have?

    A. One

    B. Two

    C. Three

    D. One for each AZ in which the VPC exists

292. You are attempting to create a VPC in an AWS account and getting an error. When you look at the console, you see that the region you're trying to create the VPC in already has five VPCs. What step should you take to create the VPC you need?

    A. You can't. Each region can only have five VPCs.

    B. Configure the VPC to be peered with an existing VPC to get around the five-VPC per-region limit.

    C. Contact AWS and explain your need for a higher number of VPCs in the region.

    D. Create the VPC in a different region.

293. What benefit does adding a second internet gateway to your VPC provide?

    A. Increased network throughput via two channels into the VPC

    B. The second VPC can be used to facilitate VPC endpoints with S3 and DynamoDB.

    C. You can't add a second internet gateway to a single VPC.

    D. You can't have two internet gateways within the same region.

294. You have created a custom VPC, created instances within that VPC, and stood up web servers on those instances. What are the simplest steps you might need to perform to serve this web content to the public Internet? (Choose two.)

    A. Add an internet gateway to the VPC.

    B. Create a NAT gateway for the instances.

    C. Create an ALB and point it at the instances.

    D. Set a public IP for the instances.

295. You have created a custom VPC, created instances within that VPC, attached an internet gateway to the VPC, and stood up web servers on those instances. However, users are unable to access the web content. What might be the problem? (Choose two.)

    A. The security group doesn't allow outbound HTTP traffic.

    B. The security group doesn't allow inbound HTTP traffic.

    C. The instances don't have elastic IP addresses.

    D. The NACL for the VPC's subnet allows all inbound traffic.

296. Which of the following statements is false?

    A. One VPC can have a single internet gateway.

    B. One VPC can have multiple subnets.

    C. A single instance retains its public IP within a VPC when stopped and restarted.

    D. A single instance does not retain its public IP within a VPC when stopped and restarted.

297. Which of the following statements is false?

    A. A subnet cannot span multiple availability zones.

    B. A VPC can peer with no more than two other VPCs.

    C. A VPC can peer with VPCs in other AWS accounts.

    D. A subnet can be public or private if a VPC has an internet gateway attached.

298. Why would you choose a NAT instance over a NAT gateway?

    A. NAT instances are faster than NAT gateways.

    B. NAT instances auto-size to accommodate traffic increases, while NAT gateways do not.

    C. NAT instances are automatically kept updated with patches by AWS, while NAT gateways are not.

    D. You wouldn't; NAT gateways are, in general, a better solution than NAT instances.

299. How do you change a VPC that is set to use dedicated hosting tenancy to use default tenancy?

    A. You can change the hosting tenancy of the VPC without affecting the running instances.

    B. Stop all instances in the VPC, and then you can change the VPC's hosting tenancy.

    C. Remove all instances in the VPC, and then you can change the VPC's hosting tenancy.

    D. You can't; you must re-create the VPC.

300. How quickly are changes made to the security group within a custom VPC applied?

    A. Immediately

    B. Within 60–90 seconds

    C. The next time each instance restarts, or within 24 hours if the instance does not restart

    D. Security groups aren't associated with VPCs.

301. You have a custom VPC with a public subnet. The VPC has an internet gateway attached to it. What else should you do to ensure that instances within the subnet can reach the Internet?

    A. Add a route to the route table that directs traffic directed at the public Internet to go through the internet gateway.

    B. Add a rule to the security group allowing outbound traffic out via HTTP.

    C. Ensure that each instance has a public IP address.

    D. The instances should have public access with this configuration already.

302. Which types of content can CloudFront cache?

    A. Static and dynamic content

    B. Static content, but not dynamic content

    C. Dynamic content, but not static content

    D. CloudFront is not a caching mechanism.

303. You have web applications that are serving up content via a large RDS instance. You are seeing heavy database utilization and want to improve performance. What might you suggest? (Choose two.)

   A. Increase the instance size of the database.

   B. Increase the instance size of the web application servers.

   C. Set up CloudFront to handle dynamic content as well as static content.

   D. Add an additional fleet of EC2 instances to serve the web content.

304. You are tasked with creating a new VPC for a large company, hosting a fleet of instances within the VPC, and ensuring that they can write to the company's S3 buckets and also be accessed via a REST API that they each host. Which of the following would be part of your proposed solution? (Choose two.)

   A. A customer gateway

   B. An internet gateway

   C. A VPC endpoint

   D. A new NACL

305. You are tasked with hosting a fleet of instances within the default VPC of a company's AWS account and ensuring that the instances can write to the company's S3 buckets and also be accessed via a REST API that they each host. Which of the following would be part of your proposed solution? (Choose two.)

   A. A customer gateway

   B. An internet gateway

   C. A VPC endpoint

   D. An updated set of rules for the NACL

306. You have been asked to troubleshoot a Direct Connect connection between your company's on-site data center and a subnet within a public VPC. You have confirmed that you can reach the instances in the VPC from your data center, but those instances cannot reach back to your data center. What would you investigate? (Choose two.)

   A. The VPC subnet's routing table

   B. The on-site storage gateway

   C. The NAT instance in your VPC

   D. The virtual private gateway configuration

307. What is route propagation with respect to a virtual private gateway?

   A. It copies all routes from an on-site network to an AWS VPC's subnets routing tables.

   B. It helps avoid manually entering VPN routes into your VPC routing tables.

   C. It automatically allows inbound traffic from your on-premises connection.

   D. It enables storage-based traffic from a customer's storage gateway.

308. What URL provides you with the public and private IP addresses of running EC2 instances?

    A. `http://169.254.169.254/meta-data/`

    B. `http://169.254.169.254/latest/meta-data/`

    C. `http://169.254.169.254/instance-data/`

    D. `http://169.254.169.254/latest/instance-data/`

309. Which of the following is a highly durable key-value store?

    A. S3

    B. EFS

    C. EBS

    D. ElastiCache

310. Which of the following is a valid Glacier use case?

    A. Storing insurance documents accessed once or twice a day by mobile clients

    B. Storing medical records in case of annual audits

    C. Storing patient images used in the scheduling department's web-based software

    D. Storing X-rays used in teaching exercises at the local college

311. You have been called in to mitigate a disastrous loss of data on S3 at a bioethics company. After investigating, it is determined that the data was deleted accidentally by a developer. The company wants to ensure that data cannot be accidentally deleted like this in the future. What would you suggest? (Choose two.)

    A. Enable S3 versioning on all S3 buckets.

    B. Create an IAM policy that disallows developers from deleting data in S3.

    C. Replace the current access pattern with signed URLs.

    D. Enable MFA Delete on the buckets.

312. How many instances can you launch in a given AWS region?

    A. 20

    B. 40

    C. 20, but this is a soft limit and can be increased by AWS

    D. 40, but this is a soft limit and can be increased by AWS

313. You are using a NAT instance inside of a VPC to support routing out to the public Internet from private instances within that VPC. As traffic has increased, the performance of any operations involving the outbound Internet traffic has degraded to unacceptable levels. How would you mitigate this problem?

    A. Add an additional internet gateway so the NAT instance can split outbound traffic over two gateways.

    B. Add an additional elastic IP to the NAT instance to increase throughput.

    C. Increase the instance size of the NAT instance by one or more instance size classes.

    D. All of these are valid solutions.

314. What is the simplest way to reduce frequent scaling in an application? For example, if an application is showing that it's scaling up and down multiple times in an hour, how would you reduce the number of "ups and downs" you are seeing?

- **A.** Set up scheduled times with proactive cycling for the scaling so that it is not occurring all the time.
- **B.** Increase the cooldown timers so that scaling down requires greater thresholds of change in your triggers.
- **C.** Update CloudWatch to use a FIFO termination policy, only terminating the oldest instances in a scaledown.
- **D.** None of these will improve the issue.

315. Which of these steps are required to get a NAT instance working? (Choose two.)

- **A.** Update the routing table for EC2 instances accessing the public Internet to go through the NAT instance.
- **B.** Locate the NAT instance within the private subnet that it will be serving.
- **C.** Disable source/destination checks on your instance.
- **D.** Set the NAT instance to allow port forwarding from the private subnet.

316. Which of these is not a default CloudWatch metric?

- **A.** Disk read operations
- **B.** Memory usage
- **C.** CPU usage
- **D.** Inbound network traffic

317. You have an existing fleet of EC2 instances in a public subnet of your VPC. You launch an additional instance from the same AMI as the existing instances, into the same public subnet. What steps might you need to take to ensure that this instance can reach the public Internet? (Choose two.)

- **A.** Assign an elastic IP address to the instance.
- **B.** Add the instance to the ELB serving the existing instances.
- **C.** Add the instance into a private subnet.
- **D.** Ensure that the instance has a route out to the Internet.

318. Which of the following is the destination address for the public Internet?

- **A.** 192.168.1.255/0
- **B.** 0.0.0.0/16
- **C.** 169.254.169.254/0
- **D.** 0.0.0.0/0

319. Which of the following would you use to route traffic from your subnet to the public Internet?

- **A.** Destination: 0.0.0.0/0 ➤ Target: your internet gateway
- **B.** Destination: 0.0.0.0/16 ➤ Target: your internet gateway
- **C.** Destination: your internet gateway ➤ Target: 0.0.0.0/0
- **D.** Destination: 0.0.0.0/0 ➤ Target: your virtual private gateway

Chapter

2

Domain 2: Define Performant Architectures

✓ **Subdomain: 2.1 Choose performant storage and databases.**

✓ **Subdomain: 2.2 Apply caching to improve performance.**

✓ **Subdomain: 2.3 Design solutions for elasticity and scalability.**

Review Questions

1. When replicating data from a primary RDS instance to a secondary one, how much will you be charged, in relation to the standard data transfer charge?

    A. Your data will be transferred at the standard data transfer charge.

    B. Your data will be transferred at half of the standard data transfer charge.

    C. Your data will be transferred at half of the standard data transfer charge up to 1 GB of transfer per day and then additional data at the standard data transfer charge.

    D. There is no charge for primary-to-secondary data replication.

2. Which of the following are valid options for where an RDS read replica is set up in relation to the primary instance? (Choose two.)

    A. In the same region as the primary instance

    B. In a separate region from the primary instance

    C. In an instance running on premises

    D. Both A and B

3. What is the primary purpose of a read replica RDS configuration?

    A. Disaster recovery

    B. Fault tolerance

    C. Performance

    D. Security

4. Which of the following databases support read replicas?

    A. MariaDB

    B. MySQL

    C. PostgreSQL

    D. All of the above

5. Which of the following databases support read replicas?

    A. Oracle

    B. MySQL

    C. DynamoDB

    D. All of the above

6. Which of the following is true about a read replica? (Choose two.)

    A. It is a read-only instance of a primary database.

    B. It can only exist in the same region as the primary database, although it can be in a different availability zone.

    C. It is updated via asynchronous replication from the primary instance.

    D. It is updated via synchronous replication from the primary instance.

7. Which of the following is true about an RDS read replica configuration? (Choose two.)

   A. Only three read replicas can be set up for a single primary database instance.

   B. Only MariaDB, MySQL, and Aurora are supported.

   C. A read replica replicates all databases in the primary instance.

   D. A read replica can exist in a different region than the primary instance.

8. You have a primary database set up to use read replicas running on an instance in US East 1. You have three read replicas also in US East 1 and two additional replicas in US West 2. You are trying to create a new replica in EU West 1 and are getting an error. What do you need to do to resolve this error and successfully create a new read replica in EU West 1?

   A. Turn on the Multi-AZ option for your primary instance.

   B. You can't create the replica in EU West 1. Instead, create the replica in another US region to avoid regulations about read replicas in the EU.

   C. Contact AWS about raising the number of read replicas allowed from 5 to 8.

   D. Turn off one of the read replicas in US East 1 and then you can create the instance in EU West 1.

9. Which of the following are true about a read replica setup? (Choose two.)

   A. Backups are configured by default when you set up read replicas.

   B. They provide a highly scalable solution for your on-premises databases.

   C. They can exist within a single AZ, cross-AZ, or cross-region.

   D. A read replica can be promoted to a stand-alone database instance.

10. Which of the following are true about a read replica setup? (Choose two.)

    A. Automated backups are taken from the read replicas rather than the primary instance.

    B. The database engine on all instances is active.

    C. Each read replica instance can upgrade its database engine separate from the primary instance.

    D. Replication is synchronous.

11. Which of the following statements are false? (Choose two.)

    A. Both read replicas and Multi-AZ configurations ensure that you have database instances in multiple availability zones.

    B. Both read replicas and Multi-AZ configurations provide disaster recovery options for your primary instance.

    C. A single database can both have a read replica and be part of a Multi-AZ setup.

    D. A read replica can be promoted to be a stand-alone database instance.

12. Which of the following statements is true?

    A. A Multi-AZ setup is aimed at fault tolerance, while a read replica setup is aimed at scalability.

    B. Both read replicas and Multi-AZ configurations are aimed at fault tolerance.

    C. A Multi-AZ setup is aimed at scalability, while a read replica setup is aimed at fault tolerance.

    D. Both read replicas and Multi-AZ configurations are aimed at scalability.

13. How do applications communicate with read replica instances?

    A. Through the read replica REST API provided by RDS

    B. ELBs and ALBs will automatically translate requests to a read replica to use the read replica REST API provided by RDS.

    C. Each read replica provides a read replica key that allows applications to communicate with the instance as if it were a normal database instance.

    D. Applications communicate with a read replica exactly as they would with a non-read replica.

14. Which of the following are valid reasons to use read replication? (Choose two.)

    A. You have a read-heavy database that is peaking in traffic.

    B. You have a large number of errors reported by applications trying to update user entries in your current database and want to reduce these errors.

    C. You want an automated disaster recovery solution in case you lose an AZ.

    D. You have a large number of business reporting queries that are currently interfering with customer application performance.

15. Does a read replica provide any assistance at all in creating a fault-tolerant database setup?

    A. Yes, it provides automated backups to the read replicas.

    B. Yes, if the primary instance fails, one of the replicas can be manually promoted to a stand-alone database instance.

    C. Yes, if the primary instance fails, one of the replicas will be automatically promoted to a stand-alone database instance.

    D. No

16. Which of the following are valid reasons to use read replication? (Choose two.)

    A. You have customers in a region geographically distant from your primary instance and want to improve their read performance when they access your applications hosted in regions closer to them.

    B. Your current database instance is showing memory saturation with current traffic loads.

    C. Your boss has asked for an automated backup solution that takes advantage of AWS managed services.

    D. You need to perform additional OLTP queries and want to improve the performance of those queries.

17. Can you configure a database instance to be both a read replica and a primary database instance for the original instance?

    A. Yes, as long as the instances are all in the same availability zone.

    B. Yes, if you turn on circular replication in both primary database instances.

    C. Yes, as long as the instances are not in the same availability zone.

    D. No, AWS does not support circular replication.

18. In which of the following ways can you create a read replica? (Choose two.)

    A. Through the AWS console

    B. Through the AWS online support system

    C. Through the AWS API

    D. Through Elastic Beanstalk

19. How are automated backups related to read replicas?

    A. They are not; read replicas and automated backups have no relationship at all.

    B. Read replicas do not create automatic backups, but the primary database instance must have automatic backups enabled to create read replicas.

    C. Read replicas cause the primary database instance to automatically begin backing up.

    D. Each read replica is automatically backed up after an initial read from the primary database instance.

20. Can a database instance be a read replica of one database and the source instance for another read replica?

    A. Yes, as long as the source and replicant database are not the same instance.

    B. No, a database cannot be both a read replica and a source database.

    C. Yes, as long as the source and replicant database are in the same availability zone.

    D. Yes, as long as you enable circular replication on both databases.

21. How quickly can you make changes to the backup window used by your RDS instance?

    A. Changes to the window via the console take place within 1 hour; changes made via the API take place immediately.

    B. Changes to the window take place after the next complete backup occurs.

    C. Changes to the window via the API take place within 1 hour; changes made via the console take place immediately.

    D. Changes to the window take place immediately.

22. What is the longest backup retention window that Amazon RDS allows?

    A. 30 days

    B. 35 days

    C. 45 days

    D. 365 days

23. You have an Oracle installation using a custom geospatial plug-in. You also want to ensure the maximum throughput for database operations once those operations are begun by the plug-in. How would you set up Oracle to meet these requirements?

 A. Set up Oracle using RDS with provisioned IOPS.

 B. Set up Oracle using RDS with magnetic storage.

 C. Install Oracle on an EC2 instance with a provisioned IOPS EBS volume.

 D. Install Oracle on an EC2 instance with a magnetic EBS volume.

24. In what scenarios would you install an Oracle database on an EC2 instance rather than using RDS? (Choose two.)

 A. You want to use an ALB to support multiple instances and round-robin request distributions.

 B. Your database size is greater than 80% of the maximum database size in RDS.

 C. You have custom plug-ins that will not run in RDS.

 D. You want to ensure that your database is only accessible through your private subnet in a VPC.

25. Which of the following are SQL-based options in RDS? (Choose two.)

 A. Aurora

 B. DynamoDB

 C. MariaDB

 D. Redshift

26. You are a new architect at a company building out a large-scale database deployment for web applications that receive thousands of requests per minute. The previous architect suggested a Multi-AZ deployment in RDS to ensure maximum responsiveness to the web tier. Is this a good approach for high performance?

 A. No, because a Multi-AZ deployment is no faster in responding to requests than a standard RDS deployment.

 B. Yes, because the additional databases in a Multi-AZ deployment will share the request load from the web tier.

 C. Yes, because a Multi-AZ deployment will ensure that if the primary database goes down, a secondary database will be current and available.

 D. No, because a Multi-AZ deployment can only field requests from the availability zone in which each database resides.

27. You launch an EC2 instance that has two volumes attached: a root and an additional volume, both created with default settings. What happens to each volume when you terminate the instance?

 A. The root volume is deleted and the additional volume is preserved.

 B. Both volumes are deleted.

 C. Both volumes are preserved.

 D. The instance is unable to terminate until the root volume is deleted.

28. How many S3 buckets can you add to an account?

   A. 100

   B. 100 by default, but this can be increased by contacting AWS.

   C. It depends on the default set for the new account by AWS.

   D. It depends on how the account is configured at account creation.

29. What type of replication occurs in a Multi-AZ RDS setup?

   A. Sequential replication

   B. Synchronous replication

   C. Asynchronous replication

   D. Synchronous replication for full backups and asynchronous replication for incremental backups

30. What type of replication occurs in a read replica RDS setup?

   A. Sequential replication

   B. Synchronous replication

   C. Asynchronous replication

   D. Synchronous replication for full backups and asynchronous replication for incremental backups

31. Which of the following protocols and routing approaches does a classic load balancer support? (Choose two.)

   A. IPv4

   B. IPv6

   C. HTTP/2

   D. Registering targets in target groups and routing traffic to those groups

32. How many elastic IP addresses can you create per region by default in a new AWS account?

   A. 5

   B. 10

   C. 20

   D. There is no preset limit.

33. To how many EBS volumes can a single EC2 instance attach?

   A. 1

   B. 2

   C. 27

   D. Unlimited

34. How many EC2 instances can be attached to a single EBS volume at one time?

   A. 1

   B. 2

   C. 27

   D. Unlimited

35. Which of the following protocols are supported by an application load balancer? (Choose two.)

   A. SSH

   B. HTTP

   C. HTTPS

   D. FTP

36. Which of the following provide ways to automate the backup of your RDS database? (Choose two.)

   A. Automated snapshots

   B. S3 lifecycle management policies

   C. Automated backups

   D. Data pipeline

37. You have an EC2 instance running a heavy compute process that is constantly writing data to and from a cache on disk. How and when should you take a snapshot of the instance to ensure the most complete snapshot?

   A. Take a snapshot of the instance from the AWS console.

   B. Shut down the instance and take a snapshot of the instance.

   C. Take a snapshot of the instance from the AWS CLI.

   D. Detach the EBS volume attached to the instance and take a snapshot of both the EC2 and EBS instance.

38. Your web-based application uses a large RDS data store to write and read user profile information. The latest marketing campaign has increased traffic to the application by an order of magnitude. Users are reporting long delays when logging in after having signed up. Which solutions are valid approaches to addressing this lag? (Choose two.)

   A. Set up a Multi-AZ configuration for your RDS and round-robin requests between the two RDS instances to spread out traffic.

   B. Employ ElastiCache to cache users' credentials after their initial visit to reduce trips to the database from the web application.

   C. Set up a read replica configuration for your RDS and round-robin requests between all the replicas to spread out traffic.

   D. Increase the number of EC2 instances allocated to your Auto Scaling group to spread out traffic on the web application tier.

39. Your users are now storing all of their photos in your cloud-based application. Cloud-Watch metrics suggests that photos are written an average of 5 times per user per day and read 100 times per user per day. If photos are lost, user surveys indicate that users are not typically upset and simply re-upload the missing photo or ignore the missing photo altogether. What is the most cost-effective recommendation for the S3 storage class to use?

   A. Standard S3

   B. S3-IA

   C. S3 One Zone-IA

   D. S3 RRS

40. You are consulting for a company that wants to migrate its 85TB data store into S3. It is willing to upload the data into S3 every night in small batches but is concerned that overseas customers using its other applications might experience network latency as they are transferring files into S3. What solution should you recommend to move the company's data?

   A. Enable Transfer Acceleration on S3.

   B. Direct Connect

   C. Snowball

   D. Set up a VPN that uses a virtual private gateway for transferring the data.

41. Which of the following are valid reasons for using Multipart Upload for uploading objects to S3? (Choose two.)

   A. You need a solution that recovers from network issues.

   B. You need a solution to upload files larger than 10 GB.

   C. You need a solution for increasing the security around uploaded objects.

   D. You need a solution to decrease the time required to upload large files.

42. In which of the following situations would you recommend using a placement group?

   A. Your fleet of EC2 instances requires high disk IO.

   B. Your fleet of EC2 instances requires high network throughput across two availability zones.

   C. Your fleet of EC2 instances requires high network throughput within a single availability zone.

   D. Your fleet of EC2 instances requires high network throughput to S3 buckets.

43. Which of the following statements are true about cluster placement groups? (Choose two.)

   A. All instances in the group must be in the same availability zone.

   B. Instances in the group will see lowered network latency in communicating with each other.

   C. Instances in the group will see improved disk write performance when communicating with S3.

   D. Instances in the group must all be of the same instance class.

44. Which of the following statements are true about spread placement groups? (Choose two.)

   A. All instances in the group must be in the same availability zone.

   B. Instances in the group will see lowered network latency in communicating with each other.

   C. You can have up to seven instances in multiple availability zones in the group.

   D. AWS provisions the hardware rather than having you specify the distinct hardware for the group.

45. Which of the following storage classes has the lowest durability?

   A. S3 standard

   B. S3-IA

   C. Glacier

   D. They all have equal durability.

46. Which of the following storage classes has the highest availability?

   A. S3 standard

   B. S3-IA

   C. Glacier

   D. They all have equal availability.

47. Which of the following storage classes support automated lifecycle transitions?

   A. S3 standard

   B. S3-IA

   C. Glacier

   D. They all support lifecycle transitions.

48. Where is data stored when placed into S3-IA? (Choose two.)

   A. In the region specified at bucket creation

   B. In a special AWS "global" region for S3 storage

   C. In at least three availability zones

   D. In a single availability zone within at least three regions

49. You need to perform a large amount of OLAP. Which AWS service would you choose?

   A. DynamoDB

   B. RDS Aurora

   C. Redshift

   D. Oracle installed on EC2 instances

50. What is the maximum allowable RDS volume size when using provisioned IOPS storage?

   A. 8 TB

   B. 16 TB

   C. 12 TB

   D. 1 PB

51. Which of the following EBS volumes is the most performant?

    A. Provisioned IOPS

    B. Throughput optimized HDD

    C. Cold HDD

    D. General SSD

52. Which of the following is a valid reason to use a cold HDD EBS volume?

    A. You need a performant solid-state drive.

    B. You are trying to choose the lowest-cost EBS volume possible.

    C. You are performing data warehousing using the volume.

    D. You need an inexpensive boot volume.

53. Which of the following are available to use as an EBS boot volume? (Choose two.)

    A. General SSD

    B. Cold HDD

    C. Throughput optimized HDD

    D. Provisioned IOPS

54. Which of the following is a valid reason to use a General Purpose SSD EBS volume? (Choose two.)

    A. You need to support large database workloads.

    B. You want a blend of a performant SSD and a cost-sensitive SSD volume.

    C. You are performing data warehousing using the volume.

    D. You have low-latency apps and want to run them on a bootable volume.

55. Which of the following is a valid reason to use a magnetic EBS volume? (Choose two.)

    A. You want a low-cost option for your EBS volume.

    B. You have a set of data that is infrequently accessed but want it stored on an EBS volume rather than S3.

    C. You need to perform processing to support Oracle installed on a fleet of EC2 instances.

    D. You have low-latency apps and want to run them on a bootable volume.

56. Which of the following is a valid reason to use a provisioned IOPS EBS volume? (Choose two.)

    A. You want a low-cost option for your EBS volume.

    B. You need to support a large MongoDB database workload.

    C. You need massive performance and throughput for your applications.

    D. You have applications that need a bootable environment but can fail from time to time and be re-created.

57. Which of the following are characteristics of SSD-backed volumes? (Choose two.)

    A. Transactional workloads

    B. Streaming workloads

    C. Small I/O size

    D. Throughput-focused

58. Which of the following are characteristics of HDD-backed volumes? (Choose two.)

    A. Transactional workloads

    B. Streaming workloads

    C. Small I/O size

    D. Throughput-focused

59. You are charged with installing Oracle on a fleet of EC2 instances due to custom Java-based plug-ins you need to install along with Oracle. Which EBS volume type would you choose to best support your Oracle installation?

    A. Magnetic

    B. Throughput-optimized HDD

    C. Provisioned IOPS SSD

    D. General SSD

60. You are the solutions architect for a company installing a web application on a set of EC2 instances. The application writes a small amount of user profile data to attached EBS volumes, and accesses that data an average of once every five minutes if the user is still using the web application. Additionally, because of the high cost of the application's RDS instance, you would like to minimize your EBS volume costs. Which EBS volume type would you choose to support these applications?

    A. Magnetic

    B. Throughput-optimized HDD

    C. Provisioned IOPS SSD

    D. General SSD

61. Which of the following can be an EBS boot volume? (Choose two.)

    A. Magnetic

    B. Throughput-optimized HDD

    C. Provisioned IOPS SSD

    D. Cold HDD

62. Which of the following cannot be used as an EBS boot volume? (Choose two.)

    A. General SSD

    B. Throughput-optimized HDD

    C. Cold HDD

    D. Magnetic

63. Which of the following is not an Elastic Load Balancing option?
    A. Classic load balancer
    B. Application load balancer
    C. Weighting load balancer
    D. Network load balancer

64. Which of the following are valid Elastic Load Balancing options? (Choose two.)
    A. ELB
    B. MLB
    C. ALB
    D. VLB

65. At what level of the TCP stack does an ALB operate?
    A. Level 1
    B. Level 4
    C. Level 7
    D. Level 8

66. At what level of the TCP stack does a network load balancer operate?
    A. Level 1
    B. Level 4
    C. Level 7
    D. Level 8

67. At what levels of the TCP stack does a classic load balancer operate? (Choose two.)
    A. Level 1
    B. Level 4
    C. Level 7
    D. Level 8

68. Which of the following is a valid reason to use an application load balancer?
    A. You want your applications to automatically scale.
    B. You want to balance load across your applications, which reside in containers.
    C. You want to achieve better fault tolerance for your applications.
    D. All of the above

69. Can you use an elastic load balancer to balance load within a VPC?
    A. Yes, as long as the VPC has an internet gateway.
    B. Yes, by setting the ELB to be internal to the VPC.
    C. No, load balancers can only route traffic from the Internet.
    D. No, load balancers cannot operate inside a VPC.

70. You are an architect working on adding scalability to an application based on EC2 instances within a public-facing VPC. You want the maximum amount of flexibility in weighting and load balancing options, as you plan to experiment with various routing types to see which handles load most evenly. Which type of load balancer should you use?

    A. Classic ELB

    B. Application load balancer

    C. Network load balancer

    D. Either an ALB or ELB would be suitable.

71. You have a host of EC2 instances all with dedicated IP addresses serving results from complex computations. You want to load balance across these instances, each of which receives hundreds of thousands of requests a second currently. Which load balancer would you employ?

    A. Classic ELB

    B. Application load balancer

    C. Network load balancer

    D. Either an ALB or ELB would be suitable.

72. You have a fleet of web-hosting EC2 instances. Currently, you have SSL certificates installed for each EC2 instance, but the cost of maintaining these certificates and installing new ones has become higher over recent years. You want to architect a solution for SSL termination that doesn't involve multiple certificates. Which load balancer would you suggest?

    A. Classic ELB

    B. Application load balancer

    C. Network load balancer

    D. Either an ALB or ELB would be suitable.

73. You need a load balancer that supports SSL termination. Which type of load balancer would you choose?

    A. Classic ELB

    B. Application load balancer

    C. Network load balancer

    D. Either an ALB or ELB would be suitable.

74. How many domains can you register and manage with Route 53?

    A. 50

    B. 100

    C. There is no limit.

    D. There is a limit of 50, but it can be raised upon request.

75. Which of the following record sets are supported by Route 53?

    A. A records

    B. MX records

    C. Alias records

    D. All of the above

76. Are zone apex records supported by Route 53?

    A. Yes

    B. No

    C. Yes, as long as they point to AWS resources.

    D. Not by default, but you can request support by AWS and then support them.

77. What engines does ElastiCache provide for caching? (Choose two.)

    A. memcached

    B. redis

    C. cacherm

    D. gitcache

78. Which of the following do you need to handle when setting up ElastiCache?

    A. Patching

    B. Backups

    C. Monitoring

    D. None of the above

79. For which of the following would ElastiCache offer performance improvements? (Choose two.)

    A. Gaming

    B. ElastiCache can improve any application's performance when used properly.

    C. Financial services

    D. A and C

80. Which of the following accurately describe ElastiCache? (Choose two.)

    A. An in-memory data store

    B. A runtime engine for data distribution

    C. A mechanism for sharding application demands

    D. A monitoring solution for large datasets

81. Which of the following would you use to interact with a CloudFront distribution?

    A. CloudFormation

    B. The AWS CLI

    C. The AWS REST APIs

    D. Any of these

82. Which of the following are origin sources usable with a CloudFront distribution? (Choose two.)

   A. An ALB

   B. DynamoDB

   C. AWS Shield

   D. An Oracle RDS instance

83. Which of the following are origin sources usable with a CloudFront distribution? (Choose two.)

   A. DynamoDB

   B. A fleet of EC2 instances

   C. S3 buckets

   D. RedShift

84. Which of the following are origin sources usable with a CloudFront distribution? (Choose two.)

   A. Lambda@Edge

   B. A static website on S3

   C. Aurora on RDS

   D. ElastiCache instances

85. Which of the following two are advantages of using a CloudFront distribution? (Choose two.)

   A. Performance

   B. Fault tolerance

   C. Integration with AWS managed services

   D. Disaster recovery

86. How does CloudFront increase the security of content at the edge? (Choose two.)

   A. Required HTTPS at all edge locations

   B. Integration with AWS WAF (if configured)

   C. Automatic client keys encrypted with KMS

   D. Automatic deployment of AWS Shield

87. Choose the true statements about edge locations. (Choose two.)

   A. There are fewer edge locations than regions.

   B. There are more edge locations than regions.

   C. There are fewer edge locations than availability zones.

   D. There are more edge locations than availability zones.

88. Which of the following can you do with CloudFront? (Choose two.)

    A. Quickly deploy a global network for your content without contracts or startup requirements.

    B. Quickly create websites that are dynamic and low latency.

    C. Distribute content with low latency and high data transfer rates.

    D. Provide storage for static files that are frequently accessed.

89. Which of the following can be origin servers for CloudFront? (Choose two.)

    A. S3 buckets

    B. EC2 instances

    C. RedShift workloads

    D. SNS notifications

90. Which domain name should you use to take advantage of CloudFront?

    A. The domain name registered to your S3 buckets in Route 53

    B. The domain name registered in CloudFront as the origin for your static and dynamic content

    C. The domain name registered in your ALB or ELB pointing to your content

    D. The domain name from the AWS console for your CloudFront distribution

91. Which of the following might occur when content is requested from a CloudFront edge location? (Choose two.)

    A. Cached content at the edge location is returned.

    B. The request is passed directly to an origin server without CloudFront processing.

    C. A request is made to an origin server for the requested content.

    D. A redirect is returned to the client.

92. Which of the following statements about CloudFront are not true? (Choose two.)

    A. CloudFront edge locations are geographically distributed across the world.

    B. CloudFront maintains persistent connections with origin servers.

    C. A request will be routed by CloudFront to the nearest edge location to the origin server, which will serve that request.

    D. CloudFront can use an RDS instance of PostgreSQL as an origin server.

93. How is data transferred out from a region to a CloudFront edge location charged?

    A. At normal egress data rates

    B. At half the price of normal egress rates

    C. At the lowest available rate for the region from which the data originates

    D. There is no charge.

94. Which of the following are true about both S3 and CloudFront? (Choose two.)

  A. They both store files.

  B. They both support encryption of their content.

  C. They both cache files.

  D. They both provide low-latency distribution of content to clients.

95. Which of the following content types can be served by CloudFront? (Choose two.)

  A. The returned rows from a SQL query

  B. The response from a PHP script

  C. A Lambda function

  D. HTML and CSS

96. Which of the following can be CloudFront origin servers? (Choose two.)

  A. A web server hosted on another cloud provider

  B. An EC2 instance fleet spread across two regions

  C. A MySQL RDS instance

  D. An SNS topic

97. What is an edge location?

  A. A specific node within a worldwide network of data centers that deliver CloudFront content

  B. A virtual cloud of caching stations

  C. A fleet of EC2 instances managed by AWS

  D. An EC2 instance in a remote region from your primary content

98. What is a CloudFront distribution?

  A. A worldwide network of data centers

  B. A set of origin servers whose content is served by CloudFront via various edge locations

  C. The cached content on CloudFront edge locations at any given time

  D. The cached content from your account stored on CloudFront edge locations at any given time

99. How long is content cached at an edge location?

  A. 24 hours

  B. 12 hours

  C. 12 hours by default, but this value can be changed.

  D. 24 hours by default, but this value can be changed.

100. What is the shortest expiration period allowed for a CloudFront edge location?

    A. 0 seconds

    B. 5 seconds

    C. 30 seconds

    D. 1 minute

101. You have a CloudFront distribution setup, but you are not seeing any performance benefit to your users. What might be possible causes for the lack of benefit? (Choose two.)

    A. Users do not have CloudFront enabled in their client applications and are therefore not getting the benefits of the CloudFront distribution. Enable CloudFront in their client applications.

    B. The expiration period is set so low that caching is not happening enough to benefit users. Raise the expiration period time.

    C. Your set of origin servers is too small and being flooded by requests from Cloud-Front. Consider increasing the number or processing power of origin servers.

    D. Users are not close enough to edge locations to see a benefit from CloudFront.

102. Why would you set the expiration period to 0 on a CloudFront distribution?

    A. To expire all content on all existing edge locations

    B. To ensure caching does not occur for maximum throughput

    C. To reduce the chances of a DDoS attack on your edge locations

    D. To ensure the most up-to-date content is served at all edge locations

103. How can you delete a file from an edge location? (Choose two.)

    A. Use the AWS console to navigate to the edge location and delete the file.

    B. Set the expiration period to 0 on your distribution.

    C. Remove the file from your origin servers.

    D. Delete the file from your CloudFront distribution using the AWS CLI.

104. Which is the correct order of the steps below to remove a file from an edge location immediately with the least interruption to existing service?

    A. First set the expiration time on a CloudFront distribution to 0; then remove the file from the origin servers.

    B. First take the CloudFront distribution offline; then remove the file from the origin servers.

    C. First remove the file from the origin servers; then set the expiration time on the CloudFront distribution to 0.

    D. First, remove the file from the origin servers; then take the CloudFront distribution offline.

105. Which of the following immediately removes an object from all edge locations?

    A. Removing the object from all origin servers

    B. Removing all CloudFront edge locations with the object cached

    C. Removing the object using the invalidation API

    D. Invalidating the CloudFront distribution

106. Which of the following provides the highest availability for critical files?

    A. S3

    B. S3-IA

    C. S3 One Zone-IA

    D. Glacier

107. Which of the following storage classes has the lowest first byte latency?

    A. S3

    B. S3-IA

    C. S3 One Zone-IA

    D. They are all identical.

108. Which of the following storage classes provides the fastest data retrieval speeds?

    A. S3

    B. S3-IA

    C. S3 One Zone-IA

    D. They are all identical.

109. How long does a typical Glacier data retrieval take?

    A. 1 hour

    B. 1–3 hours

    C. 3–5 hours

    D. 5–10 hours

110. Why would you choose S3-IA over S3?

    A. You want to save money and don't need your data as quickly.

    B. You want to save money and don't need your data as frequently.

    C. You want to save money and don't need data in multiple availability zones.

    D. You want to save money and don't need fault tolerance of your data.

111. Which of the following statements are not true? (Choose two.)

    A. There are more edge locations than availability zones.

    B. An edge location is separate from an availability zone.

    C. An RDS instance can be an origin server.

    D. The default expiration period is 12 hours.

112. Which of the following is a valid origin server for a CloudFront distribution?

    A. An S3 bucket

    B. An EC2 instance

    C. An ALB

    D. All of the above

113. What does AWS call a collection of edge locations?

    A. CloudFront

    B. An edge zone

    C. Lambda@Edge

    D. A distribution

114. What type of distribution should you use for media streaming?

    A. Web distribution

    B. Media distribution

    C. RTMP distribution

    D. Edge distribution

115. Which of the following are valid media distributions for CloudFront? (Choose two.)

    A. Wcb distribution

    B. Media distribution

    C. RTMP distribution

    D. Edge distribution

116. Which of the following are valid direct operations on an edge location? (Choose two.)

    A. Read an object.

    B. Write an object.

    C. Delete an object.

    D. Update an object.

117. Which of the following are valid use cases for using ElastiCache? (Choose two.)

    A. Real-time transactions

    B. Offline transactions

    C. Record storage

    D. Business intelligence

118. Which of the following can ElastiCache be used for? (Choose two.)

    A. Web server

    B. Database cache

    C. Object storage

    D. Message broker

119. Which of the following can ElastiCache be used for? (Choose two.)

    A. Ephemeral storage

    B. Long-term storage

    C. Message Queue

    D. Logging store

120. What is an ElastiCache shard?

    A. A collection of multiple nodes that make up a cluster

    B. A collection of clusters in an ElastiCache distribution

    C. A collection of edge locations in an ElastiCache distribution

    D. A single node in a cluster

121. Which of the following provides low latency access to most frequently accessed data while storing all data in the cloud?

    A. Storage gateway – snapshot

    B. Storage gateway – virtual tape library

    C. Storage gateway – stored volume

    D. Storage gateway – cached volume

122. Which of the following provides low latency access to all data while still storing the dataset in the cloud?

    A. Storage gateway – snapshot

    B. Storage gateway – virtual tape library

    C. Storage gateway – stored volume

    D. Storage gateway – cached volume

123. Which of the following provides the fastest access to a customer dataset?

    A. S3 with Transfer Acceleration

    B. Storage gateway – virtual tape library

    C. Storage gateway – stored volume

    D. S3 standard

124. Which of the following provides access to frequently accessed data at top speeds while still maintaining disaster recovery options?

    A. Storage gateway – stored volume

    B. Storage gateway – virtual tape library

    C. S3-IA

    D. S3 standard

125. You are creating a user data storage system by using an S3 bucket with multiple folders, one folder per user. You want to then tag each folder with the username of the staff member and build IAM permissions based on these tags. Which of the following is a problem with this approach?

A. S3 buckets cannot be permissioned using IAM.

B. Folders in an S3 bucket cannot have individual tags associated with them.

C. Buckets in S3 cannot be tagged with multiple tags.

D. IAM cannot operate based on individual S3 buckets.

126. You are in charge of a data migration your company is preparing to undertake. Your company wants to store files on AWS and see if the costs are lower than on-premises storage, but your company is being very cautious. In this first phase, it wants to ensure the lowest possible latency of the majority of the files. Which storage gateway configuration would you recommend?

A. Cached volumes

B. Virtual tape library

C. Snapshot

D. Stored volumes

127. Why would you choose to configure read replicas across all available AZs as opposed to configuring them in the same region as your primary database source?

A. You have a global customer base.

B. You want to ensure disaster recovery.

C. You want to maximize network throughput.

D. You should never configure read replicas outside of the region of the primary database instance.

128. Why would you choose to configure read replicas across all available AZs in the same single region as your primary database instance as opposed to configuring them across all AWS regions?

A. You have a global customer base.

B. You want to ensure disaster recovery.

C. You have a localized customer base close to the target region.

D. You should never configure all read replicas within the same region of the primary database instance.

129. All your customers are in a single geographical region, and you have created a database instance and multiple read replicas across the AZs in that region. Is there any value in also creating replicas in additional regions?

A. No, there is no value in that approach.

B. Yes, as you gain some disaster recovery benefits from a replica in another region.

C. Yes, as customers may be routed to different regions when they request data from your databases.

D. Yes, as S3 buckets are in different regions as well.

130. Which of the following can be done to a read replica? (Choose two.)

    A. Read from it.

    B. Write to it.

    C. Fail over to it.

    D. Back it up.

131. Which of the following will tend to cause performance improvements in an RDS instance that is currently severely taxed? (Choose two.)

    A. Create RDS read replicas of the instance.

    B. Switch from RDS to DynamoDB.

    C. Configure the instance to use Multi-AZ.

    D. Upgrade the RDS instance.

132. You have a number of large PDF files stored in an RDS instance. These PDFs are accessed infrequently, but when they are accessed, they need to respond quickly to requests. As the user base increases, the load is beginning to overwhelm the database. What suggestions would you make to improve performance? (Choose two.)

    A. Move the PDFs to S3.

    B. Install ElastiCache in front of the database.

    C. Create read replicas of the primary database.

    D. Consider increasing the available memory for the database instance.

133. You have a number of large PDF files stored in an RDS instance used by a company's internal staff, of which 80% are on-site. These PDFs are accessed infrequently, but when they are accessed, they need to respond quickly to requests. As the company's support staff has increased, the load is beginning to overwhelm the database. What suggestions would you make to improve performance? (Choose two.)

    A. Set up a CloudFront distribution.

    B. Upgrade the instance running the RDS database.

    C. Consider installing a storage gateway with stored volumes at the customer's on-premises site.

    D. Install ElastiCache in front of the database.

134. You have a number of large PDF files stored in an RDS instance used by a company's geographically distributed user base. These PDFs are accessed infrequently, but when they are accessed, they need to respond quickly to requests. As the company's user base has increased, the load is beginning to overwhelm the database. What is the best option for improving database performance?

    A. Set up a CloudFront distribution.

    B. Create read replicas across the regions in which the user base accesses the application.

    C. Consider installing a storage gateway with stored volumes at the customer's on-premises site.

    D. Install ElastiCache in front of the database.

135. You have a number of large images stored in an RDS instance used by a company's geographically distributed user base. Each of these images is accessed several thousand times a day and needs to respond quickly to requests. As the company's user base has increased, the load is beginning to overwhelm the database. What is the best option for improving database performance?

    A. Upgrade the instance running the RDS database.

    B. Create read replicas across the regions in which the user base accesses the application.

    C. Consider installing a storage gateway with stored volumes at the customer's on-premises site.

    D. Install ElastiCache in front of the database.

136. Which of the following are valid routing policies for Route 53? (Choose two.)

    A. Simple routing

    B. Fault recovery routing

    C. Latency-based routing

    D. Cached routing

137. Which of the following are valid routing policies for Route 53? (Choose two.)

    A. Geolocation routing

    B. Weighted routing

    C. Round-robin routing

    D. Distributed routing

138. Which of the following are valid routing policies for Route 53? (Choose two.)

    A. FIFO routing

    B. Multivalue answer routing

    C. Geoproximity routing

    D. Distributed routing

139. Which of the following routing policies sends traffic to a single resource, such as a web server?

    A. Geolocation routing

    B. Weighted routing

    C. Simple routing

    D. Latency-based routing

140. Which of the following routing policies sends traffic to a single resource, unless that resource is unhealthy, and then routes to a backup resource?

    A. Health-based routing

    B. Failover routing

    C. Simple routing

    D. Latency-based routing

141. Which of the following routing policies chooses a route for a user based on the user's geographic location?

   A. Health-based routing

   B. Failover routing

   C. Geolocation routing

   D. Region-based routing

142. Which of the following routing policies chooses a route for a user based on the latency of the available region to which traffic can be directed?

   A. Health-based routing

   B. Latency-based routing

   C. Geolocation routing

   D. Region-based routing

143. Which of the following routing policies can direct traffic to multiple resources as long as those resources are healthy?

   A. Health-based routing

   B. Latency-based routing

   C. Multivalue answer routing

   D. Region-based routing

144. Which of the following routing policies uses assigned weights to shape traffic to different resources?

   A. Health-based routing

   B. Latency-based routing

   C. Multivalue answer routing

   D. Weighted routing

145. Which of the following routing policies is ideal for routing traffic to a single web server?

   A. Simple routing

   B. Latency-based routing

   C. Multivalue answer routing

   D. Weighted routing

146. Which of the following Route 53 routing policies are ideal for a geographically distributed user base? (Choose two.)

   A. Geolocation routing

   B. Geographical routing

   C. Geoproximity routing

   D. Weighted routing

147. Which of the following values is an invalid weight for a weighted routing policy?

    A. 1

    B. 255

    C. 125

    D. These weights are all valid.

148. How does a weight of 0 affect routing on Route 53 when using a weighted routing policy?

    A. 0 is an invalid weight.

    B. All traffic is directed to the resource with a weight of 0, as long as that resource is healthy.

    C. No traffic is directed to the resource with a weight of 0.

    D. Traffic is routed to the resource, but health checks are not performed.

149. You have three resources in a weighted routing policy. Resource A has a weight of 100, resource B has a weight of 100, and resource C has a weight of 200. How will traffic be routed in this scenario?

    A. 25% of traffic to resource A, 25% of traffic to resource B, and 50% of traffic to resource C

    B. 10% of traffic to resource A, 10% of traffic to resource B, and 20% of traffic to resource C

    C. 33% of traffic to resource A, 33% of traffic to resource B, and 33% of traffic to resource C

    D. There is not enough information to know how routing will occur in this scenario.

150. Which of the following statements concerning Route 53 routing policies are true? (Choose two.)

    A. You can have multiple primary resources in a simple routing policy.

    B. A weighted routing policy uses weights for routing, but not health checks.

    C. You can have multiple secondary resources in a simple routing policy.

    D. Health checks are ignored if a resource has a weight of over 100 in a routing policy.

151. You are responsible for a media-serving website backed by a database that has a global user base. The fleet of EC2 instances serving the website is responding well to requests from the US, but requests from the EU are taking nearly five times as long to receive a response. Database CPU utilization stays between 70% and 90% throughout the day. What suggestions would you make to attempt to improve performance of this website? (Choose two.)

    A. Install ElastiCache in front of the RDS instance to cache common queries and reduce database reads and therefore overall load.

    B. Set up CloudFront to enable caching of data at edge locations closer to the EU user base.

    C. Set up an Auto Scaling group with low CPU thresholds to scale up the EC2 instances.

    D. Create additional EC2 instances that will serve the website, and locate them in a South Asia region.

152. Which of the following are not valid instance types? (Choose two.)

    A. T3

    B. E1

    C. M5

    D. Q2

153. What is the primary purpose of IAM?

    A. Deployment of applications

    B. Management of permissions in AWS

    C. User authentication for applications

    D. Configuration of applications

154. Which of the following statements about IAM are accurate? (Choose two.)

    A. IAM manages access from one AWS resource to another.

    B. IAM manages the authentication interface for the AWS console.

    C. IAM manages access from a user to the AWS console.

    D. IAM manages single sign-on for users to AWS applications.

155. What does IAM stand for?

    A. Improved Access Management

    B. Identity and Access Management

    C. Information and Access Management

    D. Identity and Authorization Management

156. Which of the following does IAM manage? (Choose two.)

    A. Management of users accessing the AWS platform

    B. Management of permissions for hosted application features

    C. Management of roles affecting resources within AWS

    D. Management of cost controls for user actions

157. Which of these is not managed by IAM? (Choose two.)

    A. Groups of users that share permissions in AWS

    B. Groups of users that can log in to a hosted web application

    C. Which resources receive notifications from SNS

    D. A role that allows EC2 instances to access S3 buckets

158. Which of the following is not a feature of IAM?

    A. Multi-Factor Authentication for AWS console access

    B. Multi-Factor Authentication for object deletion in S3

    C. Centralized control of AWS resource access

    D. Integration with Active Directory accounts

159. Which of the following is a security risk as you grow your AWS developer base?

   A. Turning on MFA for AWS console access

   B. Using a single developer account across your team

   C. Creating an account for each developer

   D. Requiring passwords with 12 or more characters

160. Which of the following is required when you create additional IAM users beyond the root user?

   A. Turning on MFA for all accounts

   B. Turning on MFA for the root account

   C. Creating a customized sign-in link for users in addition to the AWS root account sign-in link

   D. Creating IAM groups for each new user

161. Which of the following are components of IAM? (Choose two.)

   A. Users

   B. Groups

   C. Organizations

   D. Organizational units

162. Which of the following are components of IAM? (Choose two.)

   A. Roles

   B. User policies

   C. Connections

   D. Permissions

163. You are tasked with ensuring that a fleet of EC2 instances can retrieve data from S3 buckets. Which of the following might you need to create? (Choose two.)

   A. Role

   B. User

   C. Policy

   D. Group

164. Which types of access can you give a user via IAM? (Choose two.)

   A. Console

   B. Application

   C. Organizational

   D. Programmatic

165. Which of the following are valid AWS and IAM policy types? (Choose two.)

    A. Access control lists

    B. Application-based

    C. Resource-based

    D. Permission-based

166. In what language do you write IAM policies?

    A. YAML

    B. JSON

    C. PHP

    D. ACSCII

167. To which of the following can an IAM policy be attached? (Choose two.)

    A. Users

    B. Database entries

    C. Groups

    D. Passwords

168. What does MFA stand for?

    A. Multi-Fraction Authentication

    B. Multi-Factor Authentication

    C. Multi-Factor Authorization

    D. Multi-Fraction Authorization

169. How does IAM provide scalability benefits to your application deployments? (Choose two.)

    A. It allows assignment of permissions to users en masse via groups.

    B. It handles allowing users access to hosted applications en masse.

    C. It allows consistency in access from instances to managed AWS services across large numbers of instances.

    D. It ensures that users do not accidentally delete objects from S3 stores.

170. Which of the following provide centralized user management across your AWS resources? (Choose two.)

    A. KMS

    B. S3 SSE-C

    C. IAM

    D. AWS Organizations

171. What is power user access, as it relates to IAM roles?

   A. The AWS name for the root user

   B. All IAM users are considered power users.

   C. A type of user that has full access to all AWS services and resources but not group or user management

   D. A user that can access application deployment profiles

172. Which of the following can the root user not do?

   A. Create users.

   B. Remove user access to the console.

   C. Delete a role.

   D. The root user can do all of these.

173. Which of the following can a power user not do?

   A. Create users.

   B. Create a new SNS topic.

   C. Stop a running EC2 instance created by another user.

   D. The power user can do all of these.

174. Which of the following is a best practice for handling root user access keys?

   A. Store them only in an instances-protected `.aws/` directory.

   B. Delete them and instead use different user IAM credentials.

   C. Only use them for API access but avoid console access.

   D. Enable MFA Delete for when they are used in association with S3.

175. Which of the following require root user credentials? (Choose two.)

   A. Close an AWS account.

   B. Delete IAM users.

   C. Create a CloudFront key pair.

   D. Create an IAM policy.

176. Which of the following do not require root user credentials? (Choose two.)

   A. Resizing an existing RDS instance

   B. Deploying an application via a CloudFormation template

   C. Restoring revoked permissions for a user

   D. Changing support options for an AWS account

177. How do you remove the AWS account root user's access to your application EC2 instances?

   A. Delete all the keys in the instance's `.aws/` directory.

   B. Switch the instance to only accept SSH logins.

   C. Remove any keys from the instance's `.ssh/` directory.

   D. You can't remove access for an AWS account root user.

178. In a typical single-account AWS environment, which group of users should have root-level account access?

   A. Developers and managers

   B. Account auditors and developers

   C. 2 to 3 developers or engineers responsible for account management

   D. Nobody

179. Which of the following is not a predefined AWS IAM policy?

   A. Administrator

   B. Power User

   C. Billing

   D. These are all predefined policies in IAM.

180. You want to set your DevOps team up quickly in IAM. You have created users for each member of the team. What additional steps should you take? (Choose two.)

   A. Create sign-in URLs for the users.

   B. Check the DevOps option for each user in the console.

   C. Attach the Developer Power User policy to each user.

   D. Attach the View-Only User policy to each user.

181. Which of the following policies would be the best fit for a manager who wants access to the company's main AWS account?

   A. Administrator

   B. Power User

   C. Security Auditor

   D. View-Only User

182. Which of the following policies would be the best fit for a team member running Hadoop jobs and queries to determine application usage patterns?

   A. Administrator

   B. Power User

   C. Security Auditor

   D. Data Scientist

183. Which of the following policies would be the best fit for a team member responsible for setting up resources for the development team, working with AWS directory service, and potentially setting up DNS entries?

   A. System Administrator

   B. Power User

   C. Security Auditor

   D. Data Scientist

184. Which of the following are not possible to do with IAM policies and permissions? (Choose two.)

    A. Remove access for a user from EC2 instances.

    B. Remove access for the root user from EC2 instances.

    C. Give the root user access to a hosted web application.

    D. Add an additional user with access to all EC2 instances.

185. What does logging out of the AWS console and then logging back in accomplish?

    A. Applies any IAM policies attached to the user since their last login

    B. Applies any IAM policies attached to groups that the user was added to since their last login

    C. Applies any updates to IAM policies via JSON or the AWS REST API that have been made since the user's last login

    D. Nothing, all changes to an account are immediate and do not require logging in or back out.

186. You have created a new user for a new developer at your company. What permissions will this user have before you take any additional actions?

    A. They will not have any access to any AWS services.

    B. They will have read-only access to all AWS services.

    C. They will have administrator-level access to all AWS services.

    D. They will have the same permissions as the root user until restricted.

187. You have created a new user for a new developer at your company. What steps do you need to take to ensure they can work with EC2 instances? (Choose two.)

    A. Set the user up as part of the AWS-defined EC2 Users group.

    B. Set the user up as a Developer user in the AWS console.

    C. Provide the user with a URL for signing in.

    D. Add the user to a group such as Administrators or power users.

188. How can you ensure that the new users you have created only can access AWS via the API rather than through the console? (Choose two.)

    A. Do not create a sign-in URL for the users.

    B. Only provide the users with an access key ID and secret access key.

    C. Uncheck the Log In To Console box next to the user in the AWS console.

    D. Turn off MFA for the user.

189. To what degree do usernames have to be unique across AWS?

    A. Across the region in which the user exists

    B. Across all AWS accounts

    C. Across the AWS account in which the user exists

    D. Usernames don't have to be unique, but email addresses do.

190. Which of the following does a user need in order to access AWS resources programmatically? (Choose two.)

   A. Username

   B. Access key ID

   C. Password

   D. Secret access key pair

191. Which of the following does a user need in order to access the AWS console? (Choose two.)

   A. Username

   B. Access key ID

   C. Password

   D. Secret access key pair

192. In what language are policy documents written?

   A. JavaScript

   B. JSON

   C. Node.js

   D. Ruby

193. Which of the following would apply to giving federated users access to the AWS console via single sign-on?

   A. SAML

   B. JSON

   C. SSO

   D. IAM

194. You have a large user base in an Active Directory and want to give these users access to the AWS console without creating individual users in AWS for each. What approach would you take?

   A. Set the AWS console to use the Read Users From Another Authentication Source feature.

   B. Use the database migration tool to migrate the Active Directory database into RDS.

   C. Set up AWS to federate the users from the Active Directory into AWS.

   D. You cannot use a non-AWS Active Directory for access to AWS.

195. Which of the following is a collection of permissions?

   A. Group

   B. Role

   C. Topic

   D. Policy

196. You want to add a small group of developers located in a different region than your main development office. How would you handle scaling out users and permissions to this new region?

    A. Create the new users in the second region.

    B. Create the new users in the primary region and then replicate them to the new region.

    C. Create the new users in the primary region, set up IAM replication, and then apply correct permissions to the replicated users in the new region.

    D. Create the new users and they will apply to all regions.

197. What considerations do you need to take to ensure that your policy documents will scale across your entire organization and set of AWS resources?

    A. Make sure each policy has a name unique within the region to which it applies.

    B. Make sure each policy document has the *region: * * attribute so it applies to all regions.

    C. Nothing, policy documents are automatically applicable across all AWS resources within an account.

    D. When you create the policy document, ensure that you select the Avoid Regional Conflicts option.

198. Which of the following does Auto Scaling address? (Choose two.)

    A. Application monitoring

    B. Capacity management

    C. Cost limiting

    D. Permissions management

199. Which of the following are benefits of Auto Scaling? (Choose two.)

    A. Pay for only what you need.

    B. Improve network performance.

    C. Set up scaling quickly.

    D. Reduce VPC management overhead.

200. Which of the following can be scaled using the Auto Scaling interface? (Choose two.)

    A. DynamoDB

    B. Route 53 domains

    C. Aurora read replicas

    D. ALBs

201. Which of the following can be scaled using the Auto Scaling interface? (Choose two.)

    A. ECS containers

    B. SNS topics

    C. Redshift

    D. EC2 instances

202. What does AWS call a collection of components that can grow or shrink to meet user demand?

    A. Auto Scaling policy

    B. Launch configuration

    C. Auto Scaling group

    D. Capacity group

203. Which of the following can you not specify in an Auto Scaling group? (Choose two.)

    A. Minimum size

    B. Instances to add

    C. Desired capacity

    D. Desired cost

204. Which of the following can you specify in an Auto Scaling group? (Choose two.)

    A. Maximum size

    B. Scaling policy

    C. Minimum processing threshold

    D. Memory allocation

205. Which of the following are part of an Auto Scaling launch configuration? (Choose two.)

    A. Application language

    B. AMI ID

    C. Security group

    D. API endpoint

206. Which of the following are not part of an Auto Scaling launch configuration? (Choose two.)

    A. Instance type

    B. Maximum memory utilization

    C. Cluster size

    D. Security group

207. Which of the following are valid scaling options for an Auto Scaling group? (Choose two.)

    A. Manual scaling

    B. Memory-based scaling

    C. Schedule-based scaling

    D. Security-based scaling

208. Which of the following are valid scaling options for an Auto Scaling group? (Choose two.)

    A. Demand-based scaling

    B. Instance-based scaling

    C. Resource-based scaling

    D. Maintain current instance levels

209. Which Auto Scaling policy would you use to ensure that a specific number of instances is running at all times?

A. Demand-based scaling

B. Instance-based scaling

C. Resource-based scaling

D. Maintain current instance levels

210. Which Auto Scaling policy would you use to add and remove instances based on CPU utilization?

A. Demand-based scaling

B. Schedule-based scaling

C. Resource-based scaling

D. Maintain current instance levels

211. Which Auto Scaling policy would you use to add and remove instances at a certain time of day when usage is regularly high?

A. Demand-based scaling

B. Schedule-based scaling

C. Resource-based scaling

D. Maintain current instance levels

212. Which Auto Scaling policy would you use to control scaling yourself, within a specified maximum and minimum number of instances?

A. Demand-based scaling

B. Schedule-based scaling

C. Manual-based scaling

D. Maintain current instance levels

213. Which of these would you supply for a manual Auto Scaling policy?

A. Desired capacity

B. Time to scale up

C. Maximum CPU utilization

D. Scaling condition

214. Which of the following can be used to trigger scaling up or down for an Auto Scaling group? (Choose two.)

A. CloudWatch

B. SNS

C. The AWS console

D. Route 53

215. You have an Auto Scaling group with an instance that you believe is passing its health checks but is not responding properly to requests. What is the best approach to trouble-shoot this instance?

    A. Restart the instance.

    B. Remove the instance from the Auto Scaling group and then trouble shoot it.

    C. Put the instance into the Standby state and troubleshoot it normally.

    D. Add a CloudWatch metric to the instance to trigger Auto Scaling.

216. Which of the following are valid instance states for instances in an Auto Scaling group? (Choose two.)

    A. Deleted

    B. ReadyForService

    C. InService

    D. Standby

217. What is the correct order of tasks to create an Auto Scaling group?

    A. Verify your group, create an Auto Scaling group, create a launch configuration.

    B. Create a launch configuration, create an Auto Scaling group, verify your group.

    C. Create an Auto Scaling group, create a launch configuration, verify your group.

    D. Create a launch configuration, verify your group, create an Auto Scaling group.

218. How many AMIs can you use within a single Auto Scaling group launch configuration?

    A. None, you do not specify an AMI for a launch configuration.

    B. One for all instances within the group

    C. One for each instance in the group

    D. One for each class of instance in the group

219. How many security groups can you use within a single Auto Scaling group launch configuration?

    A. None, you do not specify a security group for a launch configuration.

    B. One security group for all instances within the group

    C. One security group for incoming requests and 1 security group for all outgoing requests

    D. As many as you like

220. From which of the following can you create an Auto Scaling group?

    A. An EC2 instance

    B. A launch configuration

    C. A launch template

    D. Any of these

221. You have an EC2 instance running a web application. You've lately seen large increases in traffic and the application is responding slowly several times a day. What are the best steps to take to ensure consistent performance? (Choose two.)

    A. Create a launch configuration with an AMI ID and instance parameters.

    B. Create an Auto Scaling group from the current EC2 instance.

    C. Set up an Auto Scaling group with demand-based scaling.

    D. Set up an Auto Scaling group with manual scaling.

222. You have an application that is peaking daily. You have determined that a large user base on the East Coast is accessing the application every evening, causing the application's performance to degrade during those hours. What steps would you take to level out performance? (Choose two.)

    A. Create an Auto Scaling group with schedule-based scaling.

    B. Consider hosting your Auto Scaling group in a US East region.

    C. Implement CloudFront to cache responses to user requests.

    D. Set up an Auto Scaling group with manual scaling.

223. You are in charge of the backup processes for converting an in-house network storage system to S3 on AWS. You want to minimize the costs of cloud storage but preserve the lowest possible latency for requests to the cloud-hosted files. What storage class would you suggest?

    A. S3 standard

    B. S3-IA

    C. S3 One Zone-IA

    D. Glacier

224. Which of the following will take the longest to retrieve data from?

    A. S3 standard

    B. S3-IA

    C. S3 One Zone-IA

    D. Glacier

225. Which of the following will take the longest to retrieve data from?

    A. S3 standard.

    B. S3-IA.

    C. S3 One Zone-IA.

    D. They are all equal.

226. You are in charge of a CPU-intensive application that has been refactored to perform the most compute-heavy portions of processing separate from normal daily operations. These compute-heavy tasks must finish every month but can be stopped and started without affecting the overall progress of the job. You want to reduce costs associated with this processing; which instance pricing model would you suggest?

A. Reserved instances

B. On-demand instances

C. Dedicated hardware instances

D. Spot instances

Chapter

3

Domain 3: Specify Secure Applications and Architectures

✓ **Subdomain: 3.1 Determine how to secure application tiers.**

✓ **Subdomain: 3.2 Determine how to secure data.**

✓ **Subdomain: 3.3 Define the networking infrastructure for a single VPC application.**

Review Questions

1. When creating a new security group, which of the following are true? (Choose two.)

    A. All inbound traffic is allowed by default.

    B. All outbound traffic is allowed by default.

    C. Connections that are allowed in must also explicitly be allowed back out.

    D. Connections that are allowed in are automatically allowed back out.

2. You have a government-regulated system that will store a large amount of data on S3 standard. You must encrypt all data and preserve a clear audit trail for traceability and third-party auditing. Security policies dictate that encryption must be consistent across the entire data store. Which of the following encryption approaches would be best?

    A. SSE-C

    B. SSE-KMS

    C. SSE-C

    D. Encrypt the data prior to upload to S3 and decrypt the data when returning it to the client.

3. You are creating a bastion host to allow SSH access to a set of EC2 instances in a private subnet within your organization's VPC. Which of the following should be done as part of configuring the bastion host? (Choose two.)

    A. Ensure that the bastion host is exposed directly to the Internet.

    B. Place the bastion host within the private subnet.

    C. Add a route from the bastion host IP into the private subnet into the subnet's NACLs.

    D. Ensure that the bastion host is within the same security group as the hosts within the private subnet.

4. Which of the following are invalid IAM actions? (Choose two.)

    A. Limiting the root account SSH access to all EC2 instances

    B. Allowing a user account SSH access to all EC2 instances

    C. Removing console access for the root account

    D. Removing console access for all non-root user accounts

5. Which of the following statements is true?

    A. You should store application keys only in your application's .aws file.

    B. You should never store your application keys on an instance, in an AMI, or anywhere else permanent on the cloud.

    C. You should only store application keys in an encrypted AMI.

    D. You should only use your application key to log in to the AWS console.

6. Your company is setting up a VPN connection to connect its local network to an AWS VPC. Which of the following components are *not* necessary for this setup? (Choose two.)

    A. A NAT instance

    B. A virtual private gateway

    C. A private subnet in the AWS VPC

    D. A customer gateway

7. You have a private subnet in a VPC within AWS. The instances within the subnet are unable to access the Internet. You have created a NAT gateway to solve this problem. What additional steps do you need to perform to allow the instances Internet access? (Choose two.)

    A. Ensure that the NAT gateway is in the same subnet as the instances that cannot access the Internet.

    B. Add a route in the private subnet to route traffic aimed at 0.0.0.0/0 at the NAT gateway.

    C. Add a route in the public subnet to route traffic aimed at 0.0.0.0/0 at the NAT gateway.

    D. Ensure that the NAT gateway is in a public subnet.

8. Which of the following statements regarding NAT instances and NAT gateways are false? (Choose two.)

    A. Both NAT instances and NAT gateways are highly available.

    B. You must choose the instance type and size when creating a NAT gateway but not when creating a NAT instance.

    C. It is your responsibility to patch a NAT instance and AWS's responsibility to patch a NAT gateway.

    D. You assign a security group to a NAT instance but not to a NAT gateway.

9. Which of the following statements is true?

    A. A VPC's default NACLs allow all inbound and outbound traffic.

    B. NACLs are stateful.

    C. Security groups are stateless.

    D. Traffic allowed into a NACL is automatically allowed back out.

10. You have changed the permissions associated with a role, and that role is assigned to an existing running EC2 instance. When will the permissions you updated take effect for the instance?

    A. Immediately

    B. Within 5 minutes

    C. Within 1 hour

    D. The next time the EC2 instance is restarted

11. Which of the following statements is true?

    A. When creating a new security group, by default, all traffic is allowed in, including SSH.

    B. If you need inbound HTTP and HTTPS access, create a new security group and accept the default settings.

    C. You must explicitly allow any inbound traffic into a new security group.

    D. Security groups are stateless.

12. Which of the following statements is not true?

    A. When creating a new security group, by default, no inbound traffic is allowed.

    B. When creating a new security group, by default, all traffic is allowed out, including SSH.

    C. When creating a new security group, by default, all traffic is allowed out, with the exception of SSH.

    D. When creating a new security group, inbound HTTPS traffic is not allowed.

13. How would you enable encryption of your EBS volumes?

    A. Use the AWS CLI with the aws security command.

    B. Take a snapshot of the EBS volume and copy it to an encrypted S3 bucket.

    C. Select the encryption option when creating the EBS volume.

    D. Encrypt the volume using the encryption tools of the operating system of the EC2 instance that has mounted the EBS volume.

14. What types of rules does a security group allow? (Choose two.)

    A. Allow rules

    B. Prevent rules

    C. Deny rules

    D. Inbound rules

15. Which of the following are true about security groups? (Choose two.)

    A. You can specify deny rules, but not allow rules.

    B. By default, a security group includes an outbound rule that allows all outbound traffic.

    C. You can specify specific separate rules for inbound and outbound traffic.

    D. Security groups are stateless.

16. Which of the following are not true about security groups? (Choose two.)

    A. Allow rules take priority over deny rules.

    B. Responses to allowed inbound traffic are allowed to flow back out.

    C. You can specify specific separate rules for inbound and outbound traffic.

    D. If there are no outbound rules, then all outbound traffic is allowed to flow out.

17. Which of the following must a security group have when you create it? (Choose two.)

    A. At least one inbound rule

    B. A name

    C. A description

    D. At least one outbound rule

18. Which of the following is a security group associated with?

    A. An ELB

    B. A network interface

    C. An ALB

    D. A network access list

19. Which of the following are default rules on a default security group, such as the one that comes with the default VPC? (Choose two.)

    A. Outbound: 0.0.0.0/0 for all protocols allowed

    B. Inbound: 0.0.0.0/0 for all protocols allowed

    C. Outbound: ::/0 for all protocols allowed

    D. Inbound: ::/0 for all protocols allowed

20. Which of the following are parts of a security group rule? (Choose two.)

    A. A protocol

    B. A subnet

    C. An instance ID

    D. A description

21. Which of the following allows you to securely upload data to S3? (Choose two.)

    A. HTTP endpoints using HTTP

    B. SSL endpoints using HTTPS

    C. HTTP endpoints using HTTPS

    D. SSL endpoints using HTTP

22. Which of the following describes client-side encryption for S3 bucket data?

    A. You encrypt and upload data to S3, managing the encryption process yourself.

    B. You encrypt and upload data to S3, allowing AWS to manage the encryption process.

    C. You request AWS to encrypt an object before saving it to S3.

    D. You encrypt an object, but AWS uploads and decrypts the object.

23. Which of the following describes server-side encryption for S3 bucket data?

    A. You encrypt and upload data to S3, managing the encryption process yourself.

    B. You encrypt and upload data to S3, allowing AWS to manage the encryption process.

    C. You request AWS to encrypt an object before saving it to S3.

    D. You encrypt an object, but AWS uploads and decrypts the object.

24. Which of the following are valid steps in enabling client-side encryption for S3? (Choose two.)

   A. Download the AWS CLI and SSH to your S3 key store.

   B. Use a KMS-managed customer master key.

   C. Download an AWS SDK for encrypting data on the client side.

   D. Turn on bucket encryption for the target S3 buckets.

25. Which of the following is not a way to manage server-side encryption keys for S3?

   A. SSE-S3

   B. SSE-KMS

   C. SSE-E

   D. SSE-C

26. Which of the following encryption key management options is best for ensuring strong audit trails?

   A. SSE-S3

   B. SSE-KMS

   C. Client-side encryption keys

   D. SSE-C

27. Which of the following encryption key management options is best for managing keys but allowing S3 to handle the actual encryption of data?

   A. SSE-S3

   B. SSE-KMS

   C. Client-side encryption keys

   D. SSE-C

28. You have a customer that has a legacy security group that is very suspicious of all things security in the cloud. The customer wants to use S3, but doesn't trust AWS encryption, and you need to enable its migration to the cloud. What option would you recommend to address the company's concerns?

   A. SSE-S3

   B. SSE-KMS

   C. Client-side encryption keys

   D. SSE-C

29. You want to begin encrypting your S3 data, but your organization is new to encryption. Which option is a low-cost approach that still offloads most of the work to AWS rather than the organization new to encryption?

   A. SSE-S3

   B. SSE-KMS

   C. Client-side encryption keys

   D. SSE-C

30. You are the architect for a company whose data must comply with current EU privacy restrictions. Which of the following S3 buckets are valid options? (Choose two.)

  A. Buckets in EU Central 1

  B. Buckets in US East 2

  C. Buckets in EU West 1

  D. Buckets in SA East 1

31. Which of the following options could be used to provide availability-zone-resilient fault-tolerant storage that complies with EU privacy laws? (Choose two.)

  A. S3 buckets in US West 1

  B. S3 buckets in EU West 2

  C. S3-IA buckets in EU Central 1

  D. S3 One Zone-IA buckets in EU-West-1

32. What type of replication will your Multi-AZ RDS instances use?

  A. Offline replication

  B. Synchronous replication

  C. Push replication

  D. Asynchronous replication

33. You want to provide maximum protection against data in your S3 object storage being deleted accidentally. What should you do?

  A. Enable versioning on your EBS volumes.

  B. Turn on MFA Delete on your S3 buckets.

  C. Set up a Lambda job to monitor and block delete requests to S3.

  D. Turn off the DELETE endpoints on the S3 REST API.

34. You want to provide maximum protection against data in your S3 object storage being deleted accidentally. What steps should you take? (Choose two.)

  A. Enable versioning on your S3 buckets.

  B. Turn on MFA Delete on your S3 buckets.

  C. Enable versioning in CloudWatch's S3 API.

  D. Remove IAM permissions for deleting objects for all users.

35. You want to enable MFA Delete on your S3 buckets in the US East 1 region. What step must you take before enabling MFA Delete?

  A. Disable the REST API for the buckets on which you want MFA Delete.

  B. Enable cross-region replication on the buckets on which you want MFA Delete.

  C. Move the buckets to a region that supports MFA Delete, such as US West 1.

  D. Enable versioning on the buckets on which you want MFA Delete.

36. What is AWS Trusted Advisor?
    - **A.** An online resource to help you improve performance
    - **B.** An online resource to help you reduce cost
    - **C.** An online resource to help you improve security
    - **D.** All of the above

37. On which of the following does AWS Trusted Advisor not provide recommendations?
    - **A.** Reducing cost
    - **B.** Improving fault tolerance
    - **C.** Improving security
    - **D.** Organizing accounts

38. Which of the following are included in the core AWS Trusted Advisor checks? (Choose two.)
    - **A.** S3 bucket permissions
    - **B.** MFA on root account
    - **C.** Quantity of CloudWatch alarms
    - **D.** Use of VPC endpoints

39. Which of the following recommendations might AWS Trusted Advisor make? (Choose two.)
    - **A.** Turn on MFA for the root account.
    - **B.** Turn on antivirus protection for EC2 instances.
    - **C.** Update S3 buckets with public write access.
    - **D.** Update NAT instances to NAT gateways.

40. Which of the following is not possible using IAM policies?
    - **A.** Requiring MFA for the root account
    - **B.** Denying the root account access to EC2 instances
    - **C.** Disabling S3 access for users in a group
    - **D.** Restricting SSH access to EC2 instances to a specific user

41. Which of the following are not true about S3 encryption? (Choose two.)
    - **A.** S3 applies AWS-256 encryption to data when server-side encryption is enabled.
    - **B.** S3 encryption will use a client key if it is supplied with data.
    - **C.** Encrypted EBS volumes can only be stored if server-side encryption is enabled.
    - **D.** S3 will accept locally encrypted data if client-side encryption is enabled.

42. What types of data are encrypted when you create an encrypted EBS volume? (Choose two.)

    A. Data at rest inside the volume

    B. Data moving between the volume and the attached instance

    C. Data inside S3 buckets that store the encrypted instance

    D. Data in an EFS on instances attached to the volume

43. What types of data are not automatically encrypted when you create an encrypted EBS volume? (Choose two.)

    A. A snapshot created from the EBS volume

    B. Any data on additional volumes attached to the same instance as the encrypted volume

    C. Data created on an instance that has the encrypted volume attached

    D. Data moving between the volume and the attached instance

44. What of the following types of data is not encrypted automatically when an encrypted EBS volume is attached to an EC2 instance?

    A. Data in transit to the volume

    B. Data at rest on the volume

    C. Data in transit from the volume

    D. All of these are encrypted.

45. What encryption service is used by encrypted EBS volumes?

    A. S3-KMS

    B. S3-C

    C. KMS

    D. Customer-managed keys

46. How can you access the private IP address of a running EC2 instance?

    A. `http://169.254.169.254/latest/user-data/`

    B. `http://169.254.169.254/latest/instance-data/`

    C. `http://169.254.169.254/latest/meta-data/`

    D. `http://169.254.169.254/latest/ec2-data/`

47. If you take a snapshot of an encrypted EBS volume, which of the following will be true? (Choose two.)

    A. The snapshot will be encrypted.

    B. All data on the bucket on which the snapshot is stored will be encrypted.

    C. Any instances using the snapshot will be encrypted.

    D. Any volumes created from the snapshot will be encrypted.

48. If you take a snapshot of an encrypted EBS volume, which of the following must you do to use that snapshot as a volume in a separate region? (Choose two.)

    A. Copy the snapshot to the new region.

    B. Delete the snapshot from the old region.

    C. Unencrypt the snapshot once it is in the new region.

    D. Create a new volume from the snapshot in the new region.

49. How do you encrypt an RDS instance?

    A. Enable encryption on the running instance via the CLI.

    B. Enable encryption on the running instance via the console.

    C. Run the encryption process on the running instance via the console.

    D. Enable encryption when creating the instance.

50. Which of the following will ensure that data on your RDS instance is encrypted?

    A. Use client-side encryption keys.

    B. Enable encryption on the running RDS instance via the AWS API.

    C. Encrypt the instance on which RDS is running.

    D. None of these will encrypt all data on the instance.

51. Which of the following will allow you to bring a non-encrypted RDS instance into compliance with an "all data must be encrypted at rest" policy?

    A. Snapshot the RDS instance and restore it, encrypting the new copy upon restoration.

    B. Use the AWS Database Migration Service to migrate the data from the instance to an encrypted instance.

    C. Create a new encrypted instance and manually move data into it.

    D. None of these will encrypt all data on the instance.

52. Which of the following will allow you to bring a non-encrypted EBS volume into compliance with an "all data must be encrypted at rest" policy?

    A. Stop the volume, snapshot it, and encrypt a copy of the snapshot. Then restore from the encrypted snapshot.

    B. Stop the volume, select "Turn on encryption," and restart the volume.

    C. Encrypt the volume via the AWS API and turn on the "encrypt existing data" flag.

    D. None of these will encrypt all data on the volume.

53. Which of the following will allow you to bring a non-encrypted EBS volume into compliance with an "all data must be encrypted at rest" policy?

    A. Stop the volume, create a snapshot, and restart from the snapshot, selecting "Encrypt this volume."

    B. Stop the volume, select "Turn on encryption," and restart the volume.

    C. Encrypt the volume via the AWS API and turn on the "encrypt existing data" flag.

    D. None of these will encrypt all data on the volume.

54. Which of the following will allow you to bring a non-encrypted EBS volume into compliance with an "all data must be encrypted at rest" policy?

    A. Create a new volume, attach the new volume to an EC2 instance, copy the data from the non-encrypted volume to the new volume, and then encrypt the new volume.

    B. Create a new volume with encryption turned on, attach the new volume to an EC2 instance, and copy the data from the non-encrypted volume to the new volume.

    C. Create a new volume, attach the new volume to an EC2 instance, and use the encrypted-copy command to copy the data from the non-encrypted volume to the new volume.

    D. None of these will encrypt all data on the volume.

55. Which of the following are valid options on an EBS volume? (Choose two.)

    A. Encrypt the volume.

    B. Encrypt a snapshot of the volume.

    C. Encrypt a copy of a snapshot of the volume.

    D. Restore an encrypted snapshot to an encrypted volume.

56. Which of the following are not true about EBS snapshots? (Choose two.)

    A. Snapshots of encrypted volumes are automatically encrypted.

    B. When you copy an encrypted snapshot, the copy is not encrypted unless you explicitly specify.

    C. You cannot copy an encrypted snapshot unless you unencrypt the snapshot first.

    D. Volumes that are created from encrypted snapshots are automatically encrypted.

57. Can you copy a snapshot across AWS accounts?

    A. Yes

    B. Yes, but you first have to modify the snapshot's access permissions.

    C. Yes, but you have to be the owner of both AWS accounts.

    D. No

58. You have a snapshot of an EBS volume in US East 2. You want to create a volume from this snapshot in US West 1. Is this possible?

    A. Yes, create the volume in US West 1 based upon the snapshot in US East 2.

    B. Yes, but you'll need to copy the snapshot to US West 1 first.

    C. Yes, but you'll need to create the instance in US East 2 and then move it to US West 1.

    D. No

59. Can you copy an EBS snapshot across regions?

    A. Yes, as long as the snapshot is not encrypted.

    B. Yes, as long as the snapshot is marked for multi-region use.

    C. Yes

    D. No

60. Which of the following does a security group attached to an instance control? (Choose two.)

    A. Inbound traffic

    B. HTTP error messages

    C. Outbound traffic

    D. Access control lists

61. How many security groups can you attach to a single instance in a VPC?

    A. None, security groups aren't attached to instances.

    B. 1

    C. 1 or more

    D. 2 or more

62. Which of the following can be added to a VPC, in addition to security groups on included instances, to further secure the VPC?

    A. A NACL

    B. A port filter

    C. An ALB

    D. A flow log

63. Which of the following statements is true about a custom, user-created NACL?

    A. A NACL by default allows all traffic out of a VPC.

    B. A NACL by default allows all traffic into a VPC.

    C. A NACL is a virtual firewall for associated subnets.

    D. A NACL functions at the instance level.

64. What do you use to permit and restrict control of a NACL?

    A. VPC

    B. WAF

    C. AWS Organizations

    D. IAM

65. Which of these are true about security groups? (Choose two.)

    A. Support allow and deny rules

    B. Evaluate all rules before deciding whether to allow traffic

    C. Operate at the instance level

    D. Apply to all instances in the associated subnet

66. Which of these are true about security groups? (Choose two.)

    A. Stateful

    B. Stateless

    C. Process rules in order

    D. Associated with an instance

67. Which of these are true about NACLs? (Choose two.)

    A. Stateful

    B. Stateless

    C. Process rules in order

    D. Associated with an instance

68. Which of these are true about NACLs? (Choose two.)

    A. Apply to all instances in an associated subnet

    B. Only apply if no security group is present

    C. Support allow and deny rules

    D. Evaluate all rules before deciding whether to allow or disallow traffic

69. In which order are NACLs and security groups evaluated?

    A. NACLs and security groups are evaluated in parallel.

    B. A NACL is evaluated first, and then the security group.

    C. A security group is evaluated first, and then the NACL.

    D. It depends on the VPC setup.

70. Which of these statements are true? (Choose two.)

    A. A security group can apply to two instances at the same time.

    B. A NACL applies to all instances within a subnet at the same time.

    C. A security group can apply to only one instance at the same time.

    D. A NACL can apply to only one instance at the same time.

71. With which of the following is a NACL associated?

    A. An instance

    B. A subnet

    C. A VPC

    D. A NACL can be associated with all of these.

72. Which of the following are true about the default NACL that comes with the default VPC? (Choose two.)

    A. It allows all inbound traffic.

    B. It allows all outbound traffic.

    C. It disallows all inbound traffic.

    D. It disallows all outbound traffic.

73. Which of the following are true about a user-created NACL? (Choose two.)

    A. It allows all inbound traffic.

    B. It allows all outbound traffic.

    C. It disallows all inbound traffic.

    D. It disallows all outbound traffic.

74. In which order are rules in a NACL evaluated?

    A. From low to high, using the number on the rule

    B. From high to low, using the number on the rule

    C. From low to high, using the port of the rule

    D. From high to low, using the port of the rule

75. Which of the following statements is not true? (Choose two.)

    A. A network ACL has separate inbound and outbound rules.

    B. Network ACLs are stateful.

    C. Each subnet in your VPC must be associated with a NACL.

    D. A network ACL can only be associated with a single subnet.

76. With how many subnets can a NACL be associated?

    A. One

    B. One or more

    C. A NACL is associated with instances, not subnets.

    D. A NACL is associated with VPCs, not subnets.

77. With how many NACLs can a subnet be associated?

    A. One

    B. One or more

    C. A subnet is associated with security groups, not NACLs.

    D. A subnet is associated with VPCs, not NACLs.

78. What happens when you associate a NACL with a subnet that already is associated with a different NACL?

    A. Nothing, both NACLs are associated with the subnet.

    B. You receive an error. You must remove the first NACL to associate the new one.

    C. You receive an error. You must first merge the two NACLs to apply them to a subnet.

    D. The new NACL replaces the previous NACL, and the subnet still only has one NACL association.

79. Which of the following are part of a network ACL rule? (Choose two.)

    A. An ASCII code

    B. A rule number

    C. An IAM group

    D. A protocol

80. Which of the following are part of a network ACL rule? (Choose two.)

    A. An ALLOW or DENY specification

    B. A CIDR range

    C. An IP address

    D. A VPC identifier

81. Which of the following inbound rules of a custom NACL would be evaluated first?

    A. Rule #800 // HTTP // TCP // 80 // 0.0.0.0/0 -> ALLOW.

    B. Rule #100 // HTTPS // TCP // 443 // 0.0.0.0/0 -> ALLOW.

    C. Rule * // All // All // All // 0.0.0.0/0 -> DENY.

    D. Rule #130 // RDP // TCP // 3389 // 192.0.2.0/24 -> ALLOW.

82. If all of the following inbound rules existed on a custom NACL, would SSH traffic be allowed?

Rule #800 // HTTP // TCP // 80 // 0.0.0.0/0 -> ALLOW

Rule #100 // HTTPS // TCP // 443 // 0.0.0.0/0 -> ALLOW

Rule * // All // All // All // 0.0.0.0/0 -> DENY

Rule #130 // RDP // TCP // 3389 // 192.0.2.0/24 -> ALLOW

    A. Yes, SSH is included as a default protocol on NACLs.

    B. Yes, SSH is included in the HTTPS protocol.

    C. Only if the SSH access permission in IAM is granted.

    D. No

83. If all of the following inbound rules existed on the default VPC's default NACL, would SSH traffic be allowed?

Rule #800 // HTTP // TCP // 80 // 0.0.0.0/0 -> ALLOW

Rule #100 // HTTPS // TCP // 443 // 0.0.0.0/0 -> ALLOW

    A. Yes, the default VPC's default NACL allows all inbound traffic by default.

    B. Yes, SSH is included in the HTTPS protocol.

    C. Only if the SSH access permission in IAM is granted.

    D. No

84. If all of the following inbound rules existed on a custom NACL, would SSH traffic be allowed?

Rule #800 // HTTP // TCP // 80 // 0.0.0.0/0 -> ALLOW

Rule #100 // HTTPS // TCP // 443 // 0.0.0.0/0 -> ALLOW

Rule #140 // All // All // All // 0.0.0.0/0 -> DENY

Rule #120 // SSH // TCP // 22 // 192.0.2.0/24 -> ALLOW

    A. Yes

    B. Yes, but only from the CIDR block 192.0.2.0/24.

    C. Only if the SSH access permission in IAM is granted.

    D. No

85. If all of the following inbound rules existed on a custom NACL, would SSH traffic be allowed?

    Rule #800 // HTTP // TCP // 80 // 0.0.0.0/0 -> ALLOW

    Rule #100 // HTTPS // TCP // 443 // 0.0.0.0/0 -> ALLOW

    Rule #110 // All // All // All // 0.0.0.0/0 -> DENY

    Rule #120 // SSH // TCP // 22 // 192.0.2.0/24 -> ALLOW

    A. Yes

    B. Yes, but only from the CIDR block 192.0.2.0/24.

    C. Only if the SSH access permission in IAM is granted.

    D. No

86. Which of the following is the most accurate statement about what the following inbound rule on a NACL will do?

    Rule #120 // SSH // TCP // 22 // 192.0.2.0/24 -> ALLOW

    A. Allows inbound SSH traffic to the associated subnets

    B. Allows inbound TCP traffic to the associated subnets

    C. Allows inbound TCP traffic to the associated subnets from the CIDR block 192.0.2.0/24

    D. Allows inbound SSH traffic to the associated subnets from the CIDR block 192.0.2.0/24

87. Which of the following is the most accurate statement about what the following inbound rule on a NACL will do?

    Rule #120 // HTTP // TCP // 80 // 0.0.0.0/0 -> ALLOW

    A. Allows inbound HTTP traffic to the associated subnets

    B. Allows inbound IPv4 HTTP traffic to the associated subnets as long as it is not prevented by lower-numbered rules

    C. Allows inbound IPv4 HTTP traffic to the associated subnets

    D. Allows inbound IPv4 TCP traffic to the associated subnets

88. What does the CIDR block 0.0.0.0/0 represent?

    A. The entire Internet

    B. The entire Internet, limited to IPv4 addresses

    C. The entire Internet, limited to IPv6 addresses

    D. Inbound traffic from the entire Internet

89. What does the CIDR block ::/0 represent?

    A. The entire Internet

    B. The entire Internet, limited to IPv4 addresses

    C. The entire Internet, limited to IPv6 addresses

    D. Inbound traffic from the entire Internet

90. Which of the following rules allows IPv6 outbound traffic to flow to the entire Internet through a NAT gateway with the ID nat-123456789?

   A. 0.0.0.0/0 -> NAT -> nat-123456789

   B. ::/0 -> nat-123456789

   C. 0.0.0.0/0 -> nat-123456789

   D. ::/0 -> NAT -> nat-123456789

91. How many availability zones in a single region does a single VPC span?

   A. None, VPCs do not span availability zones.

   B. One

   C. At least two

   D. All of them

92. Which of these must be specified when creating a new VPC? (Choose two.)

   A. An availability zone

   B. A region

   C. A CIDR block

   D. A security group

93. How many subnets can be added to an availability zone within a VPC?

   A. None

   B. One

   C. One or more

   D. At least two

94. To how many availability zones within a region can a single subnet in a VPC be added?

   A. None

   B. One

   C. One or more

   D. At least two

95. How many availability zones can a subnet span?

   A. None

   B. One

   C. One or more

   D. At least two

96. How many IPv6 CIDR blocks can be assigned to a single VPC?

   A. None

   B. One

   C. One or more

   D. At least two

97. How many IPv4 CIDR blocks can be assigned to a single VPC?

A. None

B. One

C. One or more

D. At least two

98. You have a VPC in US East 1 with three subnets. One of those subnets' traffic is routed to an internet gateway. What does this make the subnet?

A. A private subnet

B. A restricted subnet

C. The master subnet of that VPC

D. A public subnet

99. You have a public subnet in a VPC and an EC2 instance serving web traffic within that public subnet. Can that EC2 instance be reached via the Internet?

A. Yes

B. Yes, as long as it has a public IPv4 address.

C. Yes, as long as the VPC is marked as public.

D. No

100. You have a public subnet within your VPC. Within that subnet are three instances, each running a web-accessible API. Two of the instances are responding to requests from Internet clients, but one is not. What could be the problem?

A. The VPC needs to be marked as public-facing.

B. The three instances should be moved into an Auto Scaling group.

C. There is no internet gateway available for the VPC.

D. The unavailable instance needs an elastic IP.

101. Which of the following are allowed when creating a new VPC? (Choose two.)

A. An IPv4 CIDR block

B. VPC description

C. An IPv6 CIDR block

D. A security group

102. Which of the following is not a required part of creating a custom VPC? (Choose two.)

A. An IPv6 CIDR block

B. A VPC name

C. A set of VPC tags

D. An IPv4 CIDR block

103. Which of the following defines a subnet as a public subnet? (Choose two.)
    A. A security group that allows inbound public traffic
    B. A routing table that routes traffic through the internet gateway
    C. Instances with public IP addresses
    D. An internet gateway

104. Which of the following defines a VPN-only subnet? (Choose two.)
    A. A routing table that routes traffic through the internet gateway
    B. A routing table that routes traffic through the virtual private gateway
    C. A virtual private gateway
    D. An internet gateway

105. Which of the following are required components in a VPN-only subnet? (Choose two.)
    A. A routing table
    B. A virtual private gateway
    C. An elastic IP address
    D. An internet gateway

106. By default, how many VPCs can you create per region?
    A. 1
    B. 5
    C. 20
    D. 200

107. By default, how many subnets can you create per VPC?
    A. 1
    B. 5
    C. 20
    D. 200

108. By default, how many IPv4 CIDR blocks can you create per VPC?
    A. 1
    B. 5
    C. 20
    D. 200

109. By default, how many elastic IPs can you create per region?
    A. 1
    B. 5
    C. 20
    D. 200

110. Which of the following is not true? (Choose two.)

   A. A subnet can have the same CIDR block as the VPC within which it exists.

   B. A subnet can have a larger CIDR block than the VPC within which it exists.

   C. A subnet can have a smaller CIDR block than the VPC within which it exists.

   D. A subnet does not have to have a CIDR block specified.

111. A VPC peering connection connects a VPC to which of the following?

   A. A subnet within another VPC

   B. A specific instance within another VPC

   C. Another VPC

   D. A virtual private gateway

112. An Amazon VPC VPN connection links your on-site network to which of the following?

   A. A customer gateway

   B. An internet gateway

   C. An Amazon VPC

   D. A virtual private gateway

113. Which of the following are required for a VPC VPN connection? (Choose two.)

   A. A customer gateway

   B. An internet gateway

   C. A virtual private gateway

   D. A public subnet

114. Which of the following would you use to secure a VPC and its instances? (Choose two.)

   A. A customer gateway

   B. A NACL

   C. A virtual private gateway

   D. A security group

115. You want to ensure that no incoming traffic reaches any instances in your VPC. Which of the following is your best option to prevent this type of traffic?

   A. A blacklist

   B. A NACL

   C. A virtual private gateway

   D. A security group

116. You want to ensure that no incoming traffic reaches just the database instances in a particular subnet within your VPC. Which of the following is your best option to prevent this type of traffic?

A. A blacklist

B. A NACL

C. A virtual private gateway

D. A security group

117. You have a subnet with five instances within it. Two are serving public APIs and three are providing backend compute power through database instances. What is the best way to secure these instances? (Choose two.)

A. Apply NACLs at the subnet level.

B. Attach a single security group to all the instances.

C. Move the two backend database instances into a different subnet.

D. Attach an internet gateway to the VPC.

118. Security groups operate most like which of the following?

A. A blacklist

B. A NACL

C. A whitelist

D. A greylist

119. If you have a NACL and a security group, at what two levels is security functioning? (Choose two.)

A. The VPN level

B. The service level

C. The subnet level

D. The instance level

120. What type of filtering does a security group perform?

A. Stateful

B. Synchronous

C. Whitelist

D. Stateless

121. What type of filtering does a network ACL perform?

A. Stateful

B. Synchronous

C. Whitelist

D. Stateless

122. With which of the following can you create a VPC peering connection?

   A. A VPC in the same AWS account and same region

   B. A VPC in another AWS account

   C. A VPC in the same AWS account but in another region

   D. All of these

123. With which of the following can you not create a VPC peering connection? (Choose two.)

   A. A VPC in another AWS account

   B. An instance in the same region

   C. A VPC in the same region

   D. An internet gateway

124. You have an instance within a custom VPC, and that instance needs to communicate with an API published by an instance in another VPC. How can you make this possible? (Choose two.)

   A. Enable cross-VPC communication via the AWS console.

   B. Configure routing from the source instance to the API-serving instance.

   C. Add a security group to the source instance.

   D. Add an internet gateway or virtual private gateway to the source VPC.

125. Which of the following could be used to allow instances within one VPC to communicate with instances in another region? (Choose two.)

   A. VPN connections

   B. NACLs

   C. Internet gateways

   D. Public IP addresses

126. Which region does not currently support VPCs?

   A. US East 1

   B. EU West 1

   C. SA East 1

   D. VPC is supported in all AWS regions.

127. How many availability zones can a VPC span?

   A. None, VPCs don't exist within availability zones.

   B. One

   C. Two or more

   D. All the availability zones within a region

128. When you launch an instance within a VPC, in which availability zone is it launched?

    A. The default availability zone

    B. You must specify an availability zone.

    C. The first availability zone without an instance

    D. The availability zone with the least resources utilized

129. You are the architect at a company that requires all data at rest to be encrypted. You discover several EBS-backed EC2 instances that will be commissioned in the next week. How can you ensure that data on these volumes will be encrypted?

    A. Use OS-level tools on the instance to encrypt the volumes.

    B. Specify via the AWS console that the volumes should be encrypted when they are created.

    C. You cannot enable encryption on a specific EBS volume.

    D. Start the instances with the volumes and then encrypt them via the AWS console.

130. Which of the following is required to use a VPC endpoint?

    A. An internet gateway

    B. A VPN connection

    C. A NAT instance

    D. A VPC endpoint does not require any of these.

131. Which of the following is not true about a VPC endpoint?

    A. A VPC endpoint can attach to an S3 bucket.

    B. A VPC endpoint is a hardware device.

    C. A VPC endpoint does not require an internet gateway.

    D. Traffic to a VPC endpoint does not travel over the Internet.

132. To which of the following can a VPC endpoint *not* attach?

    A. S3

    B. SNS

    C. Internet gateway

    D. DynamoDB

133. Which of the following might you need to create for using a VPC endpoint attached to S3?

    A. A NAT instance

    B. A NAT gateway

    C. An IAM role

    D. A security group

134. Is it possible to SSH into a subnet with no public instances?

    A. Yes

    B. Yes, as long as you have a bastion host and correct routing.

    C. Yes, as long as you have an AWS Direct Connect.

    D. No

135. Where should a bastion host be located?

    A. In a private subnet

    B. In a public subnet

    C. In a private VPC

    D. In a VPC with a virtual private gateway

136. What is another name for a bastion host?

    A. A remote host

    B. A box host

    C. A jump server

    D. A bastion connection

137. To which of the following might a bastion host be used to connect?

    A. A public instance in a public subnet

    B. A public instance in a private subnet

    C. A private instance in a public subnet

    D. A private instance in a private subnet

138. Which of these would you use to secure a bastion host?

    A. A network ACL

    B. A security group

    C. OS hardening

    D. All of the above

139. For a bastion host intended to provide shell access to your private instances, what protocols should you allow via a security group?

    A. SSH and RDP

    B. Just SSH

    C. Just RDP

    D. Just HTTPS

140. Which of the following statements about internet gateways is false?

    A. They scale horizontally.

    B. They are automatically redundant.

    C. They are automatically highly available.

    D. They scale vertically.

141. To which of the following does an internet gateway attach?
    A. An AWS account
    B. A subnet within a VPC
    C. A VPC
    D. An instance within a subnet

142. Which of the following destination routes would be used for routing IPv4 traffic to an internet gateway?
    A. 0.0.0.0/24
    B. 0.0.0.0/0
    C. ::/0
    D. 192.168.1.1

143. Which of the following destination routes would be used for routing IPv6 traffic to an internet gateway?
    A. 0.0.0.0/24
    B. 0.0.0.0/0
    C. ::/0
    D. 192.168.1.1

144. Which of the following is not necessary for an instance to have IPv6 communication over the Internet?
    A. A VPC with an associated IPv6 CIDR block
    B. A public IPv6 assigned to the instance
    C. A subnet with an associated IPv6 CIDR block
    D. A virtual private gateway with IPv6 enabled

145. Which of the following are possible options for assigning to an instance that needs public access? (Choose two.)
    A. A public IP address
    B. An elastic IP address
    C. An IAM role
    D. A NACL

146. Which of the following will have internet gateways available? (Choose two.)
    A. A public subnet
    B. An IPv6 elastic IP address
    C. The default VPC
    D. An ALB

147. What does ALB stand for?

    A. Access load balancer

    B. Application load balancer

    C. Adaptive load balancer

    D. Applied load balancer

148. At what OSI layer does an application load balancer operate?

    A. 4

    B. 7

    C. 4 and 7

    D. 6

149. At what OSI layer does a network load balancer operate?

    A. 4

    B. 7

    C. 4 and 7

    D. 6

150. At what OSI layer does a classic load balancer operate?

    A. 4

    B. 7

    C. 4 and 7

    D. 6

151. Which type of load balancer operates at the Transport layer?

    A. Classic load balancer

    B. Application load balancer

    C. Network load balancer

    D. Both classic and network load balancers

152. Which type of load balancer operates at the Application layer?

    A. Classic load balancer

    B. Application load balancer

    C. Network load balancer

    D. Both classic and application load balancers

153. What type of subnets are the default subnets in the default VPC?

    A. Private

    B. Hybrid

    C. Public

    D. Transport

154. What type of subnets are the default subnets in a custom VPC?

   A. Private

   B. Hybrid

   C. Public

   D. Transport

155. Which of the following is not automatically created for an instance launched into a non-default subnet?

   A. A private IPv4 address

   B. A security group

   C. A public IPv4 address

   D. A route to other instances in the subnet

156. Which of the following would be needed to allow an instance launched into a non-default subnet Internet access? (Choose two.)

   A. A private IPv4 address

   B. A security group

   C. An elastic IP address

   D. An internet gateway

157. Which of the following would you need to add or create to allow an instance launched into a default subnet in the default VPC Internet access?

   A. A public IPv4 address

   B. An internet gateway

   C. An elastic IP address

   D. None of these

158. Which of the following would you use to allow outbound Internet traffic while preventing unsolicited inbound connections?

   A. A NAT device

   B. A bastion host

   C. A VPC endpoint

   D. A VPN

159. What does a NAT device allow?

   A. Incoming traffic from the Internet to reach private instances

   B. Incoming traffic from other VPCs to reach private instances

   C. Outgoing traffic to other VPCs from private instances

   D. Outgoing traffic to the Internet from private instances

160. Which of the following are NAT devices offered by AWS? (Choose two.)

   A. NAT router

   B. NAT instance

   C. NAT gateway

   D. NAT load balancer

161. Which of the following requires selecting an AMI? (Choose two.)

   A. Launching an EC2 instance

   B. Backing up an EBS volume

   C. Creating an EBS volume

   D. Launching a NAT instance

162. For which of the following do you not need to worry about operating system updates?

   A. NAT instance

   B. NAT gateway

   C. EC2 instance

   D. ECS container

163. Which of the following does not automatically scale to meet demand?

   A. DynamoDB

   B. NAT instance

   C. SNS topic

   D. NAT gateway

164. Which of the following, without proper security, could be most dangerous to your private instances?

   A. Bastion host

   B. VPC endpoint

   C. Internet gateway

   D. NAT instance

165. Which of the following could be used as a bastion host?

   A. NAT gateway

   B. VPC endpoint

   C. Internet gateway

   D. NAT instance

166. You are building out a site-to-site VPN connection from an on-site network to a private subnet within a custom VPC. Which of the following might you need for this connection to function properly? (Choose two.)

    A.   An internet gateway

    B.   A public subnet

    C.   A virtual private gateway

    D.   A customer gateway

167. You are building out a site-to-site VPN connection from an on-site network to a custom VPC. Which of the following might you need for this connection to function properly? (Choose two.)

    A.   A NAT instance

    B.   A DynamoDB instance

    C.   A private subnet

    D.   An internet gateway

168. With which of the following is an egress-only internet gateway most closely associated?

    A.   IPv4

    B.   IPv6

    C.   A NAT instance

    D.   A NAT gateway

169. You are responsible for securing an EC2 instance with an IPv6 address that resides in a public subnet. You want to allow traffic from the instance to the Internet but restrict access to the instance. Which of the following would you suggest?

    A.   VPC endpoint

    B.   Internet gateway

    C.   Egress-only internet gateway

    D.   A NAT gateway

170. You have just created a NAT instance and want to launch the instance into a subnet. Which of these need to be true of the subnet into which you want to deploy? (Choose two.)

    A.   The subnet is public.

    B.   The subnet is private.

    C.   The subnet has routing into the private subnets in your VPC.

    D.   The subnet has routing to the public subnets in your VPC.

171. Which of the following are true about an egress-only internet gateway? (Choose two.)

    A.   It only supports IPv4 traffic.

    B.   It is stateful.

    C.   It only supports IPv6 traffic.

    D.   It is stateless.

172. Which of these would be used as the destination address in a routing table for a VPC that uses an egress-only internet gateway?

    A. 0.0.0.0/0

    B. 0.0.0.0/16

    C. ::/0

    D. ::/24

173. Which of the following are true about IPv6 addresses? (Choose two.)

    A. They are globally unique.

    B. They are in the format x.y.z.w.

    C. They require underlying IPv4 addresses.

    D. They are public by default.

174. What is an elastic network interface? (Choose two.)

    A. A hardware network interface on an EC2 instance

    B. A virtual network interface

    C. An interface that can have one or more IPv6 addresses

    D. An interface that does not have a MAC address

175. Which of the following is not part of an elastic network interface?

    A. A primary IPv4 address

    B. A MAC address

    C. A source/destination check flag

    D. A NACL

176. How many network interfaces can a single instance have?

    A. None

    B. One and only one

    C. One or more

    D. At least two, up to five

177. If an elastic network interface is moved from one instance to another, what happens to network traffic directed at the interface?

    A. It is redirected to the elastic network interface that has moved to the new instance.

    B. It is redirected to the primary network interface on the original instance.

    C. It is redirected to the primary network interface on the new instance.

    D. It is lost and must be re-sent to the elastic network interface on the new instance.

178. To how many instances can an elastic network interface be attached?

    A. One and only one

    B. One or more

    C. One at a time, but it can be moved from one instance to another.

    D. Up to five

179. Which of these is not a reason to attach multiple network interfaces to an instance?

    A. You are creating a management network.

    B. You are attempting to increase network throughput to the instance.

    C. You need a high-availability solution and have a low budget.

    D. You need dual-homed instances.

180. Which of the following can you not do with regard to network interfaces?

    A. Detach a secondary interface from an instance.

    B. Attach an elastic network interface to an instance with an existing interface.

    C. Detach a primary interface from an instance.

    D. Attach an elastic network interface to a different instance than originally attached.

181. Which of the following is not a valid attribute for an elastic network interface?

    A. An IPv6 address

    B. An IPv4 address

    C. A source/destination check flag

    D. A routing table

182. Why might you use an elastic IP address?

    A. You need an IPv4 address for a specific instance.

    B. You need an IPv6 address for a specific instance.

    C. You want to mask the failure of an instance to network clients.

    D. You want to avoid making changes to your security groups.

183. Which of the following can you not do with an elastic IP address?

    A. Change the IP address associated with it while it is in use.

    B. Move it from one instance to another.

    C. Move it across VPCs.

    D. Associate it with a single instance in a VPC.

184. Which of the following are advantages of an elastic IP? (Choose two.)

    A. Reduces the number of IP addresses your VPC uses

    B. Provides protection in case of an instance failure

    C. Allows all attributes of a network interface to be moved at one time

    D. Provides multiple IP addresses for a single instance

185. Which of the following would you need to do to create an elastic IP address? (Choose two.)

    A. Allocate an elastic IP address for use in a VPC.

    B. Allocate an IP address in Route 53.

    C. Detach the primary network interface on an instance.

    D. Associate the elastic IP to an instance in your VPC.

186. Which of these is not a valid means of working with an Amazon EBS snapshot?

    A. The AWS API

    B. The AWS CLI

    C. The AWS console

    D. The AWS EBS management tool

187. Where are individual instances provisioned?

    A. In a VPC

    B. In a region

    C. In an availability zone

    D. In an Auto Scaling group

188. How are EBS snapshots backed up to S3?

    A. Incrementally

    B. In full, every time they are changed

    C. EBS snapshots are backed up to RDS.

    D. Sequentially

189. You have an existing IAM role in use by several instances in your VPC. You make a change in the role, removing permissions to access S3. When does this change take effect on the instances already attached to the role?

    A. Immediately

    B. Within 60 seconds

    C. The next time the instances are restarted

    D. The instances preserve the pre-change permissions indefinitely.

190. How many IAM roles can you attach to a single instance?

    A. One

    B. One or two

    C. As many as you want

    D. None, roles are not assigned to instances.

191. How can you attach multiple IAM roles to a single instance? (Choose two.)

    A. You can attach as many roles as you want to an instance.

    B. You cannot, but you can combine the policies each role uses into a single new role and assign that.

    C. You can assign two IAM roles to an instance, but no more than that.

    D. You cannot; only one role can be assigned to an instance.

192. You need to make a change to a role attached to a running instance. What do you need to do to ensure the least amount of downtime? (Choose two.)

   A. Update the IAM role via the console or AWS API or CLI.

   B. Re-attach the updated role to the instance.

   C. Restart the instance.

   D. Other than updating the role, no additional changes are needed.

193. You have a new set of permissions that you want to attach to a running instance. What do you need to do to ensure the least amount of downtime? (Choose two.)

   A. Remove the instance's IAM role via the console or AWS API or CLI.

   B. Create a new IAM role with the desired permissions.

   C. Stop the instance, assign the role, and restart the instance.

   D. Attach the new role to the running instance.

194. How can you delete a snapshot of an EBS volume when it's used as the root device of a registered AMI?

   A. You can't.

   B. You can, but only using the AWS API or CLI.

   C. Delete the snapshot using the AWS console.

   D. Ensure that you have correct IAM privileges and delete the AMI.

195. Which of these is the best option for encrypting data at rest on an EBS volume?

   A. Configure the volume's encryption at creation time.

   B. Configure AES 256 encryption on the volume once it's been started.

   C. Configure encryption using the OS tools on the attached EC2 instance.

   D. Back up the data in the volume to an encrypted S3 bucket.

196. How can you ensure that an EBS root volume persists beyond the life of an EC2 instance, in the event that the instance is terminated?

   A. The volume will persist automatically.

   B. Configure the EC2 instance to not terminate its root volume and the EBS volume to persist.

   C. You cannot; root volumes always are deleted when the attached EC2 instance is terminated.

   D. Ensure that encryption is enabled on the volume and it will automatically persist.

197. Which of the following is not part of the well-architected framework?

   A. Apply security at all layers.

   B. Enable traceability.

   C. Use defaults whenever possible.

   D. Automate responses to security events.

198. Which of the following should you attempt to automate, according to the AWS well-architected framework? (Choose two.)

   A. Security best practices

   B. Scaling instances

   C. Responses to security events

   D. IAM policy creation

199. Which of the following statements are true? (Choose two.)

   A. You are responsible for security in the cloud.

   B. AWS is responsible for security of the cloud.

   C. AWS is responsible for security in the cloud.

   D. You are responsible for security of the cloud.

200. For which of the following is AWS responsible for security? (Choose two.)

   A. Edge locations

   B. Firewall configuration

   C. Network traffic

   D. Availability zones

201. For which of the following is AWS not responsible for security?

   A. Networking infrastructure

   B. RDS database installations

   C. S3 buckets

   D. Networking traffic

202. For which of the following are you not responsible for security?

   A. DynamoDB

   B. Operating system configuration

   C. Server-side encryption

   D. Application keys

203. Which of the following is not included in the well-architected framework's definition of security?

   A. Data protection

   B. Infrastructure protection

   C. Reduction of privileges

   D. Defective controls

204. Which of the following is a principle of the well-architected framework's security section?

   A. Encrypt the least amount of data possible.

   B. Always encrypt the most important data.

   C. Encrypt everything where possible.

   D. Encrypt data at rest.

205. Which of the following are principles of the well-architected framework's security section? (Choose two.)

    A. Encrypt data at rest.

    B. Encrypt data in transit.

    C. Encrypt data in groups rather than individually.

    D. Encrypt data at the destination.

206. Who is responsible for encrypting data in the cloud?

    A. You

    B. AWS

    C. AWS provides mechanisms such as key rotation for which they are responsible, but you are responsible for appropriate usage of those mechanisms.

    D. AWS provides an API, but you are responsible for security when using that API.

207. What is the term used to represent the resiliency of data stored in S3?

    A. 9 9s

    B. 11 9s

    C. 7 9s

    D. 99th percentile

208. Which of these statements is not true?

    A. AWS recommends encrypting data at rest and in transit.

    B. AWS will never move data between regions unless initiated by the customer.

    C. AWS will initiate moving data between regions if needed.

    D. Customers move data between regions rather than AWS.

209. Which of the following can be part of a strategy to avoid accidental data overwriting of S3 data?

    A. IAM roles

    B. MFA Delete

    C. Versioning

    D. All of these

210. Which of the following should always be done to protect your AWS environment? (Choose two.)

    A. Enable MFA on the root account.

    B. Enable MFA Delete on your S3 buckets.

    C. Set a password rotation policy for users.

    D. Create custom IAM roles for all users.

211. At what level does infrastructure protection exist in AWS?

   A. The physical hardware layer

   B. OSI layer 4

   C. The VPC layer

   D. OSI layer 7

212. Which of the following might be used to detect or identify a security breach in AWS? (Choose two.)

   A. CloudWatch

   B. CloudFormation

   C. CloudTrail

   D. Trusted Advisor

213. Which of the following AWS services is associated with privilege management?

   A. AWS Config

   B. RDS

   C. IAM

   D. VPC

214. Which of the following AWS services is associated with privilege management?

   A. Internet gateway

   B. S3-IA

   C. CloudTrail

   D. MFA

215. Which of the following AWS services is associated with identifying potential security holes?

   A. Trusted Advisor

   B. CloudFormation

   C. Security Detector

   D. Security Advisor

216. Which of the following is not one of the five pillars in the cloud defined by the AWS well-architected framework?

   A. Operational excellence

   B. Performance efficiency

   C. Organizational blueprint

   D. Cost optimization

217. Which of the following is not one of the five pillars in the cloud defined by the AWS well-architected framework?

    A. Performance efficiency

    B. Usability

    C. Security

    D. Reliability

218. Which of the following is not one of the security principles recommended by AWS's well-architected framework?

    A. Automate security best practices.

    B. Enable traceability.

    C. Apply security at the highest layers.

    D. Protect data in transit and at rest.

219. Which of the following is one of the security principles recommended by AWS's well-architected framework?

    A. Make sure all users have passwords.

    B. Only protect data at rest.

    C. Turn on MFA Delete for S3 buckets.

    D. Keep people away from data.

220. The AWS's well-architected framework defines five areas to consider with respect to security. Choose the two that are part of this set. (Choose two.)

    A. Identity and Access Management

    B. User management

    C. Virtual private networks

    D. Incident response

221. Who is responsible for physically securing the infrastructure that supports cloud services?

    A. AWS

    B. You

    C. Your users

    D. AWS and you have joint responsibility.

222. Which of the following statements about the root account in an AWS account are true? (Choose two.)

    A. It is the first account created.

    B. It is ideal for everyday tasks.

    C. It is intended primarily for creating other users and groups.

    D. It has access keys that are important to keep.

223. Which of the following are appropriate password policy requirements? (Choose two.)

A. Maximum length

B. Recovery

C. Minimum length

D. Complexity

224. What additional requirements should users that can access the AWS console have?

A. Users with console access should have more stringent password policy requirements.

B. Users with console access should have to use their access keys to log in.

C. Users with console access should be required to use MFA.

D. None. These users should be treated the same as other users.

225. Which of the following provide a means of federating users from an existing organization? (Choose two.)

A. SAML 2.0

B. Web identities

C. LDAP

D. UML 2.0

226. Which of the following principles suggests ensuring that authenticated identities are only permitted to perform the most minimal set of functions necessary?

A. Principle of lowest privilege

B. Principle of least priority

C. Principle of least privilege

D. Principle of highest privilege

227. What is an AWS Organizations OU?

A. Orchestration unit

B. Organizational unit

C. Operational unit

D. Offer of urgency

228. What is an AWS Organizations SCP?

A. Service control policy

B. Service control permissions

C. Standard controlling permissions

D. Service conversion policy

229. To which of the following constructs is an AWS Organizations SCP applied?

A. To a service control policy

B. To an IAM role

C. To an organizational unit

D. To a SAML user store

230. Which of the following can be used to centrally control AWS services across multiple AWS accounts?

   A. A service control policy

   B. An organizational unit

   C. An LDAP user store

   D. IAM roles

231. What AWS service would you use for managing and enforcing policies for multiple AWS accounts?

   A. AWS Config

   B. AWS Trusted Advisor

   C. AWS Organizations

   D. IAM

232. Which of the following does AWS provide to increase privacy and control network access?

   A. Network firewalls built into Amazon VPC

   B. Encryption in transit with TLS across all services

   C. Connections that enable private and dedicated connections from an on-premises environment

   D. All of these

233. You have an application that uses S3 standard for storing large data. Your company wants to ensure that all data is encrypted at rest while avoiding adding work to your current development sprints. Which S3 encryption solution should you use?

   A. SSE-C

   B. SSE-S3

   C. SSE-KMS

   D. Amazon S3 Encryption Client

234. You are the architect of an application that allows users to send private messages back and forth. You want to ensure encryption of the messages when stored in S3 and a strong auditing trail in case of a breach. You also want to capture any failed attempts to access data. What Amazon encryption solution would you use?

   A. SSE-C

   B. SSE-S3

   C. SSE-KMS

   D. Amazon S3 Encryption Client

235. Your company has just hired three new developers. They need immediate access to a suite of AWS services. What is the best approach to giving these developers access?

  A. Give the developers the admin credentials and change the admin password when they are finished for the day.

  B. Create a new IAM user for each developer and assign the required permissions to each user.

  C. Create a new IAM user for each developer, create a single group with the required permissions, and assign each user to that group.

  D. Create a new SCP and assign the SCP to an OU with each user's credentials within that OU.

236. Your application requires a highly available storage solution. Further, the application will serve customers in the EU and must comply with EU privacy laws. What should you do to provide this storage?

  A. Create a new EC2 instance in EU-Central-1 and set up EBS volumes in a RAID configuration attached to that instance.

  B. Create a new S3 standard bucket in EU-West-1.

  C. Create a new Glacier vault in EU-South-1.

  D. Create a new Auto Scaling group in EU-West-1 with at least three EC2 instances, each with an attached Provisioned IOPS EBS volume.

237. Which of the following provides SSL for data in transit?

  A. S3 standard

  B. S3 One Zone-IA

  C. Glacier

  D. All of these

238. Which of the following does not provide encryption of data at rest?

  A. S3 standard

  B. S3 One Zone-IA

  C. Glacier

  D. All of these encrypt data at rest.

239. What is the AWS shared responsibility model?

  A. A model that defines which components AWS secures and which you as an AWS customer must secure

  B. A model that defines which components you secure and which components your customers must secure

  C. A model that defines how connections between offices or on-premises data centers and the cloud must work together to secure data that moves between the two

  D. A model that defines how the five pillars of the AWS well-architected framework interact

240. Which of the following is not one of the types of services that AWS offers, according to the shared responsibility model?

    A. Infrastructure services

    B. Managed services

    C. Containers services

    D. Abstracted services

241. For which of the following are you not responsible for security?

    A. Operating systems

    B. Credentials

    C. Virtualization infrastructure

    D. AMIs

242. Which of the following is used to allow EC2 instances to access S3 buckets?

    A. IAM role

    B. IAM policy

    C. IAM user

    D. AWS organizational unit

243. You have a task within a Docker container deployed via AWS ECS. The application cannot access data stored in an S3 bucket. What might be the problem? (Choose two.)

    A. The IAM role associated with the task doesn't have permissions to access S3.

    B. The task is not in a security group with inbound access allowed from S3.

    C. The task does not have access to an S3 VPC endpoint.

    D. There is no policy defined to allow ECS tasks to access S3.

244. What is the default security on a newly created S3 bucket?

    A. Read-only

    B. Read and write is permitted from EC2 instances in the same region.

    C. Completely private, reads and writes are disallowed.

    D. There is no policy defined to allow ECS tasks to access S3.

Chapter 4

Domain 4: Design Cost-Optimized Architectures

✓ **Subdomain: 4.1 Determine how to design cost-optimized storage.**

✓ **Subdomain: 4.2 Determine how to design cost-optimized compute.**

Review Questions

1. You have a data analysis application that uses high compute instances along with RDS to do biological analysis on large datasets. The computations are not time sensitive and can be run anytime throughout the day. However, because of the high compute resources required, the processing is quite expensive. What could you do to defray these costs? (Choose two.)

    A. Purchase reserved instances and pay entirely up front for the instance usage charges.

    B. Use the spot market, setting a bid price lower than the current on-demand pricing.

    C. Lower the instance class to a less costly class and allow the processing to run longer at lower per-instance costs.

    D. Contact AWS and ask for discounted instance pricing based on your recurring usage.

2. Which of the following are valid payment options for reserved instances? (Choose two.)

    A. Actual usage pricing

    B. Predictive pricing

    C. All up-front pricing

    D. Nothing up-front pricing

3. How do you move a reserved instance from one region to another?

    A. Shut the instance down, change its region via the console or CLI, and restart the instance.

    B. Contact your AWS billing resource to manually move the instance and its associated billing.

    C. Make a snapshot of the instance, copy the snapshot to the new region, and start the instance from the snapshot.

    D. You cannot move reserved instances across regions.

4. Which of the following allows you the least expensive access to compute resources?

    A. On-demand instances

    B. Reserved instances

    C. Spot instances

    D. Dedicated hosts

5. Which of the following are not reasons to select an on-demand instance? (Choose two.)

    A. Applications with short-term, spiky workloads

    B. Applications that have flexible start and end times

    C. Applications with steady-state usage

    D. Applications being developed or tested on EC2 for the first time

6. Which of the following are reasons to select a spot instance? (Choose two.)

  A. Applications with short-term, spiky workloads

  B. Applications that have flexible start and end times

  C. Applications with steady-state usage

  D. Applications that are only feasible at very low compute prices

7. Which of the following are not reasons to select a reserved instance? (Choose two.)

  A. Applications that may require reserved capacity

  B. Applications with steady-state usage

  C. Users with urgent computing needs for large amounts of additional capacity

  D. Users that cannot make any up-front payment or long-term commitment

8. Which of the following are reasons to select the S3 standard storage class? (Choose two.)

  A. Need for high durability

  B. Need for highest available throughput

  C. Infrequent access of objects

  D. Objects can easily be re-created if lost.

9. You are the architect for a web application that exists on a cluster of EC2 instances all within an Auto Scaling group. During periods of high activity, the group scales up—adding instances—and then quickly scales back down. However, this occurs multiple times within a two-hour window, incurring significant costs. How could you reduce costs while ensuring that demand is still met? (Choose two.)

  A. Modify the Auto Scaling group's cool-down timers.

  B. Modify the Auto Scaling group to use scheduled scaling.

  C. Lower the CloudWatch alarm threshold that causes the Auto Scaling group to scale up.

  D. Modify the CloudWatch alarm period that causes the Auto Scaling group to scale down.

10. Your company needs a storage solution that can support millions of customers accessing billing data. The data should be instantly accessible for users, but individual bills are not accessed that often. What is the most cost-efficient storage for this use case?

  A. Glacier with expedited retrieval

  B. S3 with Transfer Acceleration

  C. Standard S3

  D. S3-IA

11. Is the S3-IA storage class less expensive than S3?

  A. Yes

  B. No

  C. Their costs are identical.

  D. It depends on how the storage class is used.

12. You have a website running on a fleet of EC2 instances behind an ELB. You also have an Auto Scaling group running across multiple availability zones. The instances are serving files from an EFS file system, but you are incurring lag and significant cost from serving these files from disk over and over. What would you recommend as a solution for reducing costs while still handling high traffic without degradation?

    A. Move the files into S3 standard.

    B. Use Elastic Transcoder to reduce the file sizes.

    C. Cache the files using CloudFront.

    D. Use reserved EC2 instances instead of on-demand instances.

13. You have a large archive of documents that must be backed up. The documents will be accessed very infrequently, if at all. However, when the documents are accessed, they must be delivered within 10 minutes of a retrieval request. What is the most cost-effective option for storing these documents?

    A. S3

    B. S3-IA

    C. Glacier

    D. Glacier with expedited retrieval

14. Your application has a 200 GB database running on an EC2 instance. You cannot move the database to RDS because of a custom spatial plug-in. The application is currently peaking in the morning and the evening, but the peaks are small and usage throughout the day is minimal. You need to ensure solid performance but keep costs low. What storage type would you use?

    A. EFS

    B. EBS with a General Purpose SSD

    C. EBS with a provisioned IOPS SSD

    D. EBS with a magnetic HDD

15. Which EBS volume type is most appropriate for use with a large database workload?

    A. EBS with a throughput optimized HDD

    B. EBS with a General Purpose SSD

    C. EBS with a provisioned IOPS SSD

    D. EBS with a magnetic HDD

16. Which of the following is the least expensive EBS volume type?

    A. Throughput optimized HDD

    B. General Purpose SSD

    C. Provisioned IOPS SSD

    D. Cold HDD

17. Your application currently stores all its data on EBS volumes. You want to ensure that these volumes are backed up durably. However, you also want to use as few different managed services as possible in order to keep backup costs low. What option would you recommend?

    A. Take regular EBS snapshots manually.

    B. Set up a Lambda function to take EBS snapshots and trigger the function through CloudWatch alarms.

    C. Create a script to copy the EBS data to S3 and run it on an EC2 instance.

    D. Mirror data across two EBS volumes.

18. You are the architect for a highly available and highly scalable accounting application. All transaction records in the application's data stores must be available for immediate retrieval for three months, but then they should be purged to reduce storage costs. How can you most easily address this requirement?

    A. Store the transaction records on EBS and delete the volume after three months.

    B. Store the transaction records in S3 and use lifecycle management to delete the records after three months.

    C. Store the transaction records in Glacier and use lifecycle management to delete the records after three months.

    D. Store the transaction records in EBS and use lifecycle management to delete the records after three months.

19. You have heavy load on an RDS data instance. You want to avoid the overhead and cost of upgrading the instance to a larger instance size. What other options should you consider? (Choose two.)

    A. RDS read replicas

    B. RDS Multi-AZ

    C. ElastiCache

    D. Kinesis

20. You are in charge of storage for large datasets at a predictive analytics firm. You are tasked with minimizing storage costs. You need to store data 30–59 days old in a storage class that makes the data immediately available and data older than 60 days in a class that makes the data available within 10 hours. You want to use the least expensive classes available. Which two storage classes would you choose? (Choose two.)

    A. S3 standard

    B. S3 Infrequent Access

    C. S3 RRS

    D. Glacier

21. You want to optimize performance and cost of your application by creating a placement group rather than hosting separate copies of your application in multiple availability zones. Across how many availability zones can a placement group span?

    A. One

    B. One or more

    C. Two or more

    D. Placement groups are not in availability zones.

22. Across how many availability zones can a spread placement group be stretched?

    A. One

    B. One or more

    C. Two or more

    D. Placement groups are not in availability zones.

23. How many instances can run in a single availability zone for a spread placement group?

    A. One

    B. Five

    C. Seven

    D. Nine

24. Which of the following are advantages of a spread placement group over using non-grouped instances? (Choose two.)

    A. A spread placement group can span peered VPCs in the same region.

    B. A spread placement group is less expensive than the same number of on-demand instances not in a group.

    C. A spread placement group allows instances to talk with negligible network lag.

    D. A spread placement group reduces IO in an instance within that group.

25. Which of the following statements about placement groups is false?

    A. A spread placement group can span peered VPCs in the same region.

    B. A clustered placement group has instances all in a single availability zone.

    C. A spread placement group allows instances to talk across regions without network lag.

    D. A clustered placement group involves fewer availability zones than a spread placement group.

26. Which of the following actions incur costs within AWS? (Choose two.)

    A. Data ingress from the Internet

    B. Data egress to the Internet

    C. Transferring data across regions

    D. Transferring data from one instance to another within the same availability zone

27. Which of the following costs the least?
    A. Retrieving a file from S3 to a local desktop client
    B. An instance retrieving data from S3 in the same region
    C. Uploading a file to S3 from a local desktop client
    D. An instance retrieving data from S3 in a different region

28. Which of the following costs the least?
    A. Retrieving a file from S3 to a local desktop client
    B. An instance retrieving data from another instance in the same availability zone
    C. An instance storing data in S3 in a different region
    D. An instance retrieving data from S3 in a different region

29. Which of the following might help reduce data transfer costs? (Choose two.)
    A. Set up CloudFront to cache content.
    B. Ensure that any instances communicating with other instances in the same region have private IP addresses.
    C. Set up an RDS instance with read replicas.
    D. Set up S3 buckets with versioning.

30. Which of the following is not a level of AWS support?
    A. Developer
    B. Free tier
    C. Enterprise
    D. Business

31. Which of the following is reduced as part of AWS's total cost of ownership approach?
    A. Developer salaries
    B. DevOps salaries
    C. Capital expenditures
    D. Organizational head count

32. Which of the following payment models does AWS employ to reduce total cost of ownership?
    A. Pay up front
    B. Pay-as-you-go
    C. Pay after use
    D. Quarterly pay

33. Which of the following is not a key tenet of the AWS pricing philosophy?
    A. Pay-as-you-go
    B. Pay less when you reserve.
    C. Pay less per unit by using more.
    D. Pay more only when AWS grows.

34. Which of the following is not a pricing model for instances?

    A. On demand

    B. Reserved

    C. Migration only

    D. Spot instance

35. When calculating total cost of ownership, what instance pricing model does AWS suggest using?

    A. On demand

    B. Reserved

    C. Dedicated hardware

    D. Spot instance

36. How does the cost of standard reserved instances compare with the cost of on-demand instances?

    A. Standard reserved instances cost significantly less than on-demand instances.

    B. Standard reserved instances cost about the same as on-demand instances.

    C. Standard reserved instances cost significantly more than on-demand instances.

    D. Standard reserved instances cost a little bit less than on-demand instances.

37. Which of the following is not a valid payment option for reserved instances?

    A. No upfront

    B. Partial upfront

    C. Half upfront

    D. All upfront

38. Which of the following is the least expensive payment model for reserved instances?

    A. No upfront

    B. Partial upfront

    C. All upfront

    D. They are all the same.

39. Which of the following are valid terms for reserved instances? (Choose two.)

    A. Six months

    B. One year

    C. Two years

    D. Three years

40. Which of the following are valid pricing models for EC2 instances? (Choose two.)

    A. Spot instances

    B. Spot market

    C. Dedicated hosts

    D. All upfront

41. Which instance type is ideal for an application that has a flexible start and end time?
    A. Spot instances
    B. On-demand instances
    C. Dedicated hosts
    D. Reserved instances

42. Which instance type is ideal for an application that suffers numerous spikes in usage at unpredictable times?
    A. Spot instances
    B. On-demand instances
    C. Dedicated hosts
    D. Reserved instances

43. Which instance type is ideal for an application that has a long-running compute job that cannot be interrupted but also suffers from significant fluctuations in usage patterns?
    A. Spot instances
    B. On-demand instances
    C. Dedicated hosts
    D. Reserved instances

44. Which of the following are valid ways to purchase dedicated hosts? (Choose two.)
    A. On-demand hourly
    B. All upfront
    C. On layaway
    D. As a reservation

45. Which of the following are reasons to consider reserved instances? (Choose two.)
    A. You are running an application that involves lots of short-running compute jobs.
    B. You are running an application with steady-state usage.
    C. Your business is guaranteed to need cloud compute for at least the next 18 months.
    D. You are looking to minimize commitments to AWS.

46. Which of the following is not a reason to consider spot instances?
    A. Your applications have flexible start and end times.
    B. Your applications can only run if compute costs are low because of CPU utilization.
    C. You expect to have significant compute needs and potentially a need for lots of additional capacity.
    D. You expect usage to increase dramatically in the evenings and need to support that usage.

47. You have been brought in to introduce an organization to the cloud. They have several applications ideal for cloud hosting but do not want to make any up-front commitments. Further, they are concerned that the cloud will be "unreliable" so you need to ensure that applications run smoothly. What instance types would you recommend?

   A. Spot instances

   B. On-demand instances

   C. Dedicated hosts

   D. Reserved instances

48. Which of the following are benefits to spot instances? (Choose two.)

   A. Applications can be paused and later resumed.

   B. Costs are reduced compared to on-demand pricing.

   C. The same hardware will be used for the life of an application.

   D. They can handle spikes in usage without issue.

49. Which of the following offers the lowest pricing for storage (per GB)?

   A. S3 standard

   B. S3-IA

   C. S3 One Zone-IA

   D. Amazon Glacier

50. Which of the following is not an actual S3 storage class?

   A. S3-SSE

   B. S3 Standard-IA

   C. S3 RRS

   D. Amazon Glacier

51. Which of the following would not incur a charge?

   A. Distributing data via S3 signed URLs to an Internet client in the same region

   B. Distributing data via CloudFront to an Internet client in a different region

   C. Uploading data to S3 via a user's web interface

   D. Transferring data from an EC2 instance to an instance in another region

52. Which of the following would not incur a charge?

   A. Transferring data from S3 to CloudFront

   B. Distributing data via CloudFront to an Internet client in a different region

   C. Transferring data from an EC2 instance to an instance in another region

   D. Importing data to S3 via Transfer Acceleration

53. What is the AWS free tier?

    A. A platform for experimenting with AWS that can never be in production

    B. A tier of AWS that allows limited access to AWS services at no cost

    C. A class of EC2 instances that never cost anything for unlimited compute

    D. A prepackaged suite of AWS services that can be used for web hosting at no cost

54. What is the AWS marketplace?

    A. A market for products, many of which can run on the AWS free tier

    B. A market for prebuilt AMIs beyond the standard AWS offerings

    C. A market for plug-ins and trials of paid third-party AWS services

    D. All of these

55. What of the following services is available in AWS free tier?

    A. DynamoDB

    B. AWS Lambda

    C. SNS and SQS

    D. All of these

56. Which of the following is an AWS support plan?

    A. Standard

    B. Free

    C. Small teams

    D. Enterprise

57. Which of the following AWS support plans offer 24/7 support? (Choose two.)

    A. Basic

    B. Developer

    C. Business

    D. Enterprise

58. What is AWS Trusted Advisor?

    A. An AWS security service

    B. An online resource to help you reduce cost

    C. A logging tool to help you detect intrusions

    D. A performance tool to help you correctly size your Auto Scaling groups

59. How many core Trusted Advisor checks does the Trusted Advisor tool provide?

    A. Three

    B. Four

    C. Five

    D. Nine

60. Which of the following might be a recommendation from Trusted Advisor? (Choose two.)
    A. Turn on MFA for the root account.
    B. Turn off global access to an S3 bucket.
    C. Turn on Transfer Acceleration for S3.
    D. Turn on MFA Delete for S3.

61. Which of the following is not an area in which Trusted Advisor makes recommendations?
    A. S3 bucket permissions
    B. IAM usage
    C. RDS public snapshots
    D. DNS usage

62. Which of the following is not a category for which Trusted Advisor makes recommendations?
    A. Security
    B. Scalability
    C. Service limits
    D. Fault tolerance

63. Which of the following are categories for which Trusted Advisor makes recommendations? (Choose two.)
    A. Performance
    B. Auto Scaling
    C. Caching
    D. Security

64. Which of the following might be an area about which Trusted Advisor makes recommendations? (Choose two.)
    A. Idle load balancers
    B. Incorrect S3 storage class
    C. No MFA on root account
    D. Underuse of DNS records

65. Which of the following are recommendations AWS makes to help you control your AWS costs? (Choose two.)
    A. Right-size your services to meet capacity at the lowest cost.
    B. Save money by reserving.
    C. Save money with on-demand resources.
    D. Buy high capacity and serve low capacity.

66. Which of the following might be a means by which you could decrease AWS costs in any standard application stack?

   A. Use DynamoDB instead of RDS.

   B. Use Route 53 instead of non-AWS registrars.

   C. Use the spot market.

   D. Use dedicated host instances.

67. What is AWS Cost Explorer?

   A. An analytics tool for evaluating instance usage

   B. An analytics tool for evaluating RDS usage

   C. An analytics tool for managing AWS costs over time

   D. An analytics tool for managing application deployments

68. You want to anticipate your costs over the next year. Which of the following tools would you use?

   A. AWS Trusted Advisor

   B. AWS Cost Explorer

   C. AWS Cost Manager

   D. AWS Savings Advisor

69. You want to determine how your instance class choices are affecting your overall AWS spending. Which tool would help?

   A. AWS Trusted Advisor

   B. AWS Cost Explorer

   C. AWS Auto Scaling groups

   D. AWS CloudTrail

70. You want to set limits on how much is spent monthly on S3 storage. Which of the following tools would be helpful?

   A. AWS Trusted Advisor

   B. AWS Cost Explorer

   C. AWS Budgets

   D. AWS CloudFormation

71. You want to cut off all access to your S3 buckets when a certain cost threshold is reached. Which tool allows you to do this?

   A. AWS Trusted Advisor

   B. AWS Cost Explorer

   C. AWS Budgets

   D. None of these

72. You need to produce media files optimized for various device types to optimize costs associated with transferring and viewing media on those devices. What AWS service would you use?

A. SWF

B. Workspaces

C. Elastic Transcoder

D. Cost Explorer

73. You want to reduce the maintenance costs of supporting Oracle on a fleet of EC2 instances. What service is well suited for offloading maintenance costs for Oracle database hosting?

A. RDS

B. EMR

C. SWF

D. Redshift

74. You want to delay the cost of hiring a large DevOps team while prototyping application hosting in the cloud. What service allows you to deploy your code with minimal oversight?

A. Elastic Beanstalk

B. CloudFormation

C. Elastic Transcoder

D. JSON

75. You are tasked with reducing cost in an organization that does several new application deployments every week. The company has a common stack of resources but is spending time each deployment re-creating this stack. What would help you reduce initial setup and deployment costs?

A. Elastic Beanstalk

B. CloudFormation

C. AWS Trusted Adviso.

D. Application load balancers

76. You need to transfer 50 TB of data into S3 and want to avoid lengthy network exchanges and network saturation. What option would provide you with inexpensive data transfer at a large scale?

A. Storage Gateway

B. S3 Transfer Acceleration

C. Glacier

D. Snowball

77. You want to take advantage of a large data store on premises that is already in use. How can you use this local storage while still interfacing with an additional cloud-based storage system and cloud-hosted EC2 instances?

   A.   Storage Gateway

   B.   S3 Transfer Acceleration

   C.   Glacier

   D.   Snowball

78. You need to transfer several petabytes of data into AWS at the lowest possible costs. What AWS services could help?

   A.   Large Data Transfer Service

   B.   S3 Transfer Acceleration

   C.   Snowball

   D.   CloudFront

79. You need an analytics solution to perform business intelligence on your large data store. What AWS managed service can provide you with OLAP that reduces cost at scale?

   A.   RDS

   B.   Oracle on an EC2 fleet with provisioned IOPS EBS volumes

   C.   Memcache

   D.   Redshift

80. You are currently running a fleet of 12 EC2 instances and processing large datasets that are uploaded by users. However, the cost of maintaining these instances is increasing, and the maintenance of the processing code is also growing. What AWS managed service would allow you to reduce these costs and still process large datasets?

   A.   EMR

   B.   Memcache

   C.   CloudFront

   D.   BigData Processing Service

81. You are in charge of building a business intelligence application that can handle multiple data sources and perform analytics at a large scale. Which of the following services and tools would allow you to build a cost-effective solution? (Choose two.)

   A.   QuickSight

   B.   Provisioned IOPS EBS volumes

   C.   EC2 instances

   D.   Redshift

82. You have been tasked with combining several data sources into a single (optionally ephemeral) data store that you can then perform analysis on. You currently have data in RDS, two DynamoDB instances, and multiple S3 buckets. What is the most cost-effective approach to handling this task?

   A. A fleet of EC2 instances with throughput optimized SSD EBS volumes

   B. A combination of CloudWatch, Lambda, and custom code

   C. Redshift

   D. QuickSight

83. Which of the following is the least expensive option for long-term data archival?

   A. EFS

   B. EBS snapshots

   C. Glacier

   D. Redshift

84. Your company is paying a high cost for a consultant whose only job is the provisioning of resources for new cloud deployments. What AWS service would allow you to reduce this expenditure and move the consulting into more of a business-serving capacity?

   A. Elastic Beanstalk

   B. CloudTrail

   C. CloudShift

   D. CloudFormation

85. You have been tasked with reducing the costs associated with a large fleet of EC2 instances that currently run several custom processes. These processes collect and collate data from a number of streaming data sources outside of your network. What AWS managed service could help replace these instances?

   A. CloudFront

   B. SDM

   C. Kinesis

   D. CloudFormation

86. You have been tasked with reducing the cost of a large group of EC2 instances that each serves a single process. The process is fired off when a user initiates it through a web interface. Because these processes are initiated often, a large fleet of EC2 instances is kept active to serve the requests, incurring significant monthly costs. What managed service could help you reduce the costs of these always-running instances?

   A. Lambda

   B. CloudFront

   C. Kinesis

   D. CloudFormation

87. You are in charge of a cloud migration from an on-premises data center to AWS. There are extensive software products used to monitor the on-premises applications, and you want to reduce the recurring costs associated with this monitoring. What AWS service would be ideal for this task?

    A. CloudTrail

    B. CloudMonitor

    C. AppMonitor

    D. CloudWatch

88. You are in charge of a cloud migration from an on-premises data center to AWS. The system currently has a number of custom scripts that process system and application logs for auditing purposes. What AWS managed service could you use to replace these scripts and reduce the need for instances to run these custom processes?

    A. CloudTrail

    B. CloudMonitor

    C. AppMonitor

    D. CloudWatch

89. You are the architect in charge of designing a database-driven application suite. As part of the project, you need to migrate a large Oracle database instance into the cloud. Further, you are migrating from Oracle to PostgreSQL. How would you most effectively accomplish this migration with the least expenditure?

    A. Copy the Oracle data to Snowball, send the data to AWS, move it into S3, and then import the data into PostgreSQL in RDS.

    B. Create an RDS Oracle instance in AWS, migrate the data from the existing Oracle instance to the new RDS instance, and then convert the RDS instance to PostgreSQL.

    C. Use the Database Migration Service to import the Oracle data directly into a new PostgreSQL instance.

    D. Create a local PostgreSQL instance, migrate the data locally from Oracle to PostgreSQL, and then move the PostgreSQL instance into AWS.

90. You need to choose a scalable, cost-effective, and highly durable solution for storing flat files. What AWS service would you use?

    A. S3

    B. Kinesis

    C. DynamoDB

    D. Aurora

91. You have been tasked with replacing a legacy LDAP directory server that manages users, groups, and permissions with a cloud-based solution in order to reduce maintenance costs for the current directory server. What AWS service should you investigate?

    A. IAM

    B. Cognito

    C. AWS Organizations

    D. AWS Directory Server

92. You have been tasked with replacing a legacy LDAP directory server that manages users, groups, and permissions and provides single sign-on capabilities with a cloud-based solution in order to reduce maintenance costs for the current directory server and codebase. What AWS services should you investigate? (Choose two.)

    A. IAM

    B. Cognito

    C. AWS Organizations

    D. AWS Directory Server

93. You are new on a project that makes heavy use of AWS. Your first priority is to reduce costs and identify security risks. What tool could you use to scan the existing environment and set initial priorities for change?

    A. CloudTrail

    B. Trusted Advisor

    C. AWS Organizations

    D. AWS Directory Server

94. You are migrating a large on-premises application suite to AWS. Your company has made a significant investment in Chef for configuration and management and doesn't want to lose the investment in time and money that the Chef tool represents. How could you preserve this functionality and keep costs low?

    A. CloudTrail

    B. CloudWatch

    C. OpsWorks

    D. Service Catalog

Chapter 5

Domain 5: Define Operationally Excellent Architectures

Review Questions

1. How many times will a message be delivered when using a standard SQS queue?

   A. Once and only once

   B. At least once

   C. Once for each request of the relevant message in the queue

   D. The answer is application dependent.

2. Which of the following services allow you to access the underlying operating system? (Choose two.)

   A. RDS

   B. EC2

   C. EMR

   D. DynamoDB

3. You are using an SQS queue in your web application. You are able to confirm that messages in the queue are being picked up by application instances for processing, but then nothing happens for over 12 hours. Then, after that period of time, the message appears in the queue again and processing restarts. What could be occurring?

   A. The SQS queue has a visibility timeout that is set too high. The timeout should be reduced so that application instances can process the message more quickly.

   B. SQS messages expire every 12 hours and must be reentered into the queue. The time that the message is invisible triggers the queue to ask for and receive the message from the original sender.

   C. Processing is failing, or not completing, in the application instance. The message disappears because the SQS queue keeps it "invisible" for 12 hours while it is being processed. The message is then returned to the queue for processing if not handled prior to that timeout.

   D. Your SQS queue needs to be restarted; it is likely not correctly queuing messages. The polling interval is also set too high, causing the long lack of visibility of the message.

4. Which of the following is a valid method of performing actions on an EBS snapshot?

   A. Use the AWS console with a username and password.

   B. Use the AWS CLI with an application key.

   C. Use the AWS REST APIs with an application key.

   D. All of the above

   E. None of the above

5. Which of the following is most like a mailing list?

    A. SQS

    B. SNS

    C. SWF

    D. S3

6. In which of the following managed services are messages not pushed?

    A. SQS

    B. SNS

    C. SWF

    D. Redshift

7. In which of the following managed services can messages be pulled by an application?

    A. SWF

    B. SQS

    C. SNS

    D. S3

8. Which of the following managed services guarantees single assignment of a message?

    A. S3

    B. SQS

    C. SNS

    D. SWF

9. Which of the following managed services calls the messages it receives tasks?

    A. S3

    B. SWF

    C. SNS

    D. SQS

10. Which of the following managed services calls the messages it receives notifications?

    A. S3

    B. SWF

    C. SNS

    D. SQS

11. Which of the following managed services calls the messages it receives "messages"?

    A. S3

    B. SWF

    C. SNS

    D. None of these

12. Which of the following managed services coordinates activities between different applications?

    A. S3

    B. SNS

    C. SWF

    D. SQS

13. What does SWF stand for?

    A. Simple Workflow Foundation

    B. Simple Workflow Service

    C. Sequential Workflow Service

    D. Synchronous Workflow Foundation

14. What services are suitable for running compute-intensive custom scripts? (Choose two.)

    A. EC2

    B. S3

    C. Redshift

    D. ECS

15. Which AWS service is ideal for hosting a website while requiring the least amount of AWS staff and knowledge?

    A. S3 website hosting

    B. Amazon Lightsail

    C. EC2

    D. ECS

16. You have a registered AMI using an EBS volume as a root device, created from a volume snapshot. However, you have detected malicious code running in the EBS volume and want to remove the AMI and delete the EBS volume and its snapshot. What steps are required? (Choose two.)

    A. Immediately delete the EBS volume snapshot.

    B. Immediately deregister the AMI.

    C. After the EBS volume has been deleted, deregister the AMI.

    D. After the AMI has been deregistered, remove the AMI, and delete the EBS volume and its snapshot.

17. Which of the following AWS CLI commands is used to operate upon EBS volumes?

    A. `aws ec2 [command]`

    B. `aws ebs [command]`

    C. `aws instance [command]`

    D. You cannot operate upon EBS volumes directly from the AWS CLI.

18. You have a website running at `applestoapples.net`. However, many of your users have mistakenly entered in `applestoapples.com` as the URL in their browser. To correct this, you've recently purchased the additional domain `applestoapples.com` and now want to point all requests to this domain to `applestoapples.net`. Which DNS record set would you use?

    A. MX

    B. AAAA

    C. CNAME

    D. A

19. Your website has mostly static content, but you are adding a new section driven by an EC2 instance fleet behind an Elastic Load Balancer. You want to create a subdomain and direct all traffic to that subdomain toward the ELB. Which DNS record set would you use?

    A. CNAME

    B. AAAA

    C. SOA

    D. MX

20. Your domain is hosted and managed by Route 53. You want to create a new subdomain and point it to a fleet of EC2 instances behind an application load balancer. What is the best approach to this?

    A. Create an A record and configure it as an alias to the ALB.

    B. Create a CNAME record pointed at the URL of the ALB.

    C. Create an A record pointed at the IP address of the ALB.

    D. Set the ALB to send a redirect header to clients with the IP addresses of the currently active EC2 instances.

21. Does Route 53 supports zone apex records?

    A. Yes, for all domains

    B. Yes, but only for domains hosted on AWS

    C. Yes, but only for services hosted on AWS

    D. No

22. Which of the following statements are false? (Choose two.)

    A. Route 53 does not allow aliases for naked domain names.

    B. Route 53 supports zone apex records.

    C. Route 53 allows aliases for domains hosted on AWS.

    D. Route 53 only supports zone apex records for AWS-hosted services.

23. Which of the following statements are true? (Choose two.)

    A. Route 53 supports Auto Scaling groups.

    B. Route 53 automatically configures DNS health checks for registered domains.

    C. Route 53 automatically sets up Auto Scaling groups for services to which it points.

    D. Route 53 is automatically highly available.

24. How many domain names can you manage using Route 53?

    A. 50

    B. 100, but you can raise that limit by contacting AWS support.

    C. Unlimited

    D. 50, but you can raise that limit by contacting AWS support.

25. Which of the following is the best approach to accessing an RDS instance to troubleshoot operating system problems?

    A. SSH

    B. RDP

    C. SFTP

    D. None of these

26. Which of the following are true about VPC peering? (Choose two.)

    A. A VPC peering connection is a networking connection between two VPCs within a single region.

    B. A VPC peering connection is a VPN-based connection.

    C. A VPC peering connection can help facilitate data transfer and file sharing.

    D. Peered VPCs can exist in different regions.

27. You have two VPCs paired across two different regions. What is another name for this type of connection?

    A. Inter-VPC peering connection

    B. Inter-region VPC peering connection

    C. Inter-VPC region connection

    D. Multi-region peering connection

28. Which of the following statements about peered VPCs is false?

    A. Both VPCs do not need to be within the same region.

    B. Both VPCs do not need to be in the same AWS account.

    C. Both VPCs will automatically have routing set up when the connection is created.

    D. Traffic can flow in both directions between peered VPCs by default.

29. Which of the following statements about peered VPCs is true?

    A. Both VPCs need to be within the same region.

    B. Both VPCs need to be in the same AWS account.

    C. Each VPC must use a unique security group.

    D. The two VPCs cannot have overlapping CIDR blocks.

30. What kind of relationship is a VPC peering connection?

    A. One-to-one between subnets

    B. One-to-one between VPCs

    C. One-to-many between subnets

    D. One-to-many between VPCs

31. VPC A is peered to both VPC B and VPC C. How can you allow traffic to flow from VPC B to VPC C?

    A. You can't; transitive peering relationships are not allowed in AWS.

    B. You must enable route forwarding in VPC A.

    C. You must peer VPC B to VPC C.

    D. You must enable route forwarding on VPC B.

32. VPC C has an overlapping CIDR block with VPC D. Given that, which of the following statements are true? (Choose two.)

    A. VPC C and VPC D can be peered as is.

    B. VPC C and VPC D cannot be peered as is.

    C. To peer VPC C and VPC D, you must remove the overlap in their CIDR block.

    D. To peer VPC C and VPC D, you must switch one to use IPv6 addresses.

33. How many peering connections are allowed between two VPCs?

    A. One

    B. Two

    C. One for each subnet in each VPC

    D. One for each NACL associated with each VPC

34. How many peering connections can a single VPC be a part of?

    A. One

    B. Unlimited, within AWS overall account limits

    C. One for each subnet in each VPC

    D. One for each NACL associated with each VPC

35. How does AWS facilitate transitive peering VPC relationships?

    A. Transitive VPC relationships are only allowed if a bastion host is used.

    B. Transitive VPC relationships are only allowed if a hub-and-spoke network model is used.

    C. It does not; transitive VPC peering is not allowed in AWS.

    D. It uses IPv4 for connection from a source VPC to a hub VPC and IPv6 from the hub to the origin VPC.

36. How does AWS support IPv6 communication in a VPC peering relationship? (Choose two.)

    A. AWS does not support IPv6 communication in VPC peering.

    B. You must associate IPv6 addresses with both VPCs and then set up routing to use these addresses.

    C. You must associate IPv6 addresses with both VPCs and then set up a security group to use these addresses.

    D. You must make sure the two VPCs are in the same region.

37. Which of the following are advantages of launching instances into a VPC as opposed to EC2-Classic? (Choose two.)

    A. You can assign multiple IP addresses to your instances.

    B. Your instances automatically run on multi-tenant hardware.

    C. You can attach multiple network interfaces to your instances.

    D. Your network is flat instead of layered.

38. Which of the following are differences between the default VPC and a custom VPC? (Choose two.)

    A. Default VPCs have an internet gateway but custom VPCs do not.

    B. Custom VPCs have public subnets but default VPCs do not.

    C. Custom VPCs have an internet gateway but default VPCs do not.

    D. Default VPCs have public subnets but custom VPCs do not.

39. How does the default VPC make instances in its public subnets available to Internet traffic? (Choose two.)

    A. Through a default routing table that provides routing to the Internet

    B. Through a virtual private gateway

    C. Through a default security group that provides access out to the Internet

    D. Through an internet gateway

40. Which of the following is assigned to instances launched into non-default subnets?

    A. A private IPv6 address

    B. A public IPv4 address

    C. A private IPv4 address

    D. A public IPv6 address

41. You want to provide Internet access for an instance in a non-default subnet. What do you need to do? (Choose two.)

    A. Assign a private IP address to the instance.

    B. Assign a public IP address to the instance.

    C. Attach an internet gateway to the VPC in which the subnet resides.

    D. Attach a NAT instance to the subnet.

42. What technology can you use to provide single sign-on to the AWS management console?

    A. JSON

    B. CloudFormation

    C. YAML

    D. SAML

43. You have created a new user in IAM. What default permissions does that user have?

    A. Read access to all AWS services

    B. Read and write access to all AWS services

    C. No access to any AWS services

    D. Read access only to the IAM service

44. What does IAM stand for?

    A. Interoperative Access Management

    B. Identity and Access Management

    C. Independent Access Management

    D. Identity and Authorization Management

45. You have created a new IAM user and created their sign-in URL. You give the user their URL. What else will they need to log in to the AWS management console? (Choose two.)

    A. Their username

    B. Their access key ID

    C. Their password

    D. Their secret access key

46. Which of the following IAM groups will allow users within it to interact with all AWS services?

    A. Administrator

    B. Power User

    C. The default IAM permissions provide this level of access.

    D. Support User

47. You have created a new IAM user and given the credentials to the user. However, she still is unable to log in to the AWS management console. What might the problem be?

A. You have not enabled Multi-Factor Authentication.

B. You have not enabled the User Login policy.

C. You have not provided the user her access key ID.

D. You have not provided the user her customized sign-in link.

48. You have been tasked with building an application that provides backend servicing for a mobile game with millions of users. Which of the following services might you use to receive and process the messages that the mobile clients send?

A. EC2, Mobile SDK

B. Amazon Kinesis, Mobile SDK

C. Amazon Kinesis, RDS

D. EC2, Lambda

49. Which of the following is required to set up a new AWS account for a company new to AWS?

A. Company name

B. Company email

C. Company account-holder username

D. Company URL

50. Which of the following AWS-defined IAM policies offer read and write access to the S3 and EC2 services? (Choose two.)

A. Administrator

B. Network Administrator

C. Support User

D. Power User

51. What does AWS call a document that defines a set of one or more permissions?

A. Program unit

B. Organizational unit

C. Policy

D. Group

52. What does the AWS service abbreviated as ECS stand for?

A. Elastic Compute Service

B. Elastic Container Service

C. Elastic Computer Service

D. Encapsulated Container Service

53. Which of the following are advantages of using containers for applications in AWS compared to using EC2 instances? (Choose two.)

    A. You can scale applications automatically.

    B. You can run larger applications in a container.

    C. You can reduce the startup time of applications.

    D. You can avoid having to explicitly manage and provision servers.

54. Which of the following sets of services are used in a typical AWS container stack?

    A. ECR, ECS, EC2

    B. ECS, EMR, EC2

    C. Fargate, ECS, S3

    D. ECR, ECS, S3

55. Which of the following services is typically associated with ECS?

    A. EMR

    B. S3

    C. ECR

    D. ECC

56. Which of the following are good reasons to consider using containers in AWS for your applications? (Choose two.)

    A. You want to reduce overall cost.

    B. You want to more effectively use your existing compute instances.

    C. You have limited resources for managing your existing EC2 instances.

    D. You need to scale up and down your applications.

57. Which of the following are differences between container-based applications and Lambda-based ones? (Choose two.)

    A. Containers scale based on load and usage; Lambda scales based on events.

    B. Containers live on underlying compute instances; Lambda code does not.

    C. Containers are not as highly scalable as Lambda.

    D. Containers can run entire application stacks; Lambda can only run isolated chunks of code.

Chapter

6

Practice Test

1. You are responsible for optimizing performance of a movie streaming website. Currently, you are working on the search functionality and have discovered that anytime the library database of titles is searched, the load on the database is reaching peak levels. Your current architecture consists of a PostgreSQL database on an extra-large instance. How would you update your architecture to better handle the load? (Choose two.)

   A. Re-create the database instance on a larger instance using EBS volumes with provisioned IOPS as the volume type.

   B. Add an RDS Multi-AZ setup to increase the read performance of the media library database.

   C. Add an ElastiCache store to cache data because searches will often return common data over multiple reads.

   D. Shard the database into multiple copies installed on multiple instances.

2. Which of the following are engines used by ElastiCache?

   A. reddit, memcached

   B. redis, memcached

   C. Sharding, redis

   D. memcached, Redshift

3. Which of the following are AWS-supported solutions for encrypting data at rest when that data is objects stored in S3 buckets? (Choose two.)

   A. ElastiCache for memcached

   B. AWS Key Management Service

   C. Customer-provided keys

   D. AWS Encryptic

4. You have been brought into a new organization with over 20 different AWS accounts. You are tasked with improving the cost management of the organization and want to recommend the use of AWS Organizations and the consolidated billing feature. Which of the following are advantages of consolidated billing that you could use to support your case? (Choose two.)

   A. Multiple accounts can be combined and, through that combination, receive discounts that may reduce the total cost of all the accounts.

   B. Traffic between accounts will not be subject to data transfer charges if those accounts are all in AWS Organizations.

   C. All accounts in AWS Organizations will receive a 5% billing reduction in consolidated billing.

   D. All accounts can be tracked individually and through a single tool.

5. You are tasked with improving security at an organization that has recently begun using the cloud. It has five developers, a financial manager, and two support engineers. Currently, all eight staff are using the AWS root user for their account. What changes would you make to improve security? (Choose two.)

   A. Get all the users to download the AWS CLI and change the root password.

   B. Create a new IAM user for each of the eight staff members and provide credentials to each user.

   C. Put the five developers in the Power Users group, the financial manager in the Billing group, and the support engineers in the Support User group.

   D. Create a new group with access to the IAM service and ensure that at least one developer is in that group.

6. You need to support a cluster of instances that will host a high-volume, high-load Oracle database installation. You cannot use RDS because of a custom plug-in that the database instances require. Which EBS volume type should you choose for the instances?

   A. Cold HDD

   B. Throughput Optimized HDD

   C. General Purpose SSD

   D. Provisioned IOPS SSD

7. You are responsible for a large AWS environment, and specifically, several subnets within a custom VPC. The VPC contains both public and private subnets. There are approximately 300 EC2 instances within one of the private subnets that uses a NAT device to reach the Internet. Each evening at 11 p.m., the instances push the day's date to an external data store outside of AWS, available via an API that is Internet accessible. However, you are seeing that not all of the data is getting out each evening, and several of the instances show failed transmissions to the external API. Assuming the API itself is not an issue, what should you consider when attempting to fix this issue? (Choose two.)

   A. The instances are saturating the VPC's internet gateway. Consider attaching an additional internet gateway to the VPC.

   B. The NAT device could be a NAT instance that is on an instance size too small to handle the traffic. Reprovision the NAT instance on a larger instance size with more CPU.

   C. Set up an SQS queue with all the desired transmissions as entries in the queue. Have the EC2 instances poll the queue and transmit data until the queue is completely empty. Add a Lambda job to detect failed transmissions and re-add the failed operation to the SQS queue.

   D. The instances cannot support the required throughput. Re-provision the instances to use EBS volumes with provisioned IOPS as the volume type.

8. Which of the following will AWS not allow with regard to EBS? (Choose two.)

   A. Encrypt an existing EBS volume.

   B. Create an unencrypted copy of an encrypted snapshot.

   C. Attach an encrypted volume to an EC2 instance.

   D. Create an encrypted copy of an unencrypted snapshot.

9. What is the URL at which an S3 bucket called photoData in the EU West 2 region is accessible for reading and writing, assuming permissions are correctly configured?

   A. `https://photoData.s3-eu-west-2.amazonaws.com`

   B. `https://s3.eu-west-2.amazonaws.com/photoData`

   C. `https://s3-eu-west-2.amazonaws.com/photoData`

   D. `https://photoData.s3.eu-west-2.amazonaws.com`

10. You are handling a logging update to a fleet of EC2 instances. You have set up a VPC flow log on the group of instances and now want to monitor these logs for a specific set of events, in particular security breaches. To where should the logs be forwarded?

    A. RDS

    B. S3

    C. CloudWatch

    D. RedShift

11. You want to provide task- and event-level tracking in a complex application. You've been asked to then attach custom code to these tasks and events. However, you are working on an MVP that needs to quickly go to market. Which AWS services would provide you with the most out-of-the-box functionality and require the least amount of infrastructure coding?

    A. SQS, Lambda

    B. SWF, CloudWatch

    C. SWF, Lambda

    D. Elastic Beanstalk, CloudWatch

12. You are troubleshooting a custom VPC with two subnets. One subnet contains database instances and is not Internet accessible. The other subnet has EC2 instances running web servers. The instances have elastic network interfaces assigned with public IP addresses. However, you are unable to access these instances from the Internet, and they cannot access Internet resources either. What might be causing these problems? (Choose two.)

    A. The instances need to use public IP addresses, but not elastic network interfaces. Remove the elastic network interfaces.

    B. The VPC needs an internet gateway. Attach an internet gateway and update the VPC's routing tables to route Internet traffic from the instances through the internet gateway.

    C. The instances are being prevented from accessing the Internet by the default security group they have been assigned. Add permissions to allow outgoing Internet traffic to the group.

    D. Update the NACL for the subnet with the EC2 instances to allow inbound HTTP and HTTPS traffic to the EC2 instances in the public subnet.

13. What common step that is often omitted in setting up a NAT instance can cause a failure in routing traffic from an EC2 instance through the NAT instance and out to the Internet?

   A. Adding a rule to the security group for the NAT instance that allows traffic out to the Internet

   B. Setting the NAT instance up to use an EBS volume with provisioned IOPS

   C. Setting the NACL on the subnet with the EC2 instances to allow in traffic from the Internet

   D. Ensuring that the Source/Destination Check option is disabled on the NAT instance

14. Which of these S3 storage classes is the most durable?

   A. S3

   B. S3-IA

   C. S3 One Zone-IA

   D. All of these classes are equally durable.

15. You have been tasked with setting up storage for an application that loads large photos from an existing RDS. These photos are then processed by a Lambda function and have metadata added, along with additional filters. The Lambda code is inexpensive and can easily be rerun if needed. You need to decide on where to store the photos once they have been processed. Each photo will likely be accessed between 1 and 5 times over the course of a month and should be quickly accessible. The chief driver for the application and your decision should be cost and user experience. What S3 storage class would you select?

   A. S3

   B. S3 IA

   C. S3 One Zone-IA

   D. Glacier

16. You have a growing fleet of EC2 instances that have been using EBS volumes for data storage. Each instance needs access to all other instances' data, and your custom replication scripts are growing increasingly taxed and complex. What would you recommend to replace the current usage of EBS volumes and replication?

   A. EBS

   B. DynamoDB

   C. EFS

   D. Service Catalog

17. You are responsible for setting up the architecture for a new web-based online dating site. You need to create a public subnet in a custom VPC and already have a subnet in the VPC with EC2 instances within it. What other steps would you need to take to make the subnet public? (Choose two.)

   A. Attach a customer gateway to the VPC.

   B. Make the subnet public using the AWS CLI and the subnet command.

   C. Attach an internet gateway to the VPC.

   D. Add a route for the instances in the subnet to the Internet through the attached gateway.

18. Which of the following are valid S3 request headers? (Choose two.)
    A. x-amz-date
    B. Content-Length
    C. x-aws-date
    D. Content-Size

19. Which of the following are support levels offered by AWS? (Choose two.)
    A. Developer
    B. Professional
    C. Business
    D. Corporate

20. Which of the following database options are available through RDS? (Choose two.)
    A. DynamoDB
    B. Aurora
    C. DB2
    D. MariaDB

21. You have an Auto Scaling group that has a number of instances spread over several availability zones. Currently, there are 10 instances running, and the Auto Scaling group has rules that allow it to grow to as many as 20 instances and shrink to as few as 3. You have been told by another architect that the group needs to scale in. When this scaling in completes, how many instances might still be running?
    A. 10
    B. 5
    C. 15
    D. 20

22. Which of the following are options for writing a CloudFormation template? (Choose two.)
    A. XML
    B. YAML
    C. MML
    D. JSON

23. You are responsible for building out an application that serves user bases in California, USA; in Tokyo, Japan; and in Sydney, Australia. The application is hosted in regions close to all three major user bases. You want to ensure that users receive localized content in their own area. Which of the following routing policies should you consider for this application in Route 53?
    A. Failover routing
    B. Latency-based routing
    C. Geolocation routing
    D. Weighted routing

24. You have four EC2 instances serving web content with an ELB in front of the instances. You are configuring Route 53 and want to ensure that the ELB is directing traffic. What sort of record should you create in Route 53?

    A. A record

    B. MX record

    C. CNAME record

    D. AAAA record

25. You are the architect for a large migration from on-premises data stores to DynamoDB. As part of this migration, you need to manage the access and authorization for users, but the organization wants all existing users to maintain their Active Directory usernames. What steps will you need to do in order to facilitate this move? (Choose two.)

    A. Select an identity provider.

    B. Create a new IAM user for each user of the data.

    C. Use the AWS security token service to create temporary tokens.

    D. Create a service control policy in AWS Organizations for the imported data.

26. You are working on increasing performance for an application that routinely sees traffic spikes between 6 and 8 p.m. Eastern time every evening. At that time, even with Auto Scaling policies, load increases so quickly that response times slow to a crawl. Without knowing anything more than this about what the traffic surge represents, how could you most easily and efficiently ensure that your application can respond to these surges?

    A. Set up a lower threshold for scaling in your Auto Scaling group; consider 50% as a starting point.

    B. Log on each evening at 7:30 p.m. and manually scale the application up.

    C. Set up CloudWatch monitors on the application. Write a Lambda function that will trigger scaling up. Attach the Lambda function to the CloudWatch monitors and set a trigger threshold.

    D. Set up scheduled scaling so that the application scales up at 7:45 p.m. each evening and scales back down at 8:30 p.m.

27. You want to improve the performance of an existing DynamoDB database. Currently, you believe that CPU utilization is the biggest concern, although you are attempting to proactively provision additional resources rather than reacting to an existing load problem. Which of the following might be your approach?

    A. Stop the database and re-provision it using provisioned IOPS SSD EBS volumes.

    B. Set up read replicas to improve read performance.

    C. Configure DynamoDB to use a Multi-AZ setup.

    D. None of these. DynamoDB scales automatically, and you cannot manage its resources at this level.

28. You have been brought in to reduce costs on a production application. You find that currently, CloudWatch has been configured using the detailed option, and is collecting metrics every minute. You suggest updating CloudWatch to use default settings. Your customer likes the idea of reducing monitoring costs but wants to know how often metrics would be collected in your recommendation. What do you tell the customer?

   A. CloudWatch collects metrics every 2 minutes using default settings.

   B. CloudWatch collects metrics every 5 minutes using default settings.

   C. CloudWatch collects metrics every 10 minutes using default settings.

   D. The default settings for CloudWatch do not specify an interval at which metrics are collected.

29. You are newly responsible for a data-driven system that performs search and discovery of a very large database. The database is an RDS MySQL installation currently showing 82% CPU utilization. You are concerned about performance; what steps would you recommend? (Choose two.)

   A. Set up RDS to use Multi-AZ and ensure that the regions chosen are geographically close to your user base.

   B. Set up read replicas of your RDS database.

   C. Add an ElastiCache instance in front of your database.

   D. Create three copies of your database and move them into regions that are geographically distributed.

30. You have been brought in to add bits of custom code attached to a number of events on an existing application. The application needs to be updated quickly, and you want to minimize the code you need to write. What AWS solution will offer you the ability to accomplish these goals most quickly?

   A. SWF

   B. SQS

   C. Kinesis

   D. Redshift

31. You are investigating an application that uses an SQS queue. Messages are making it to the queue, but those messages are not being processed in the order in which they were received by the queue. You want to ensure that ordering is preserved; what should you do?

   A. Update the queue to use standard delivery so delivery always happens at least once.

   B. Change the queue to be a FIFO queue, which will ensure that ordering is preserved.

   C. Update the queue to use the "deliver in order" option via the AWS CLI.

   D. Change the queue to be a LIFO queue, which will ensure that ordering is preserved.

32. Which of the following is not a valid routing policy for Route 53?

   A. Simple routing policy

   B. Failover routing policy

   C. Load-balancing routing policy

   D. Latency-based routing policy

33. You are responsible for a cluster of EC2 instances that service a user-facing media-rich application, all behind an elastic load balancer. The application has begun to receive spikes of activity at unpredictable times, and your instances are flooded with requests and become nonresponsive in many cases. How would you rearchitect this application to address these issues?

    A. Move your application instances to use the spot market to account for the spikes in usage.

    B. Increase the size of the EC2 instances and choose instances with higher CPU ratings.

    C. Ask AWS to pre-warm the elastic load balancer so that it will respond more quickly to spikes in traffic.

    D. Add another application component, such as an SQS queue, and have requests go to the queue. Then have the instances process requests from the queue rather than directly from user requests.

34. You have a long-running batch process that you want to move to use spot instances in order to reduce costs. Which of the following should you consider when evaluating if these batch processes will function effectively on the spot market? (Choose two.)

    A. The process must be able to stop and restart without failing or losing data.

    B. The process must be able to run at any time.

    C. The process must not trigger more than 100 API requests within any single minute of running.

    D. The process must not use an AWS services outside of S3 or RDS.

35. You are the architect for a new application that needs durable storage in the cloud. You have been asked to select an S3 storage class with the maximum available durability. Which option provides S3 storage classes with maximum durability?

    A. S3 standard

    B. S3 standard, S3-IA

    C. S3 standard, S3-IA, S3 One Zone-IA

    D. S3 standard, S3-IA, S3 One Zone-IA, Glacier

36. What differences exist between storing data from an instance on an attached root EBS volume versus storing that data in S3? (Choose two.)

    A. EBS uses block-level storage, while S3 uses object-level storage.

    B. EBS uses object-level storage, while S3 uses block-level storage.

    C. EBS volumes are ephemeral by default, while S3 storage is not.

    D. S3 storage is ephemeral by default, while EBS storage is not.

37. You have been put in charge of a set of RDS databases that are not performing at speeds required by the application cluster using those databases. You have been tasked with increasing the performance of the databases while keeping costs as low as possible. The current RDS installation uses MySQL. What recommendation would you make?

   A. Move from RDS to EC2 instances with databases installed on the instances. Right-size the instances and custom database installation for the application's needs.

   B. Move from MySQL to Aurora within RDS, as Aurora consistently shows better performance than MySQL.

   C. Move from MySQL to Oracle within RDS and add the required Oracle licenses to increase the overall RDS cluster size.

   D. Stop the RDS cluster and then resize all instances. Restart the cluster, keeping the MySQL databases intact.

38. Which of the following AWS services are components of a high-availability, fault-tolerant solution? (Choose two.)

   A. Lightsail

   B. AWS Organizations

   C. ELB

   D. DynamoDB

39. Which of the following AWS managed services are not automatically redundant and require configuration on your part to be highly available? (Choose two.)

   A. EC2

   B. S3

   C. SQS

   D. RDS

40. As a new architect on a large project, you have begun to run vulnerability scans on all public-facing API endpoints of your application. However, these scans are failing, and you have received a number of misuse warnings from AWS. What is the problem?

   A. AWS does not allow vulnerability scans on its instances.

   B. AWS allows vulnerability scans, but they must be run using AWS's own services and tools.

   C. AWS allows vulnerability scans, but they must be run from AWS instances.

   D. AWS allows vulnerability scans, but they must be run with advance notice to and permission from AWS.

41. You have recently taken on architecture at a large genomics nonprofit. Currently, the organization imports hundreds of terabytes (TB) daily and then needs to run complex queries against that data. The queries can take several hours, and at times even days, to complete. They write their state to S3 frequently so the queries can recover from failure without restarting. The organization wants to minimize costs associated with this processing. What technologies and recommendations might you suggest? (Choose two.)

   A. Create an SQS instance and queue up references to all the data that needs to be queried as it comes in. Ensure that the queue is readable via EC2 instances.

   B. Create a new IAM role that allows EC2 instances to write data to S3 stores.

   C. Set up a placement group with EC2 instances that can read from the SQS queue and run the queries against referenced data.

   D. Set up EC2 spot instances that can read from the SQS queue and S3 and run the queries on those instances.

42. You have an application that consists of worker nodes that are on-demand instances and processing nodes that are a mixture of on-demand instances and spot instances. Your application collects information and does initial processing as it comes in from users using the worker nodes. Then, the processing nodes perform analytics each evening. Your goal is to use spot instances for most of this processing and only overflow to the on-demand instances in times of high load. However, the spot instances have been terminating more often lately, causing more usage of the on-demand instances. What might you do to increase the usage of the spot instances?

   A. Convert the on-demand processing instances to spot instances so more spot instances will be available.

   B. Convert the worker node instances to spot instances so more spot instances will be available.

   C. Lower the bid price on the spot instances to ensure only lower-priced instances are used.

   D. Raise the bid price on the spot instances so that they will run longer before termination occurs.

43. You are assisting a company with moving its large data estate to the cloud and reducing its on-site storage costs. The company has serious concerns about performance of the cloud as it relates to accessing its data. What storage gateway setup would you suggest to ensure that the company's frequently accessed files do not suffer latency?

   A. File gateway

   B. Cached volume gateway

   C. Tape gateway

   D. Stored volume gateway

44. Which of the following take the place of a traditional firewall appliance in AWS?

    A. NACLs, IAM, WAF

    B. Security groups, IAM, WAF

    C. NACLs, security groups

    D. Security groups, VPCs, VPGs

45. Which of the following are created automatically as part of the default VPC that AWS sets up for all AWS accounts? (Choose two.)

    A. Internet gateway

    B. Virtual private gateway

    C. Public subnet

    D. NAT gateway

46. Rank the factors considered in terminating an instance that is part of an Auto Scaling group, from highest priority to lowest priority.

    A. Age of launch configuration, availability zone with the most instances, nearness to next billing hour

    B. Availability zone with the most instances, age of launch configuration, nearness to next billing hour

    C. Age of launch configuration, nearness to next billing hour, availability zone with the most instances

    D. Availability zone with the most instances, nearness to next billing hour, age of launch configuration

47. AWS supports two types of virtualization: paravirtual and hardware virtual machines. Why might you choose one type of virtualization over the other?

    A. Paravirtualization allows the use of hardware extensions like enhanced networking and GPU processing, but hardware virtualization does not.

    B. Hardware virtualization allows the use of hardware extensions like enhanced networking and GPU processing, but paravirtualization does not.

    C. Hardware virtualization only works with certain instance types, while paravirtualization works with all instance types.

    D. Both paravirtualization and hardware virtualization function exactly the same way; neither is a better performance choice than the other.

48. Which EBS volume type is most suited for workloads that perform OLTP and need to perform extremely well and consistently?

    A. Provisioned IOPS volumes

    B. General SSH volumes

    C. Magnetic storage

    D. Throughput Optimized HDD

49. After discovering that HTTPS was not allowed to reach instances via a security group, you have added a rule to allow in HTTPS. How long will it take for your changes to take effect on the affected instances?

   A. Immediately

   B. Approximately 30 seconds

   C. Approximately 1 minute

   D. Immediately for the instances, but longer if you have an ELB in front of the instances

50. You have discovered that your production database instance is peaking and reaching 90% CPU usage when a set of nightly scripts are run against the database. The scripts perform complex queries and gather reporting data to be distributed via email reports the next day. As a result of the load, the database is performing poorly, and the queries are beginning to take into the following work day to complete. Which option would you recommend to reduce this peak usage in the evenings?

   A. Increase the memory attached to the database instance.

   B. Set up a second database instance as a Multi-AZ database and run your queries against the Multi-AZ database.

   C. Set up read replicas of the database instance and run your queries against the read replicas.

   D. Set up an ElastiCache instance in front of the database instance.

51. Who can delete objects in an S3 bucket with versioning enabled?

   A. Anyone with IAM permissions to modify the bucket

   B. Anyone with IAM permissions to delete objects in the bucket

   C. Only the bucket owner

   D. Once versioning is enabled, no object can ever be completely removed.

52. Your customer has instructed you to encrypt all objects at rest in your application. The customer is frequently audited and must prove compliance with a selective set of government policies. Which encryption approach would you recommend?

   A. SSE-C

   B. SSE-KMS

   C. SSE-S3

   D. Client-provided encryption keys

53. You have set up three read replicas of your primary database instance. You have noticed that reads of the replicas do not always return consistent results, especially after large writes to the primary database instance. What might the problem be?

    A. This is normal; replication from a primary instance to read replicas always takes between 30 and 60 seconds.

    B. This is normal; replication from a primary instance to read replicas is asynchronous and, although sometimes nearly instant, may also at times take longer to complete.

    C. You need to switch the replication model on your read replicas from asynchronous to synchronous to ensure read consistency.

    D. You need to investigate network latency between your primary and read replicas and consider moving the replicas into the same availability zone as the primary instance.

54. By default, how many S3 buckets can you create for a single AWS account?

    A. 20

    B. 50

    C. 100

    D. There is no default limit.

55. You want to create a public subnet in a custom VPC. Which of the following do you *not* need to accomplish this?

    A. An internet gateway

    B. An elastic IP address

    C. A routing table with a route to an internet gateway

    D. You need all of these for a public subnet.

56. What is the largest allowed volume size for provisioned IOPS EBS volumes?

    A. 4TiB

    B. 12TiB

    C. 16TiB

    D. 32TiB

57. Which of the following statements regarding EBS volumes and EC2 instances is not true?

    A. You can attach multiple EC2 instances to a single EBS volume at one time.

    B. You can attach multiple EBS volumes to a single EC2 instance at one time.

    C. You can attach multiple EC2 instances to a single EBS volume, but not all at the same time.

    D. Non-root EBS volumes are not deleted when an attached instance is terminated by default.

58. Which of the following AWS services does not store data in key-value pairs?

    A. S3

    B. DynamoDB

    C. IAM programmatic credentials

    D. RDS

59. You are auditing the EBS volumes of a number of EC2 instances running three web-facing data-intensive applications. You notice that a number of the volumes are configured as throughput optimized HDDs rather than General Purpose SSD or Provisioned IOPS SSD. Why might this decision be appropriate? (Choose two.)

    A. Lowered costs is a primary consideration.

    B. Data throughput is a primary consideration.

    C. The applications primarily use large performance-critical workloads.

    D. The throughput optimized HDDs serve only a test environment rather than a production one.

60. Which of the following databases is not supported by RDS?

    A. MariaDB

    B. SQL Server

    C. Aurora

    D. InnoDB

61. Which of the following statements are true about the default subnet created with a standard AWS account? (Choose two.)

    A. The instances created within it will be public by default.

    B. The instances created within it will have public elastic IPs by default.

    C. The instances created within it will have routes to the Internet through an internet gateway by default.

    D. The VPC within which the subnet is created will have an attached virtual private gateway as well as an internet gateway.

62. Which of the following types of traffic are supported by classic load balancers? (Choose two.)

    A. HTTPS

    B. SSH

    C. FTP

    D. HTTP

63. Which S3 storage class has the same durability as it does availability?

    A. S3 standard

    B. S3-IA

    C. S3-RRS

    D. S3 One Zone-IA

64. You want to ensure that no object in S3 is ever accidentally deleted, as well as preserve audit trails for deleted files. What options would you consider? (Choose two.)

    A. SSE-KMS

    B. MFA Delete

    C. Versioning

    D. Detailed monitoring with CloudWatch

65. You have a fleet of EC2 instances serving web content. The instances typically run between 75% and 90% of capacity, and your projections show consistent usage over the next 36 months. What would you recommend to potentially reduce the costs of running these instances?

    A. Spot instances

    B. Reserved instances

    C. On-demand instances

    D. Placement groups

Appendix

Answers to Review Questions

Domain 1: Design Resilient Architectures

1. **B.** This is a common question on AWS exams, and relates to your understanding of the various S3 classes. S3 and S3-IA have the same durability, but the availability of S3 is one 9 greater than S3-IA. S3 has 99.99 availability, while S3-IA has 99.9 availability. Glacier has much greater first-byte latency than S3, so both C and D are false.

2. **B.** Anytime the primary consideration is storage with a local data presence—where data must be stored or seen to be stored locally—a storage gateway gives you the best option. This reduces the choices to B and D. B will store the files in S3 and provide local cached copies, while D will store the files locally and push them to S3 as a backup. Since management is concerned about storage in the cloud of primary files, B is the best choice; local files are the primary source of data, while still allowing the company to experiment with cloud storage without "risking" its data being stored primarily in the cloud.

3. **B.** Many of these answers are nonsensical in terms of what AWS allows. The limits on size related to S3 are for objects; an individual object can be as large as 5 TB. Both A and C, then, are not useful (or possible). D proposes to increase the maximum object size to 50 GB, but the maximum object size is already 5 TB. Option B is correct; AWS recommends using Multipart Upload for all objects larger than 100 MB.

4. **C, D.** PUTs of new objects have a read after write consistency. DELETEs and overwrite PUTs have eventual consistency across S3.

5. **C.** First, note that "on standard class S3" is a red herring, and irrelevant to the question. Second, objects on S3 can be 0 bytes. This is equivalent to using touch on a file and then uploading that 0-byte file to S3.

6. **A.** This is a matter of carefully looking at each URL. Bucket names—when not used as a website—always come after the fully qualified domain name (FQDN); in other words, after the forward slash. That eliminates C. Additionally, the region always comes earlier in the FQDN than amazonaws.com, eliminating D. This leaves A and B. Of the two, A correctly has the complete region, us-east-2.

7. **C.** This is another question that is tricky unless you work through each part of the URL, piece by piece. The first clue is that this is a website hosted on S3, as opposed to directly accessing an S3 bucket. Where website hosting is concerned, the bucket name is *part of* the FQDN; where direct bucket access is concerned, the bucket name comes *after* the FQDN. This is an essential distinction. This means that A and B are invalid. Then, you need to recall that the s3-website portion of the FQDN is always connected to the region; in other words, it is not a subdomain. The only option where this is the case is C.

8. **A.** This is another case of rote memorization. S3 and S3-IA have the same durability; however, the availability of S3 is higher (99.99 vs. the 99.9 of S3-IA). Both Glacier and S3-IA have the same durability of standard S3, so both C and D are false.

9. **B.** This is an important distinction when understanding S3 classes. Standard S3, S3-IA, and S3 One Zone-IA all are equally durable, although in One Zone-IA, data will be lost if

the availability zone is destroyed. Each class has different availability, though: S3 is 99.99, S3-IA is 99.9, and S3 One Zone-IA is 99.5. Therefore, it is false that all have the same availability (B).

10. A, C. The wording of this question is critical. S3 buckets are created within a region, but the AWS console and your account will show you *all* S3 buckets at all times. While a bucket is created in a specific region, names of buckets are also global. IAM permissions are also global and affect all regions. RDS and EC2 instances are region specific, and only appear in the regions in which they were created in the AWS console.

11. A, D. EBS volumes are block-based storage, meaning that A is correct and B is incorrect. That leaves C and D. The default EBS volume is SSD, so C is false. However, EBS volumes can be in a variety of types, including magnetic and SSD options, so D is true.

12. D. AMIs are not cross-region, regardless of account or security group. This makes B and C invalid. A is a valid choice but will not preserve any of the permissions or roles that allow the instance to connect to S3. Therefore, D is the correct option: manual configuration of the AMI *after* it has been copied is required for correct operation.

13. D. This is a bit of a trick question if you're not careful. While S3 allows for 0-byte objects, and charges as such, S3-IA charges all objects as if they are *at least* 128 KB in size. So while you can store a smaller object in S3-IA, it will be considered 128 KB for pricing and charging purposes.

14. A, D. A Multi-AZ setup is the easiest solution, and the most common. Turning on read replicas (option B) is not a guarantee, as read replicas are not automatically installed in different AZs or regions. However, with option D, a cross-region replica configuration will ensure multiple regions are used. A storage gateway (option C) is backed by S3, not RDS.

15. A, D. Launch configurations are concerned primarily with creating new instances while staying abstract from the details of what is on those instances. So the AMI and IAM role for an instance is a general configuration, applies to all created instances, and is correct (A and D). The polling time for latency isn't connected to launching new instances (although it might be a trigger configured elsewhere). Each instance is associated with a different EBS volume, so selecting an EBS volume for multiple instances doesn't actually make sense.

16. D. Launch configurations are where details are specified for creating (launching) new instances (option D). Security groups have to do more with what traffic is allowed into and out of the launched instances. The remaining two options—A and C—don't make sense in this context.

17. D. By default, EBS root volumes are terminated when the associated instance is terminated. However, this is only the default value; therefore A is not correct. Option B is not directly addressing the question; the EBS volume would still be deleted even if you take a snapshot. Option C is not relevant, but option D is: You can use the AWS CLI (or the console) to set the root volume to persist after instance termination.

18. B. EBS volumes are backed up to S3 incrementally.

19. B. EBS volumes can only attach to a single instance at one time. The other options are all simply to distract.

20. A, B. All instances and most services in AWS provide tagging for metadata. Certificates are related to SSL and help define the identity of a site or transmission, policies are related to permissions and roles, and labels are not (currently) an AWS construct.

21. A, B. Valid concerns in this list include placing storage close to your users, to reduce network latency, and distance from your operations center. This latter is a little less obvious but is centered around disaster recovery scenarios: If a disaster destroyed your operations center, you would not want your storage on AWS to be geographically in the same area.

22. B. Every EC2 instance provides the option to specify an availability zone. While you don't have to specify something other than the default, instances are always provisioned in a specific availability zone, which is user configurable.

23. C. Spread placement groups—which are relatively new to AWS—can be placed across multiple availability zones. Cluster placement groups cannot, and *placement groups* generally refers to cluster placement groups. *Cross-region placement groups* is a made-up term.

24. C. A customer gateway is the anchor on the customer side of an Amazon VPN connection. A storage gateway is for caching or storing data and connecting to S3. A virtual private gateway is an important part of a VPN connection but exists on the AWS side of the connection. A virtual private network is actually what VPN stands for.

25. B. VPN connections between an on-premises site and AWS consist of a customer gateway on the customer side and a virtual private gateway on the AWS side.

26. B. A typical VPN connection uses two different tunnels for redundancy. Both tunnels move between the customer gateway and the virtual private gateway.

27. D. Traffic begins at the on-premises site, which means starting at a customer gateway. Traffic then flows through the Internet and to the virtual private gateway at AWS. Then, from the gateway, traffic can flow into an Amazon VPC.

28. A, C. Traffic across the Internet can only flow between public IP addresses in most cases. For a VPN connection, you will need a customer gateway with a public IP address as well as a virtual private gateway with a public IP address, both of which you may be responsible for configuring. A VPC does not have an IP address of its own (making option B incorrect), and VPN tunnels do not either (option D).

29. A. A storage gateway is the correct answer, as it is used for caching or storing data and connecting to S3. A customer gateway is the anchor on the customer side of an Amazon VPN connection. A virtual private gateway is used for connecting into AWS via a VPN, and a virtual private network is actually what VPN stands for.

30. A, B. Both file and volume gateways offer solutions for connecting to cloud-based storage. A cached gateway isn't an AWS option, and a virtual private gateway is used in creating VPN connections.

31. A. Each of the options is a valid configuration for a storage gateway. Of the options, file gateway provides an NFS-style protocol for transferring data to and from the gateway and therefore is the best option.

32. D. This is relatively easy because the word *tape* actually appears in both the question and the answer. A tape gateway backs up data in Amazon Glacier while providing a virtual tape infrastructure that many existing tape backup systems can utilize.

33. C. A stored volume gateway stores data at the on-premises data store and backs up to S3 asynchronously to support disaster recovery. Most important, though, is that by storing data locally, network latency is minimal. Of the available options, only a stored volume gateway provides local data with this speed of access across an entire dataset.

34. C. Anytime very large data needs to be moved into AWS, consider Snowball. Snowball is a physical device that allows for data to be physically sent to AWS rather than transferred over a network. It is the only solution that will not potentially cause disruptive network outages or slowdowns.

35. A, C. A cached volume gateway stores the most commonly accessed data locally (option D) while keeping the entire dataset in S3. This has the effect of reducing the cost of storage on-site, because you need less (option B). Since both of these are true, you need to select the other two options as reasons to *not* use a cached volumes gateway: A and C.

36. A. Be careful here. While it might seem at a glance that a tape gateway is best, most backup solutions do not employ tape backups. They use NFS mounts and file-based backups, which is exactly what a file gateway is best used for.

37. B. A cached volume gateway is ideal when a *portion* of a dataset is at issue. The most used data will be cached, and therefore stored in the local cache on premises. If the entire dataset is needed, then a stored volume gateway is a better choice.

38. C. If the entire dataset is needed, then a stored volume gateway is a better choice than a cached volume gateway. The stored volume stores the entire dataset on premises and therefore is very fast for all data access.

39. D. A tape gateway is ideal for replacing off-site tape directories. The gateway is a virtual tape directory and avoids the costs of transporting actual tapes to an expensive off-site location.

40. D. This should be automatic: Glacier is the Amazon offering for long-term "on ice" storage.

41. B, D. Launch configurations are specific to a region, as are EC2 instances. While S3 buckets are created in a region, their names are global. IAM users also exist across all of your account.

42. A. HTTP 200 is the general return for success, and this is the case for S3 uploads as well.

43. D. This is easy to miss. All S3 storage classes (S3 standard, S3-IA, and S3 One Zone-IA) share the same durability of 11 9s.

44. D. This is easy to miss. All S3 storage classes (S3 standard, S3-IA, and S3 One Zone-IA) share the same durability of 11 9s.

45. D. All S3 storage classes (S3 standard, S3-IA, and S3 One Zone-IA) share the same durability of 11 9s.

46. A. While all S3 storage classes share the same durability, they have varying availability. S3-IA has 99.9%, while S3 One Zone-IA is less (99.5%), and S3 standard is higher (99.99%).

47. B. While all S3 storage classes share the same durability, they have varying availability. S3-IA has 99.9%, while S3 One Zone-IA is less (99.5%), and S3 standard is higher (99.99%).

48. C. While all S3 storage classes share the same durability, S3 standard has the highest availability, at 99.99%.

49. D. All of the S3 storage classes support both SSL for data in transit and encryption for data at rest.

50. D. All of the S3 storage classes support both SSL for data in transit and encryption for data at rest.

51. D. All S3 storage classes have buckets that can be created in a specific region. The objects in the buckets are then stored in availability zones within that region, depending upon the storage class.

52. D. While S3 does use availability zones to store objects in buckets, you do not choose the availability zone yourself. Even S3 One Zone-IA does not allow you to specify the AZ for use.

53. A. S3 storage is key based. Keys can be a string and the value is the uploaded object.

54. C, D. S3 does not provide SSH or SFTP access, nor standard FTP access. You can access your data through the AWS console and through a REST interface via HTTP.

55. B, C. S3 is built to automatically scale in times of heavy application usage. There is no requirement to enable Auto Scaling (A); rather, this happens automatically (so B is correct). Further, S3 tends to scale evenly across the AWS network (C). Option D is the opposite of what AWS intends.

56. B. When evaluating S3 storage, all storage classes have the same durability. For cost, though, S3 One Zone-IA is the clear winner. Only Glacier is potentially less expensive but does not provide the same quick file access that S3 One Zone-IA does.

57. D. This is nearly a trick question. S3 in general is built for scalability, and the different storage classes are not substantially different in terms of how they can scale. However, without knowing how quickly data retrieval must be, and the priorities of the data, it is impossible to choose between S3 standard and S3-IA, and in some cases, even Glacier.

58. C. By default, all AWS accounts can create up to 100 buckets. However, this limit can easily be raised by AWS if you request an upgrade.

59. B. S3 uploads are, by default, done via a single operation, usually via a single PUT operation. AWS suggests that you can upload objects up to 100 MB before changing to Multipart Upload.

60. B. Using the Multipart Upload is almost entirely a function of the size of the files being uploaded. AWS recommends using it for any files greater than 100 MB, and 10 GB is certainly large enough to benefit from Multipart Uploads.

61. A, C. Multipart Upload is, as should be the easiest answer, ideal for large objects on stable networks (A). But it also helps handle less-reliable networks as smaller parts can fail while others get through, reducing the overall failure rate (C). There is no cost associated with data ingress (B), and D doesn't make much sense at all!

62. A, C. Presigned URLs are created to allow users without AWS credentials to access specific resources (option C). And it's the creator of the URL (option A) that assigns these permissions, rather than the user (option B). Finally, these credentials are associated with the URL but are not encrypted into the URL itself.

63. D. Presigned URLs are not tied to specific AWS services. They are simply URLs that can point at anything a normal URL can point at, except that the creator can associate permissions and a timeout with the URL.

64. D. A presigned URL is always configured at creation for a valid Time to Live (often referred to as TTL). This time can be very short, or quite long.

65. B, D. Overwrite PUTs and DELETEs have eventual consistency. PUTs of new objects have write and then read consistency.

66. D. These are all consistent with S3 behavior. Option A could occur as the new object is being propagated to additional S3 buckets. B and C could occur as a result of eventual consistency, where a DELETE operation does not immediately appear.

67. C. All regions have eventual consistency for overwrite PUTs and DELETEs.

68. A, D. All S3 storage classes are object-based, while EBS and EFS are block-based.

69. B. EBS stands for Elastic Block Storage.

70. B. New objects uploaded via PUT are subject to read after write consistency. Overwrite PUTs use the eventual consistency model.

71. C. This is important because it reflects a recent change by AWS. Until 2018, there was a hard limit on S3 of 100 PUTs per second, but that limit has now been raised to 3500 PUTs per second.

72. B. S3 buckets have names based upon the S3 identifier (s3), the region (us-west-1 in this case), and the amazonaws.com domain. Then, the bucket name appears *after* the domain. That results in B, https://s3-us-west-1.amazonaws.com/prototypeBucket32. Option A has an incorrect region, and both C and D have the bucket name in the domain, which is incorrect.

73. A. S3 buckets have names based upon the S3 identifier (s3), the region (us-east-1 in this case), and the `amazonaws.com` domain. Then, the bucket name appears *after* the domain. That results in a URL like `https://s3-us-east-1.amazonaws.com/prototypeBucket32`. However, buckets in US East are a special case and should use the special, unique endpoint *s3.amazonaws.com* (option A).

74. B, C. Option A is not the correct format; s3 should be separated from the region with a dash (-). Option B is valid, and option C is the correct unique URL for US East (N. Virginia). Option D is the right format, but jp-west-2 is not an AWS region.

75. A, D. S3 supports two styles of bucket URLs: virtual-hosted-style and path-style URLs. Virtual-hosted-style URLs are of the form `http://bucket.s3-`*aws-region*`.amazonaws.com`, and path-style URLs are the traditional URLs you've seen: `https://s3-`*aws-region*`.amazonaws.com/`*bucket-name*.

76. B, D. Option A is not a valid URL for S3. Option B is, using the path-style URLs that are most common for S3 buckets. Option C uses a nonexistent region (mx-central-1). Option D is valid and uses the virtual-hosted-style URL format.

77. D. AWS storage gateway is a virtual appliance that allows on-premises sites to interact with S3 while still caching (in certain configurations) data locally.

78. B. AWS storage gateway is a virtual appliance and is not available as a hardware appliance.

79. B, D. While S3 buckets are created in a specific region (A), the names of buckets are global and must exist in a global namespace (so B is untrue). Buckets are object-based (so C is true), and while a single object is limited at 5 TB, the buckets are unlimited in total storage capacity (so D is false).

80. A, D. S3 supports read after write consistency for PUTs of new objects and eventual consistency for overwrite PUTs and DELETEs.

81. C, D. S3 objects have a key, a value, and a version ID, so the correct answers are C and D.

82. C. MFA Delete is the absolute best means of ensuring that objects are not accidentally deleted. MFA—Multi-Factor Authentication—ensures that any object deletion requires multiple forms of authentication.

83. B. All Amazon-specific request headers begin with x-amz. This is important to remember as it will help eliminate lots of incorrect answers. This leaves only x-amz-mfa.

84. B, C. MFA Delete applies to deleting objects, not buckets (so option A is incorrect). It affects changing the versioning state of a bucket or permanently deleting any object (or a version of that object); this makes B and C correct. Deleting an object's metadata while leaving the object intact does not require MFA Delete.

85. A. This answer simply has to be memorized. MFA Delete authentication codes are pulled from hardware or virtual MFA devices, like Google Authenticator on an iPhone.

86. D. This is tricky and somewhat un-intuitive. Only the root account can enable MFA Delete. Even the console user that created the bucket—if it isn't the root user—cannot enable MFA Delete on a bucket.

87. B. The bucket owner, root account, and all authorized IAM users of a bucket are allowed to enable versioning.

88. A, B. Each object in S3 has a name, value (data), version ID, and metadata. The version history of an object won't exist unless versioning is turned on, so it's not always a valid answer.

89. B. All metadata in AWS is currently entered using tags, name-value pairs available through the console.

90. D. All versions of an object are stored, regardless of how that object is deleted.

91. D. Once enabled, it is not possible to disable or turn off versioning on an S3 bucket. While you can suspend versioning, this doesn't actually turn versioning off, and old versions are preserved.

92. B, C. CloudFront is intended to cache and deliver static files from your origin servers to users or clients. Dynamic content is also servable through CloudFront from EC2 or other web servers. Object-based storage doesn't make sense in this context, as CloudFront is a distribution mechanism, not a storage facility.

93. D. CloudFront serves content from origin servers, usually static files and dynamic responses. These origin servers are often S3 buckets for static content and EC2 instances for dynamic content.

94. A, D. CloudFront serves content from origin servers, usually static files and dynamic responses. These origin servers are often S3 buckets for static content and EC2 instances for dynamic content (options A and D).

95. B, D. CloudFront serves content from origin servers, usually static files and dynamic responses. These origin servers are often S3 buckets for static content and EC2 instances for dynamic content (meaning option C is valid). Containers can also be used in place of EC2 instances, making option A valid as well. This leaves B and D as invalid origin servers.

96. B. CloudFront stores content as cached content on edge locations across the world.

97. C, D. CloudFront is able to distribute content from an ELB, rather than directly interfacing with S3, and can do the same with a Route 53 recordset. These allow the content to come from multiple instances. This means that options C and D are invalid origin servers and therefore the correct answers.

98. D. A CloudFront distribution is a collection of edge locations across the world.

99. B. First, you can eliminate any answer where fewer availability zones are indicated than regions, because each region has multiple availability zones (A and D). This leaves B and C. There are more edge locations than availability zones, which means that B is correct.

100. A, B. This question is simple if you remember that, from most to least, the ordering goes edge locations (most) to availability zones to regions (least). Knowing that, options A and B are correct.

101. B, D. Availability zones are not content storage devices; they are virtual data centers. Edge locations are used by CloudFront distributions to store cached content (so correct). Route 53 is the Amazon DNS service. EC2 instances can serve content from processes (so also correct).

102. A, D. While edge locations are typically read from by clients, they are also writeable. You can store objects on edge locations as well as read from them.

103. A, C. The obvious answer here is an S3 bucket. EC2 locations are compute, not storage, and availability zones are virtual data centers. This leaves edge locations, which allow objects to be written directly to them.

104. A. TTL is Time to Live, the amount of time an object is cached on a CloudFront edge location.

105. B, D. You must perform *both* steps B and D, and you must perform B *before* D or the banner ad could get re-cached. Also note that expiring a cached object manually incurs a cost.

106. B. The default TTL for edge locations is 24 hours.

107. B. All new S3 buckets are private by default.

108. B, C. The correct answers are ACLs—access control lists—and bucket policies (B and C). NACLs are network access lists, used for securing VPCs and individual instances, and JSON is used for writing policies.

109. C. S3 bucket policies are written in JSON, the JavaScript Object Notation. XML is not used much in AWS, and YAML is often used for CloudFormation. AML is made up!

110. A. All data is backed up to S3 asynchronously when a stored volume is used. This ensures that no lag is incurred by clients that interact with the stored volumes on-site.

111. A. This is a little harder unless you've seen the term *virtual tape library (VTL)* before. A tape volume is in fact a virtual tape library. Fortunately, even if you've never heard of a VTL, you can reason it out based on the other incorrect options: A VPC is a virtual private cloud, a VPN is a virtual private network, and NetBackup is an application, not a tape volume.

112. A. This is an easy one: Snowball is the AWS solution for transferring large datasets.

113. D. Snowball actually does not support any code. You just transfer your data to the device and send it to Amazon. Additionally, CloudFormation is not a language; you use YAML (for example) to write CloudFormation templates.

114. A. AWS Direct Connect is a dedicated high-speed connection between your on-premises network and AWS. Because of this, a direct connect is almost always a better choice than shipping out a Snowball, loading data to it, and then shipping it back.

115. A. All Snowball devices provide data transfer, but Snowball Edge offers data processing ("at the edge") before that data is returned to AWS (option A).

116. C. Snowball can serve as both an import and export device, both to and from S3.

117. C. Decoupling separates application layers, primarily in an attempt to reduce failures across an entire application. Limiting application interdependence helps limit failures "crossing" application layers.

118. D. Redshift is an OLAP (online analytics processing) service suitable for data warehousing.

119. B. While using separate VPCs and subnets offers some degree of redundancy, there's nothing in the answers that suggests that additional VPCs or subnets are separated from the original. This makes B, launching instances in separate regions, the best choice. (Option D doesn't make much sense.)

120. A. CloudFront is the only option here that uses edge locations. Note that Snowball offers Snowball Edge, but that is not to be confused with an edge location.

121. C. This should be pretty basic: Running an application in two availability zones is going to provide fault tolerance, because if one AZ fails, the application will keep running.

122. B, D. While all of the answers are storage-based services, A and C are databases, and relational ones at that. Options B and D, S3 and EBS, offer file storage.

123. B, C. This is a little tricky. S3 is an obvious choice. Redshift is suited for analysis data, so probably not large objects. EC2 is compute, which leaves Oracle. It is possible—without any better answers—to use Oracle (via RDS or installed on EC2) to store large objects in a BLOB-type field.

124. B. S3 Transfer Acceleration speeds up transfers to S3, although it does add cost to your application. Snowball is for data migration (A). AWS manages the network, so C is not an option, and D doesn't make sense in this context.

125. B. It's the users who are the farthest from your buckets that benefit most. This is because these users are incurring the longest delays in uploading and are therefore affected the most by the benefits.

126. A, C. The key here is to understand which problems *will* be solved by Transfer Acceleration versus which ones *might* be solved. With Transfer Acceleration, you're generally looking at problems related to large datasets being transferred over significant distances. In this case, that's A and C. While performance (B) and latency (D) might be connected to transfer speeds, there's no guarantee of that, so those are both incorrect answers.

127. A, C. This should be easy. You can host websites on EC2 easily, and S3 also offers static website hosting.

128. C. This is a case of memorization. While B is a valid S3 bucket URL, it is not the URL for website hosting. D is in the incorrect region, and also has a dot instead of a dash between s3-website and the region name. This leaves A and C. C is correct, as A incorrectly breaks up the s3-website and region portions of the domain name, using a dot instead of a dash between s3-website and the region name.

129. D. First, ensure that the domain name is correct. Option A incorrectly separates s3-website from the region, and C has the wrong region. B does not have the bucket name in the URL, which it should for website hosting. This leaves D, the correct answer.

130. A. First, eliminate option D; the domain is incorrect, adding a separator between s3-website and the region. Then, eliminate option C, as it adds a public_html to the portion of the URL after the domain, which is also incorrect. This leaves A and B. Here, you need to realize that the portion of a URL after the domain is case sensitive and compare the two directories to the question. A is correct, using the correct capitalization of phoneboothPhotos.

131. A, D. To minimize compute resources, you should avoid EC2 and Lambda. Enabling static website hosting on an S3 bucket is a better option. To use a custom domain, you'd need to also use Route 53 to direct traffic from your custom domain to the S3 bucket.

132. C, D. If the website was static content, S3 bucket hosting would be ideal. However, to support dynamic content, you will need some sort of compute service: EC2 or Lambda. To minimize costs and avoid incurring additional costs when requests aren't occurring, Lambda allows as-you-need-it serverless responses to requests. Route 53 allows you to direct traffic aimed at your custom domain to Lambda.

133. A, C. EC2 is, by definition, a server-driven option. Both S3—through static website hosting—and Lambda offer serverless options for serving content. Route 53 provides DNS but is not on its own capable of serving website content.

134. B, C. While S3 can serve static content, it has no capability for processing code or otherwise providing dynamic content. EC2 provides for dynamic content through server-driven compute, and Lambda provides dynamic content through serverless compute.

135. A, C. Elastic Beanstalk is focused on code deployment. It provides that, and in the process, load balancing, Auto Scaling, health monitoring, and capacity provisioning (C).

136. B, D. Elastic Beanstalk is focused on code deployment (A). It provides that, and in the process, load balancing, Auto Scaling, health monitoring (C), and capacity provisioning. It does not provide security or log inspection.

137. A, D. This is a little far off the beaten AWS path, but you should know which languages and technologies are commonly used and cited by AWS and which are not. In general, Docker and containers are always supported; and Node.js, JavaScript, Java, PHP, and Perl are commonly supported. C++ and Scala are not in that list.

138. D. The best way to work this question is to immediately recognize the common languages: Node.js and Python. While it's possible that you forget Java is supported, once you've identified two options that are valid, the answer must be D.

139. A, B. Elastic Beanstalk supports all RDS options as well as DynamoDB. Oracle running on EC2 is a nonstandard option so not suitable for the auto-provisioning of Elastic Beanstalk. Redshift is also not a database technology.

140. C. You can absolutely deploy to production using Elastic Beanstalk. You simply need to configure different Elastic Beanstalk environments to use different databases.

141. D. EC2 and ECS are compute services but require knowledge and working with the required resources. DynamoDB is a database and cannot run code. Lambda is correct: It runs code without needing an underlying set of compute resources that are user managed.

142. A, D. Elastic Beanstalk and Lambda are very different services, but in this context, both are valid answers. Elastic Beanstalk is a sort of "code deployment wizard," and Lambda allows for serverless code deployment. Both handle provisioning of the environment without user intervention.

143. A. Code deployed via Lambda absolutely runs on servers; however, AWS abstracts the details away from user management.

144. A, B. You should know which languages and technologies are commonly used and cited by AWS and which are not. In general, Node.js, JavaScript, Java, PHP, and Perl are pretty commonly supported. C++ and Scala are not in that list.

145. B, C. A is a bit nonsensical. Installing Oracle requires using EC2 instances, so is not a use case for Lambda. Both B and C are valid: Lambda is ideal for responding to triggers or changes in state from other AWS services and also handles scaling quite well without user-driven code. D is not valid; that is a use case for EC2 or the Elastic Container Service.

146. A. Conversion of files to various formats is transcoding and therefore the function of Elastic Transcoder.

147. B. QuickSight is a cloud-powered business analytics service. It provides visualizations and analysis from multiple data sources.

148. B. SNS is the Simple Notification Service and provides notifications—alerts and alarms—when certain events occur in your AWS environment.

149. A. AWS Cognito allows you to add user sign-up, sign-in, and access control to web applications, as well as single sign-on. It also allows identity providers such as Facebook and Google to be used.

150. B. Every region is a specific geographic area, but none are as big as an entire continent.

151. D. A VPC is a virtual private cloud. It is a virtual network dedicated to a single AWS account.

152. C. ECS is the Elastic Container Service. It manages containers (Docker) that are each compute resources and can be spun up and spun down quickly.

153. B. RDS is the Relational Database Service, which provides managed database services for your applications.

154. D. Route 53 is the DNS service managed by AWS. It provides domain management and registration.

155. D. A customer gateway allows an on-premises site to connect with AWS through a peer-to-peer VPN. It is a virtual networking device.

156. A. Anything related to S3 is going to be storage-related. In this case, lifecycle management handles transitioning data from one S3 storage class to another.

157. D. Amazon Lightsail is a compute solution for web applications and involves compute, storage, and networking as well as database storage when needed. It launches servers and configures them with the needed services for web hosting. Note that while AWS considers Lightsail a compute service, it absolutely interfaces and controls additional resources.

158. C. Elastic Beanstalk is an Amazon service that spins up and manages a number of other services, in particular, compute. Even though you can configure other services, though, Beanstalk is considered to primarily be a code deployment tool and therefore is focused on compute services.

159. A. EFS is the Elastic File System, a scalable file system concerned with storage.

160. C. Redshift is one of AWS's OLAP (online analytics processing) tools and is a database service. While it does processing, it is primarily intended to receive large amounts of data and operate upon that data, as a database would (in loose terms).

161. B. CloudFront is AWS's distribution network. It's a content caching system that is ultimately a networking component of your AWS buildout.

162. D. Athena is a database and available through RDS but is ultimately intended for analytics, much like Redshift and Elastic MapReduce.

163. B. EMR is Elastic MapReduce and provides data processing and analysis of large datasets.

164. C. Cloud9 is a developer environment, intended as an IDE for AWS developers.

165. D. Direct Connect is an AWS service for creating a high-speed connection between an on-premises site and AWS.

166. D. Amazon Workspaces allows you to provide a desktop service via the cloud. The service allows people throughout the world to take advantage of scalable desktop provisioning.

167. B. Kinesis is a data analytic service capable of handling large data streams and providing real-time insights.

168. C. Elastic Transcoder processes video into formats suitable for a wide variety of devices across resolutions and formats.

169. D. OpsWorks is an operational management service, which AWS often classifies as "management tools" (especially in the AWS console). It allows integration with tools like Puppet and Chef.

170. A. Lex is the Amazon service for building voice recognition and conversation bots.

171. A. CloudWatch offers the ability to set up specific metrics (network throughput, requests, disk IO, and so on) and monitor those metrics via dashboards and reports.

172. D. An availability zone (AZ) is a virtual data center within a region, separated from other AZs by a distance sufficient to provide redundancy in the case of a disaster. B is incorrect as AZs do not have redundancy within them; that is the definition of a region.

173. B. A region is an area geographically that has redundancy within it, in the form of availability zones. Each AZ (which is defined in both A and C) is separate from other AZs and each is in essence a virtual data center.

174. A, B. AWS will always ask at least a few questions related to regions and availability zones. As long as you read these carefully, they should be easy correct answers. A region is a geographical area with redundancy within it, through at least two availability zones. Option A is false as services are not tied to regions. B is false because a region contains virtual data centers; it is not itself a virtual data center.

175. B, D. Availability zones are virtual data centers (which makes D false, as AZs do not *contain* data centers) and are isolated from each other except through low-latency network links. So C is true (and therefore incorrect), and A is true, as AZs definitely host compute resources. That leaves B in addition to D. B is not describing an AZ as an AZ does not itself provide redundancy. It's the *combination* of AZs that does this work.

176. C, D. Elastic IPs are assigned to an instance in a specific availability zone, but in the event of a failure, that elastic IP can be remapped to another AZ, making A false. B is false because regions will contain *at least* two availability zones, not exactly two. C is true, as different accounts may remap AZs to different names to ensure better resource distribution, and D is correct, even though many users simply accept the defaults and don't pick a specific AZ.

177. A, C. This is admittedly a tough question, but worth working through. You need to have at least a familiarity with AWS regions and know that there are several major regions: US, EU, and AP. There are a few others (CA, SA, for example), but the major ones are US, EU, and AP. Knowing those, you can spot that A and C are likely valid. JP (presumably for Japan) isn't correct, and UK you should recognize should be EU. There is no UK-specific region.

178. B, D. This is more of a formatting question than knowing the list of AWS regions. A region identifier is the region name, which is usually the country or area (eu, us, etc.), then the geographical area (southeast, west, east, etc.), then a number. This makes B and D correct. A is the "human readable" name, and C is an availability zone, due to the letter appended to the end.

179. A. An availability zone identifier is the region identifier with a letter appended on the end. A region identifier is the region name, which is usually the country or area (eu, us, etc.), then the geographical area (southeast, west, east, etc.), then a number.

180. C. EFS, Elastic File System, provides scalable storage accessible from multiple compute instances. EBS is Elastic Block Storage and is tied to one instance at a time and therefore not like a NAS (network attached storage). DynamoDB is a NoSQL database, and tape gateway is a client device for interacting with S3, but locally rather than in the cloud.

181. C. Be careful here; while ElastiCache is an AWS service for caching, it uses memcached and redis for actual caching. Therefore, memcached is the engine, not ElastiCache.

182. A, C. ElastiCache uses two different caching engines: memcached and redis.

183. C. You can choose reserved instances for EC2 and RDS, so the correct answer here is C.

184. D. You can use reserved instances for almost anything AWS offers. This applies to RDS (in any configuration) as well as ElasticCache nodes.

185. A, B. First, you need to know that you can manually force a failover (option A). Then, realize that a Multi-AZ setup is for disaster recovery, so it would take a failure of the primary availability zone to fail over (option B). The secondary AZ does not cause a failover (C), nor does a specific number of failed reads (D).

186. A, D. You can approach this in two ways: by knowing what you can do, and knowing what you cannot. You *can* select the database type and the AZ to which you want your instance deployed (A and D). You *cannot* specify extremely detailed issues related to performance and failover (B and C).

187. A, B. This is a bit tricky. While I/O may briefly suspend, the database never goes completely offline (C). However, the I/O suspension can result in increased latency (A) and a slowing down of responses (B). However, network requests will still be fulfilled; they will not fail (D).

188. C, D. RDS supports Aurora, PostgreSQL, MySQL, MariaDB, Oracle, and Microsoft SQL Server.

189. A, D. RDS supports Multi-AZ deployments. Automated backups are turned *on* by default. Some RDS databases—notably Maria and Aurora—are only supported through a managed service like RDS. And all RDS databases provide a SQL interface.

190. D. MySQL is by default available on 3306. You can also remember that databases are typically only available on unreserved ports, above 1024. Ports below 1024 are reserved for privileged services.

191. A. OLAP is online analytics processing, often associated with business intelligence. AWS services like Redshift are ideal for OLAP.

192. D. OLTP is online transaction processing and is generally the domain of relational databases in AWS.

193. A. Redshift is the prime example of AWS providing an OLAP service.

194. D. Aurora, as a managed service via RDS, is a relational database, and relational databases are generally the best answer for OLTP in AWS.

195. B, D. In OLTP questions, look for the relational databases. In this question, those are Oracle and SQL Server, and therefore the answers. memcache is one of the engines for ElastiCache and DynamoDB is a NoSQL database.

196. D. Redshift provides data warehousing on AWS, which is closely associated with OLAP.

197. A. EMR, Elastic MapReduce, is ideal for big data processing. Is uses the Hadoop and Spark frameworks and is a managed service for processing very large datasets.

198. C. This is a little trickier. The best way to remember how to answer a question like this is to associate Kinesis with streaming data, which implies real-time analysis. Kinesis can take in streams of data and do immediate processing on that.

199. B. QuickSight doesn't come up much in AWS study guides, but there is usually a single question on many AWS exams about it. QuickSight gives you "sight" into your application, which is the easiest way to remember it's about visualization.

200. D. This is another tough question, especially if both Kinesis and Athena appear in the answer choices. Kinesis handles streams of data and does real-time analytics; Athena is more on the interactive side. Athena analyzes data but allows standard SQL queries. That's why it's a better choice than Kinesis with this question.

201. B, D. EMR, or Elastic MapReduce, is most commonly used with Hadoop and Spark. Unfortunately, this simply has to be memorized; there's no good way to get at this unless you already know that Hadoop and Spark are ideal for data processing.

202. D. Aurora actually stores a whopping six copies of your data, across three availability zones, to ensure failover and disaster recovery.

203. B. Aurora actually stores a whopping six copies of your data, across three availability zones, to ensure failover and disaster recovery.

204. C. Aurora, under the RDS managed service, is about five times as fast as MySQL and three times as fast as PostgreSQL. Still, there's an easier way to remember this: Anytime an AWS exam asks you about speed or performance, it's generally the case that the AWS offering is the right answer. AWS won't ask you to choose MySQL or Oracle as a faster option than one of its own databases!

205. A. Aurora, under the RDS managed service, stores six copies of your data by default, across three availability zones. Additionally, there's an easier way to remember this: Anytime an AWS exam asks you about resilience, it's generally the case that the AWS offering is the right answer.

206. B, C. Aurora is compatible with both PostgreSQL and MySQL. These are also easier to choose because they are both relational databases, also managed through RDS.

207. B, D. RDS provides for SQL interaction as well as access through the RDS web APIs. RDS instances do *not* allow access via SSH or RDP.

208. C. RDS allows backup retention periods up to 35 days.

209. A. You can't use RDS because the question explicitly says you are installing Oracle on EC2 rather than using the managed service. In this case, then, you want the fastest disk space available, which will be EBS, Elastic Block Storage.

210. B, D. Anytime OLTP comes up, simply look for options that are RDS-supported databases, and if that fails, look for relational databases. In this question, the answers that fit these criteria are MariaDB and Aurora.

211. A, C. Anytime OLTP comes up, simply look for options that are RDS-supported databases, and if that fails, look for relational databases. In this question, the answers that fit these criteria are PostgreSQL and SQL Server. Since the question asks which are *not* suitable options, the correct selections are Kinesis (A) and Redshift (C).

212. A, C. A Multi-AZ setup provides disaster recovery options through a secondary database. This also implicitly provides data redundancy.

213. B, D. A read replica setup is intended to reduce the load on a single database instance by providing additional databases from which to read. This also has the "side effect" of reducing network latency via spreading out traffic across multiple instances.

214. A, C. A read replica setup is intended to reduce the load on a single database instance by providing additional databases from which to read. Applications can read from the replica (A) but not write to it (B). Only the primary instance—through RDS and AWS—can "write" changes to the replica (C).

215. C. Multi-AZ setups provide disaster recovery through a secondary instance (A and B), and all RDS databases support Multi-AZ (D). This just leaves C, which is not provided (and is the correct answer). Because only the primary instance is accessible, it is not any more performant than a standard RDS setup.

216. B. Multi-AZ setups use synchronous replication (B) to back up data to the secondary instance for the purposes of disaster recovery.

217. D. Read replicas use asynchronous replication (D), pushing data to the read replicas whenever possible, for improved read performance.

218. A. Read replicas are intended to provide scalability for your application by adding additional instances for increased reads from applications.

219. C. A Multi-AZ setup is about disaster recovery, and therefore durability. They provide automatic backups (so not A), upgrades happen on the primary database and then are replicated (so not B), and there is a primary and usually a single secondary instance (so not D). That leaves C: durability.

220. B. AWS provides up to five read replicas for a single database instance, configurable via the AWS console.

221. A, B. DynamoDB is a NoSQL database, and RDS is required for read replicas (so A is correct, as it does not support read replicas). Redshift is not a database, but rather a data warehousing tool, so also should be selected. Both MySQL and MariaDB support read replicas through RDS.

222. A, C. DynamoDB is a NoSQL database and does indeed offer "push-button" scaling (A). You can scale up the size of the database at any time, *without* needing to change the instance size (as you do with RDS instances). This makes C true.

223. B, C. DynamoDB is easier to scale than RDS as it does not require either read replicas or instance size changes to scale up, making A false. DynamoDB does use SSD drives, so B is true. It is also—according to AWS documentation—spread across three geographically distinct data centers, so D is correct.

224. A. DynamoDB uses eventually consistent reads by default, meaning a read might not immediately reflect the results of a very recent write. The remaining choices are not actual consistency models.

225. A, D. DynamoDB uses eventually consistent reads by default, meaning a read might not immediately reflect the results of a very recent write. It also offers a strongly consistent reads model, always reflecting the most recent write operations.

226. A, D. Delays occur in a strongly consistent read model when recently written data cannot be returned. Since a strongly consistent read model guarantees the latest data is returned, until that data is available, no response can be sent. This is the situation described in both option A and D. Option B involves replication, which is not relevant in this context, and C involves previous reads rather than writes.

227. D. VPCs put relatively few restrictions on the types and numbers of subnets supported. They can certainly support single and multiple private and public subnets alongside each other.

228. A, D. All instances in the default VPC have IP a public and private IP address by default at launch time.

229. C, D. All of the options are val   2 instances can have public and private addresses, elastic addresses, a   v4 and IPv6 addresses.

230. B, C. There is no concept of a V   peering with itself, and VPCs can only peer with other VPCs, not subnets. This makes A and D incorrect. VPCs *can* peer with other VPCs, in the same account or different ones (B and C).

231. A. A /16 offers 65,536 IP addresses. The lower the number, the larger the pool of IP addresses when using CIDR notation.

232. A. SWF stands for Simple Workflow, and Amazon SWF is the Amazon Simple Workflow Service.

233. D. SWF places no language restraints on your workflow, as long as interactions can be managed via HTTP requests and responses.

234. B. SWF provides an API, but it is neither the AWS-specific API nor language specific. Instead, SWF supports standard HTTP requests and responses.

235. D. SWF stands for Simple Workflow, an AWS managed service. That should be a clue that the key factor here is workflow management. Tasks are handled and coordinated across application components with SWF.

236. C. SWF is typically thought of as an asynchronous service, but it also supports synchronous tasking when needed.

237. B. SES is the Simple Email Service and is used for sending and receiving emails for AWS applications and services.

238. D. SQS is the Simple Queue Service. This should be a tip-off, but it's actually *messaging* in the question that is the key word. SQS does provide queuing but is ultimately a queue-based message delivery system.

239. C, D. SNS is the Simple Notification Service and SQS is the Simple Queue Service. The two are not interchangeable (A is wrong). SNS pushes notifications, while SQS allows for pulls of its messages (so B is wrong, but D is correct). Finally, SNS handles notifications, and SQS handles messages (C is correct).

240. B, D. Worker nodes (D) can poll SQS for new messages (B) and then pull those messages when they are available. Tasks are associated with SWF, while notifications are associated with SNS.

241. B, C. SNS is a push-based service (C) that pushes notifications (B) to anything subscribed to an appropriate topic.

242. A, B. SWF is associated with tasks and is distinct from (for example) SQS, because it guarantees a single delivery of all tasks.

243. A, B. SNS provides topics that can be subscribed to; then notifications related to that topic are pushed to all the topic subscribers.

244. A. SWF tasks are assigned once and only once.

245. B. This is a bit esoteric, but even if you're unsure, you should be able to reason this one out. A topic is simply a name or "category" to which subscribers can attach and receive notifications. Therefore, a linked list and a named message don't make much sense. (They're also constructs that are never seen in AWS documentation for the most part.) An IAM role is an AWS construct, but roles are related to permissions. This leaves only B, an Amazon Resource Name, which is correct.

246. D. SQS will guarantee that a message is delivered at least once, but that message may be redelivered.

247. C. A SWF domain is a collection of related workflows.

248. D. SQS queues only make an "attempt" to deliver messages in order (more or less a FIFO approach) but do not guarantee FIFO. If strict FIFO is needed, that option can be selected.

249. B. SQS queues only make an "attempt" to deliver messages in order (more or less a FIFO approach) but do not guarantee FIFO. If strict FIFO is needed, that option can be selected. Option B will ensure that orders are processed in the order in which they were received.

250. C, D. Other than the slightly odd answer choices (which sometimes comes up!), all VPCs can communicate with the hub, so C and D cover all the options.

251. B, D. Any spoke in a hub-and-spoke model can only directly communicate with the hub (option B), as well as any other peered VPCs (option D).

252. B, C. Any spoke in a hub-and-spoke model can only directly communicate with the hub (option B is true, while A is false). And the hub (VPC G) can communicate with all spokes (so C is true, but D is false).

253. C, D. Any spoke in a hub-and-spoke model can only directly communicate with the hub. This makes A and B true and C and D false; so the right answers are C and D.

254. B. NACLs are stateless—rules and must exist for inbound and outbound. Security groups are stateful—anything allowed in is allowed back out automatically.

255. A. NACLs are stateless—rules must exist for inbound and outbound—and security groups are stateful—anything allowed in is allowed back out automatically.

256. B. NACLs are stateless—rules must exist for inbound and outbound—and security groups are stateful—anything allowed in is allowed back out automatically.

257. B. ALBs are redundant across at least two subnets.

258. A, D. This is a little tricky. While the default VPC automatically creates a subnet, additional VPCs do not. You do automatically get a security group, route table, and NACL, so in this case, you'd want to choose options A and D.

259. C, D. The key here is "default VPC." While subnets are not created in additional custom VPCs, the default VPC does get a subnet automatically (as well as an internet gateway). And all new VPCs get route tables, NACLs, and security groups.

260. A, C. The key here is "default VPC." While subnets are not created in additional custom VPCs, the default VPC does get an internet gateway automatically (as well as a subnet). And all new VPCs get route tables, NACLs, and security groups.

261. A. This is really tough and requires pure memorization. The default VPC has a CIDR block of /16, but the default subnet in each AZ is a /20.

262. B. This is a case of rote memorization. Default VPCs get a /16 CIDR block assigned to them.

263. D. There is no default CIDR block for custom VPCs. While the default VPC has a /16 CIDR block, custom VPCs must have this entered in.

264. B. In general, the smaller the number after the slash, the larger the CIDR block. /16 is the largest valid block. A /16 offers 65,536 IPv4 addresses.

265. C, D. Default VPCs have a default subnet, along with a NACL, security group, and internet gateway, and a route table as well.

266. B. The default VPC has an internet gateway, and instances are given public IP addresses, so option B is correct. You do not create the default VPC (A), and security groups control specific access, not the public or private nature of the VPC and instances within it (C).

267. A, B. The default VPC does have an internet gateway attached to it, but custom VPCs do not. This is an important exam topic!

268. A, C. Option A is true for both the default and custom VPCs: All VPCs have NACLs automatically created. While all outgoing traffic is allowed out by default (C), incoming traffic is restricted by default (B)—this includes inbound HTTP traffic (D).

269. A, D. All VPCs have NACLs, security groups, and route tables automatically created. However, only the default VPC has a default subnet and an internet gateway created as well.

270. B, D. All VPCs have NACLs, security groups, and route tables automatically created. However, only the default VPC has a default subnet and an internet gateway created as well, different from the custom VPC.

271. B, C. All EC2 instances in the default VPC have both a public and private IP address. They do *not* have an elastic IP address, and the security group that is created by default does not allow any inbound traffic (until changed manually).

272. C, D. All EC2 instances in the default VPC have both a public and private IP address. Therefore, the only addition to serve web content would be to allow the web traffic in via security group.

273. C, D. Instances in any non-default VPCs need to be made public via an elastic or public IP (A), and the VPC itself needs an internet gateway (B). Further, you need to allow in web traffic via the security group (C). So this is an "All of the above" situation, translating into options C and D.

274. B, C. A VPC endpoint provides a connection over the Amazon network between your VPC and a service, such as S3 (B). This avoids leaving the network and routing over the public Internet, which inherently provides greater security for the traffic involved (C).

275. D. A VPC endpoint does not require any of these to connect; it is a private connection outside of these constructs altogether, which is part of why it is an attractive solution for internal AWS communication.

276. B, C. A VPC endpoint is a virtual device that provides redundancy via AWS (and automatically). This makes options B and C correct, and A wrong. VPC endpoints scale horizontally, not vertically.

277. B, D. A VPC endpoint can connect to S3 and DynamoDB, as well as a host of additional AWS services, so B is true. It does not require an internet gateway or a VPN connection and does not route traffic over the public Internet (D).

278. A, C. A VPC endpoint comes in two flavors: an interface endpoint, which provides an elastic network interface and a private IP address, and a gateway endpoint, targeted for a specific route in your route table.

279. A, D. This is pretty tough and is arguably right at the boundary of what the CSA Associate exam might ask. A gateway endpoint handles all traffic for a supported AWS service. Further, it's not a specific portion of that service, so you can rule out a particular Kinesis data stream (C). That leaves A, B, and D. A and D make sense, while routing private traffic to Route 53 does not.

280. A, C. This is another tough question. An interface endpoint provides a private IP address for connecting to a specific entry point for a specific AWS service. Anything that's more general—like DynamoDB—isn't a valid candidate. Additionally, a VPN (B) doesn't make sense, as a VPN is a different type of connection altogether. In this case, that leaves a specific API gateway and a specific Kinesis data stream (A and C).

281. C, D. Instances that take advantage of a VPC endpoint do not need to have a public IP address or use a NAT instance. Instead, assuming they have a route to the endpoint (D), they send traffic over the AWS network to the connected service (C).

282. C. The best way to remember this is to consider the process for creating an instance: you must select the security group for every instance. So security groups operate at the instance level (C).

283. A. Security groups only provide for allow rules (A). All other traffic is automatically denied, so allow rules are the only means of allowing traffic in.

284. A, C. Security groups disallow all traffic unless there are specific allow rules for the traffic in the security group.

285. A. Security groups evaluate all the rules on the group before deciding how to handle traffic.

286. D. Security groups evaluate all the rules on the group before deciding how to handle traffic.

287. B. Five VPCs are allowed per region, per account, unless you contact AWS to raise this default limit.

288. B. All custom VPCs have a route table (so A is false) and a NACL (so C is false) and will *not* have an internet gateway (D is false). This leaves B, which is true: subnets can communicate with each other across availability zones by default.

289. D. Only a bastion host (D) makes SSH available to private instances. You can use a NAT gateway or NAT instance to route traffic from these instances out, but a bastion host allows for SSH into private instances.

290. A, C. Both a NAT instance and a NAT gateway provide for outgoing traffic to route to the Internet from instances within a private subnet.

291. A. A VPC can only have a single internet gateway.

292. C. A single region can only have five VPCs by default, but this limit can be raised by contacting AWS.

293. C. A single VPC can have a single internet gateway. This limit isn't based on region (D) but on VPC (C).

294. A, D. First, realize it's possible that almost any of these answers could be a part of a larger solution. However, the question asks for the simplest—or most direct—solutions. Given that, the solutions that are best are giving the instances public IP addresses (D) and adding an internet gateway to the VPC. You also will likely need routes in and out, security groups, etc.

295. B, C. Given the internet gateway, the most likely issues are the instances being accessible via IP (which C addresses) and traffic for web/HTTP being disallowed (B).

296. D. VPCs can have a single internet gateway and multiple subnets. However, instances within a VPC with a public address have that address released when it is stopped and are reassigned a new IP when restarted.

297. B. A VPC can peer with unlimited other VPCs, so B is false. A subnet cannot span AZs, a VPC can peer with VPCs in other accounts, and a VPC having an internet gateway has no bearing on the public or private status of subnets within it.

298. D. All of the statements about NAT instances are false in A through C. Further, a NAT gateway is preferable to a NAT instance because it is managed by AWS rather than you, the architect.

299. D. A VPC cannot be changed from dedicated hosting tenancy to default hosting. You have to re-create the VPC.

300. A. Changes to a security group take place immediately. As a note, option D is a bit misleading. While security groups operate at various levels, they absolutely affect VPCs, so D is false.

301. A. This is a routing question. Instances need to have their outbound traffic directed to the internet gateway on the VPC, and then that traffic can flow outward to the Internet.

302. A. CloudFront supports both static and dynamic content.

303. A, C. With only the information presented, the best options are to focus on the database and the dynamic content; the web application servers (from the question's limited information) are not the issue. That means look at the database instance size (A) and caching dynamic content (C). B and D focus on the web app instances, which would not appear to be the issue.

304. B, C. An internet gateway is required to handle Internet traffic, and a VPC endpoint is ideal for connecting the instances to S3. A customer gateway is used in setting up a VPN or site-to-site connection, and if NACL changes are required, you'd make them to the existing NACL, not a new one.

305. C, D. The key here is recalling that the default VPC already has an internet gateway attached, so you wouldn't need one (B). A customer gateway is for a VPN or direct connection. This leaves C, a VPC endpoint for communication with S3, and D, updated NACL rules for the endpoint and the gateway (potentially).

306. A, D. The most likely culprits are the routing table of the VPC subnet and the virtual private gateway. A storage gateway (B) is not part of a Direct Connect solution, nor is a NAT instance (C).

307. B. Route propagation is a routing option that automatically propagates routes to the route tables so you don't need to manually enter VPN routes. It's most common in a Direct Connect setup. A is too broad a statement—not all routes are automatically copied. C is incorrect, and in D, a storage gateway is not part of a Direct Connect solution (it can be, but isn't required).

308. B. This is a matter of rote memorization. All metadata for instances is available at `http://169.254.169.254`, at `/latest/meta-data`. `/latest/instance-data` is actually not a URL that is responsive to requests.

309. A. S3 is highly durable and stores data as key-value pairs.

310. B. B is the only answer that doesn't presume at least semi-frequent access. Glacier is best for files that are rarely accessed and do not require quick access times.

311. A, D. The best answer here is to enable MFA Delete (D). However, to do this, you'll also need versioning (A). It is not practical to disallow developers from all delete access (B), and signed URLs do not help the issue.

312. C. For all new AWS accounts, 20 instances are allowed per region. However, you can increase this limit by requesting it via AWS support.

313. C. The only one of these that makes sense is C, increasing the size of the NAT instance. It is impossible to add an additional internet gateway to a VPC that already has one (A), and adding an additional elastic IP requires using a newer EC2 instance, and it will not affect performance in this case (B).

314. B. If instances are scaling up and down quickly, this means that the thresholds for adding and removing instances are being met frequently. Since you don't want to reduce the scaling up to meet demand, you should increase what it takes for the system to scale down; that's what B suggests. Proactive cycling (A) won't help the situation and C is completely made up.

315. A, C. Routing is one of the most important steps (A); you must set the route to the public Internet to go to the NAT instance. Additionally, you need to disable source/destination checks, a commonly forgotten step (C). The NAT instance *cannot* be in a private subnet (B), and D doesn't make sense in this context.

316. B. This is a tough one because it must simply be memorized. CloudWatch provides disk read operations, CPU usage, and inbound network traffic but does *not* provide memory usage by default.

317. A, B. The instance will need an elastic IP for public communication (A) and should be behind the same ELB as the other instances (B). Adding it into a private subnet (C) will remove its ability to communicate with the public Internet. D looks good, but if the instance is in the same subnet as the other instances, it automatically gets their routes; routing tables apply to the subnet, not a specific instance.

318. D. The public Internet is addressed via 0.0.0.0/0.

319. A. The public Internet is addressed via 0.0.0.0/0, so if that's the destination, the target should be the internet gateway within the VPC.

Domain 2: Define Performant Architectures

1. D. There is no way to reason through this; it is a matter of memorization. There is no charge associated with data replication in this scenario.

2. C, D. All of these are valid options. Although it's not particularly common, you can set up a read replica in an on-premises instance. Additionally, read replicas are often created in separate regions from the primary instance, to improve performance for clients closer to different regions than the primary instance.

3. C. A read replica configuration is aimed squarely at increasing database performance, specifically the performance of reading data from an RDS instance.

4. D. All three of these databases support read replicas. Most other databases supported by RDS (Oracle, for example, or Aurora) offer other approaches to gain similar functionality to read replicas but do not support the AWS read replica functionality.

5. B. Currently, read replicas in RDS are only supported by MariaDB, MySQL, and PostgreSQL.

6. A, C. A read replica is a read-only instance of a database created from a snapshot of the primary instance (A). Read replicas can be in the same instance, or a different one, as the primary instance (so B is false). Read replicas are updated via asynchronous replication—the most performant approach—from the primary database.

7. C, D. Read replicas can be in a different region than the primary instance (D), and they replicate all the databases in the primary instance (C). You can have up to five read replicas at a time for a single instance (so A is false). While MySQL and MariaDB are supported (B), Aurora is not.

8. D. The root issue here is that a read replica setup only allows for five read replicas. This is not a limit that can be raised by AWS either (so C is out). Option A won't address the issue, and option B isn't accurate; there are no EU limitations affecting the issue here. The only answer that would result in being able to create the instance is D: By turning off an existing instance, you can create a new fifth replica in the desired region.

9. C, D. Read replicas are focused on performance, so you can generally eliminate any answers related to disaster recovery—in this case, A. Read replicas work with RDS databases, as well, so B is out; on-premises databases aren't supported. This leaves C and D, which are both valid.

10. B, C. No backups are taken from any instance automatically, including the primary instance, so A is false. Since each read replica has its own database instance running, both B and C are valid. Replication is asynchronous rather than synchronous (so D is false).

11. A, B. A is false because you can create read replicas in the same AZ as the primary instance. There is no requirement to use multiple AZs, as there is with a Multi-AZ setup. B is also false; read replicas provide no disaster recovery options. Both C and D are true.

12. A. Only A is correct. A Multi-AZ setup is focused on disaster recovery and fault tolerance, while read replicas provide performance and scalability.

13. D. There is no difference in how applications communicate with read replicas as compared to the communication with non-replica instances. In fact, applications don't "know" that they're communicating with a read replica other than an inability to make writes.

14. A, D. A and D are both solutions that would be aided by additional read-only instances. B is not a valid answer because updating records would still only be possible with the primary instance; read replicas don't support writes. C is incorrect because read replicas do not provide automated fault recovery.

15. B. You need to be careful here. While read replicas are not advertised or even suggested as solutions for disaster recovery, option B does provide a somewhat manual process to use them in that manner. While you get no automated backups or failover (A or C), you can manually promote a read replica instance to a stand-alone instance if you have to. Still, a Multi-AZ setup is almost always a more robust solution for fault tolerance.

16. A, B. Both A and B are ideal situations for read replicas. C is the usual incorrect answer: read replicas don't provide automated backups. And D is not accurate; the actual database processing doesn't improve; you are merely adding more sources for reading data for clients.

17. D. AWS does not support circular replication through RDS. While some of the databases supported by RDS do, RDS itself does not provide access to this functionality.

18. A, C. You can create a read replica through the AWS console (A), the AWS API (C), and the AWS CLI (not mentioned, but still true).

19. B. As has been said numerous times, read replicas are not a backup strategy, nor do they cause automatic backups to be set up. However, you must turn on automatic backups for the primary database instance to enable read replicas.

20. A. This bears careful reading. Amazon RDS does not support circular replication, which means one database reads from a second database but then is replicated back by that second database. However, it is absolutely permissible for one database to replicate another database and then be the source for a third database. This makes option A correct.

21. D. There is no difference in response to a change in the backup window based on how that window is changed (API, console, etc.). All changes take place immediately.

22. B. This is another straight memorization question: Amazon RDS backups can be retained for up to 35 days, and no longer.

23. C. There are two components to this question: using RDS or EC2 for Oracle hosting and the class of storage to select. While RDS is a better option in the general case, it is likely not possible to use RDS in this scenario due to the custom plug-in required. This eliminates A and B. Given an installation on EC2, then, the question becomes which storage class is faster: provisioned IOPS or magnetic. The answer here is always provisioned IOPS.

24. B, C. Option C should be the immediately obvious first choice. Anytime you have custom plug-ins, you will likely need to install your database on an EC2 instance rather than using RDS. Options A and D are really both about network routes and services around your database, and both can be accomplished without affecting your EC2 vs. RDS decision. This leaves B, which also logically makes sense: If you have a very large database, and it will grow (as almost all databases do), then sizing restraints on RDS can be a limiting factor.

25. A, C. This should be an easy question if you're prepared. While it's easy to forget if Aurora and MariaDB are RDS options—they are!—you should know that DynamoDB is AWS's NoSQL database, and Redshift is a data-warehousing solution.

26. A. This is not particularly difficult as long as you understand that a Multi-AZ deployment is concerned with failover, not performance. Option A is correct: There is no particular performance increase in a Multi-AZ deployment, unless read replicas are also turned on (which isn't specified). B is false because only the primary database responds to requests in a Multi-AZ deployment. C is actually a true statement but does not have a bearing on the subject of the question: performance. And D doesn't actually make sense in the context of the question at all!

27. A. This one is a little tricky as it requires understanding what default options AWS puts in place. By default, root volumes are terminated on instance deletion, and by default, additional EBS volumes attached to an instance are not. This makes option A true. However, note that these settings can be changed! Also note that option D is not true in any configuration.

28. B. The default for all new accounts is 100 allowed S3 buckets; this is consistent across AWS and does not change via configuration (meaning that C and D are not correct). However, this value can be raised through asking AWS for an exception and providing a reasonable justification, making B the correct answer.

29. B. Replication occurs synchronously from a primary instance to a secondary instance in a Multi-AZ setup. Asynchronous replication only occurs in a read replica setup (which can be enabled in addition to a Multi-AZ setup).

30. C. Replication occurs asynchronously from a primary instance to the various read replicas in a read replica setup. As a result, updates are not guaranteed to be instant on the read replicas. Synchronous replication occurs in a Multi-AZ setup.

31. A, B. Classic load balancers support both IPv4 and IPv6. They support HTTP/1 and HTTP/1.1, but only application load balancers support HTTP/2. Further, you must register individual instances, rather than target groups, with classic load balancers; registering target groups is a functionality only available with application load balancers.

32. A. AWS accounts allow you five elastic IP addresses per region by default. As with most AWS defaults, this can be raised by contacting AWS and providing a reasonable justification.

33. C. Officially, instances can have up to 28 attachments. One of those attachments is the network interface attachment, leaving 27 attachments available for EBS volumes. However, the better approach is to remember that an instance can attach to a root volume and several more volumes (more than two); this eliminates options A and B. Additionally, instances cannot have unlimited attachments. This leaves the correct answer, C.

34. A. Be careful with the wording, to ensure that you do not misread this as asking how many EBS volumes can be attached to an EC2 instance (a different question altogether). A single EBS volume can only be attached to one instance at a time.

35. B, C. This should be an easy answer: Application load balancers, as well as classic load balancers, only support HTTP and HTTPS.

36. A, C. RDS provides two (and only two) methods for backing up RDS databases at this point: automated backups and automated snapshots. S3 lifecycle management policies are not applicable to RDS databases, and data pipeline is not relevant in this context.

37. B. Data written to and from cache is ephemeral, and if your instance is reading and writing that data frequently, the only way to ensure that your snapshot isn't missing data is to stop the instance from running altogether and to then take a snapshot (B). Both A and C will take snapshots but will likely miss any cached data. With option D, you cannot detach a root volume from an instance (it's unclear from the question if the cached data is being written to EBS, EFS, or another storage mechanism in any case), and so it is not a safe choice.

38. B, C. Option A is invalid because Multi-AZ is a disaster recovery solution; the primary database is the only instance that can respond to traffic in normal operation (unless read replicas are also set up). Option B is valid; caching user data would reduce round trips to the database and should reduce lag for users. Option C also makes sense, as having additional databases from which to read should decrease network latency to a single RDS instance. Option D is not helpful as the problem appears to be in retrieving credentials, not in the web tier itself.

39. C. Standard S3 (A) is not a bad choice, but is the most expensive, and both it and S3-IA (B) are more expensive than S3 One Zone-IA because of their increased availability and resilience. The key here is that photos can be lost without an issue, making S3 One Zone-IA the better option. S3 RRS is no longer recommended by AWS.

40. C. This should be automatic: Anytime a large data transfer is involved (especially on an AWS exam!), the answer should be Snowball. This comes up a lot and should be an easy correct answer.

41. A, D. The only tricky answer here is B. While Multipart Upload absolutely would improve the experience of uploading large files (larger than 10 GB, for example), it is not required; therefore, option B is not the best option to choose. Options A and D both are only possible with Multipart Upload enabled. Option C is false, as security is not related to Multipart Upload.

42. C. A placement group is concerned primarily with network throughput and reducing latency among EC2 instances within a single availability zone. AWS does support a placement group spanning multiple AZs via spread placement groups, but unless "spread" is specifically mentioned, you should assume the question references a "normal" (or "cluster") placement group.

43. A, B. Cluster placement groups (the default type of placement group) must be made up of instances that exist within a single availability zone (A). This results in increased throughput for network activity (B) but does not affect actual disk performance when writing to S3 (C). Instances can also be of different types, so D is also false.

44. B, C. Spread placement groups can span availability zones and support up to seven instances per zone (C). Like cluster groups, this results in increased throughput for network activity (B). You must specify the distinct underlying hardware for spread placement groups, which means that D is false.

45. D. This is a question where the answer is nonintuitive. All the S3 storage classes have the same durability. Even S3 One Zone-IA has 11 9s of durability in the single availability zone in which it resides.

46. A. Availability starts at 99.99% for S3 and then decreases to 99.9% for S3-IA, 99.5% for S3 One Zone-IA, and finally N/A for Glacier.

47. D. This question is easy if you recall that lifecycle transitions are concerned with moving between these storage classes. Therefore, all of these classes support those transitions.

48. A, C. All S3 and S3-IA data is stored in a single region and within at least three availability zones within that region. There is no "global" region for S3 storage.

49. C. Redshift is the only database or service in this list suitable for online analytics processing (OLAP). DynamoDB is an object database (NoSQL), and both Aurora and Oracle are relational databases, better suited for transaction processing.

50. B. All the major databases supported by RDS—MariaDB, SQL Server, MySQL, Oracle, and PostgreSQL—allow up to 16 TB of storage for a provisioned IOPS volume.

51. A. A provisioned IOPS EBS volume is a solid-state drive that provides the highest performance volume.

52. B. A cold HDD is the cheapest EBS option, so B is correct. It is not solid state (A), it is not appropriate for data warehousing (C), and it is not available to be used as a boot volume.

53. A, D. This is easiest to remember by noting that HDD types are not available to use as boot volumes. The SSD types (A, D) are, and are correct.

54. B, D. A General Purpose SSD is the less-expensive SSD (compared to provisioned IOPS), so B is a valid answer. It also provides low-latency performance and is bootable. Option A is more suitable for provisioned IOPS, and C is better for a throughput-optimized HDD.

55. A, B. Magnetic volumes are older and generally not used much. They are ideal for saving money (A) or for infrequently accessed data (B).

56. B, C. Provisioned IOPS volumes are not inexpensive (A) but are well-suited for critical database workloads and throughput (B and C).

57. A, C. An SSD volume is best for transactional workloads (A) with a large number of small I/O sized read/write operations.

58. B, D. An HDD-backed volume is best for streaming workloads where throughput needs to be maximized over IOPS.

59. C. While it is possible that a General Purpose SSD might be sufficient to support an Oracle installation that doesn't do a lot of processing, the best option is C, a provisioned IOPS SSD. Provisioned IOPS handles transaction processing well and will handle the large number of reads and writes that an Oracle installation would need.

60. A. This use case is one where access needs to be minimal, as does cost. If you have infrequently accessed data and cost is a major driver, magnetic drives might be a good option. While throughput-optimized HDDs are still cheaper than SSDs, magnetic is the cheapest option and would work fine for a set of data that is accessed without high performance needs.

61. A, C. You can boot an EC2 instance off any SSD type, as well as the magnetic type. HDD options are not available to use as boot volumes.

62. B, C. The HDD EBS volume types are not available to use as boot volumes, so B and C are the correct answers.

63. C. There is no such thing as a weighting load balancer. The other options are actual options.

64. A, C. An ELB is an elastic load balancer and generally refers to a classic load balancer. An ALB is an application load balancer. So A and C are valid; MLB and VLB are not acronyms or abbreviations for load balancers.

65. C. An ALB operates at Level 7, the individual request (application) level. Network load balancers operate at Level 4, the connection (transport) level. No load balancers operate at Level 1, and there is no Level 8 in the TCP/OSI stack.

66. B. An ALB operates at Level 7, the individual request (application) level. Network load balancers operate at Level 4, the connection (transport) level. No load balancers operate at Level 1, and there is no Level 8 in the TCP/OSI stack.

67. B, C. Classic load balancers operate at both the connection (Level 4) and the request (Level 7) layer of the TCP stack. An ALB operates at Level 7, the individual request level. Network load balancers operate at Level 4, the connection (transport) level.

68. D. With the newer features of an ALB, all of these use cases are supported. It is important to recognize that ALBs can balance across containers, making B true, and pointing you to D: all of the above.

69. B. This is a difficult question, and right at the edges of what the Architect exam might ask. However, it is possible to use a load balancer to operate within a VPC. It can be pointed internal, instead of Internet-facing, and distribute traffic to the private IPs of the VPC.

70. B. ALBs offer the most flexibility in routing and load distribution.

71. C. Network load balancers can handle the extremely high request load mentioned in the question as well as route between static IP addressed instances.

72. B. An ALB offers SSL termination and makes the SSL offload process very simple through tight integration with SSL processes. While an ELB will handle SSL termination, it does not offer the management features that ALBs do.

73. D. Both ALBs and ELBs offer SSL termination. While an ALB is a better choice when considering the management of SSL certificates—due to its ACM integration—both ELBs and ALBs are correct when considering just SSL termination.

74. D. Route 53 supports up to 50 domain names by default, but this limit can be raised if requested.

75. D. Route 53 supports all of the records mentioned, including alias records.

76. A. Route 53 does support zone apex (naked) domain records.

77. A, B. ElastiCache offers two engines: memcached and redis. Neither C nor D are even real things!

78. D. ElastiCache, when used through AWS, handles all of these tasks and more: hardware provisioning, software patching, setup, configuration, monitoring, failure recovery, and backups.

79. B, D. This is another example of an odd answer set, which sometimes appears on the AWS exam. In this case, all answers are valid, which means choosing two: B and D (D references the remaining two, A and C)!

80. A, C. ElastiCache is an in-memory data store (A) that shards across instances (C). It is not in itself a data distribution mechanism, which is why B is not correct. And it is not a monitoring solution at all (D).

81. D. CloudFront allows interaction via CloudFormation, the AWS CLI, the AWS console, the AWS CLI, the AWS APIs, and the various SDKs that AWS provides.

82. A, C. CloudFront can front a number of AWS services: AWS Shield, S3, ELBs (including ALBs), and EC2 instances.

83. B, C. CloudFront can front a number of AWS services: AWS Shield, S3, ELBs (including ALBs), and EC2 instances.

84. A, B. CloudFront can front a number of AWS services: AWS Shield, S3, ELBs (including ALBs), and EC2 instances. It also most recently supports Lambda@Edge as an origin.

85. A, C. This is a bit difficult, as CloudFront is typically associated with performance (A), and not a lot else. However, CloudFront also provides deep integration with many managed AWS services, such as S3, EC2, ELBs, and even Route 53.

86. B, D. CloudFront automatically provides AWS Shield (standard) to protect from DDoS, and it also can integrate with AWS WAF and AWS Shield advanced. These combine to secure content at the edge. HTTPS is not required (so A is incorrect), and there is no KMS involvement with CloudFront (C).

87. B, D. Edge locations number more than both regions and availability zones.

88. A, C. CloudFront is easy to set up and lets you create a global content delivery network without contracts (A). It's also a mechanism for distributing content at low latency (C). Creating websites and the actual file storage reference in B and D are not features of CloudFront but of LightSail (for example) and S3, respectively.

89. A, B. CloudFront can serve static content from S3 and dynamic content generated by EC2 instances.

90. B. When you create a CloudFront distribution, you register a domain name for your static and dynamic content. This domain should then be used by clients.

91. A, C. CloudFront will always handle requests that it receives. It will either return the requested content if cached (A) or retrieve that content by requesting it from an origin server (C). It will not redirect the client (D), nor will it pass the request on directly (B).

92. C, D. Both A and B are true. C is not, as routing will occur to the nearest edge location to the client, not the origin server. D is false; RDS is not a valid origin server for CloudFront.

93. D. There is no charge associated with data moving from any region to a CloudFront edge location.

94. A, B. S3 stores files and CloudFront stores copies of files, so A is true. Both also encrypt their files (B) as needed. Only CloudFront caches files (C), and only CloudFront can guarantee low-latency distribution (D).

95. B, D. CloudFront can store and serve both static (HTML and CSS, option D) and dynamic (PHP, option B) content. SQL queries cannot be directly returned, nor can an actual Lambda function. You can front the result of a Lambda@Edge function, but not the function itself.

96. A, B. CloudFront supports a variety of origin servers, including a non-AWS origin server (A). It supports EC2 (B), regardless of region, as well. It does not support RDS or SNS.

97. A. An edge location is a data center that delivers CloudFront content. Edge locations are spread across the world.

98. B. A distribution is the setup including your origin servers and how the content from those servers is distributed via CloudFront. It does not specifically refer to cached content at any given point in time.

99. D. Edge locations check for updated content every 24 hours by default, but this value can be changed.

100. A. Edge locations can be set to have a 0-second expiration period, which effectively means no caching occurs.

101. B, C. The most obvious culprit is a very low expiration period (B). Ensure that time is not close to 0. Beyond that, it's possible that—especially in conjunction with a very low expiration period—your compute resources or storage resources are getting flooded with requests. Consider using additional origin servers.

102. A. Setting an expiration period to 0 expires all content (A). It actually would slow down response time and has nothing to do with DDoS attacks. While it would technically always return the most current content (D), that's not a good reason to take this step; it defeats the purpose of CloudFront if the period is left at that value.

103. B, C. First, there is no mechanism either in the AWS console (A) or the AWS CLI (D) to interact directly with files on CloudFront distributions or edge locations. Second, the correct solution is to remove the file and then wait for the expiration period to cause a reload—which can be forced by setting that time to 0.

104. C. You need to remove a file from CloudFront's origin servers before doing anything else, because files are replicated from the origin server. If the file exists, it will end up on an edge location. Then, with the file removed, the expiration period can be set to 0, and the cache will be updated—resulting in the file being removed.

105. C. The invalidation API is the fastest way to remove a file or object, although it will typically incur additional cost.

106. A. S3 will always be the most available S3 storage class. This should be an easy correct answer.

107. D. This can be a bit tricky. While S3 is more available, all the S3-based storage classes provide the same first byte latency: milliseconds. Remember that performance is identical; availability is not.

108. D. This is another semi-trick question. With the exception of Glacier, retrieving data from the various S3 storage classes should be virtually identical (network issues notwithstanding). The classes differ in availability, but not in how fast data can be accessed. (They also differ in terms of charging for the number of accesses of that data.)

109. C. Glacier data retrieval, using the standard class, takes 3–5 hours on average.

110. B. The difference between S3 and S3-IA is cost, and frequency of access (B). Retrieval is just as fast as S3 (so A is wrong), and data in S3-IA is stored redundantly (C and D).

111. C, D. C and D are both false. RDS instances cannot be origin servers, and the default expiration period is 24 hours, not 12.

112. D. CloudFront allows all of these as origin servers: S3, EC2 instances, ALBs, etc.

113. D. A collection of edge locations is a distribution.

114. C. An RTMP distribution is the Adobe Real-Time Messaging Protocol and is suitable for using S3 buckets as an origin server to serve streaming media.

115. A, C. CloudFront supports both web distributions and RTMP distributions. Media and edge distributions are not valid distribution types.

116. A, B. You can read and write objects directly to an edge location. You cannot delete or update them directly; only the CloudFront service can handle that.

117. A, D. ElastiCache is ideal for high-performance and real-time processing as well as heavy-duty business intelligence. It does not shine as much with offline transactions, where speed is less essential, and it's not at all suitable for long-term or record storage.

118. B, D. Consider ElastiCache as only useful for storing transient data. Further, it's not a persistent store; therefore, it's great for caching data from a database or message service.

119. A, C. Consider ElastiCache as only useful for storing transient data. Further, it's not a persistent store; therefore, it's great for caching data from a message queue or providing very fast ephemeral storage.

120. A. ElastiCache uses shards as a grouping mechanism for individual redis nodes. So a single node is part of a shard, which in turn is part of a cluster (option A).

121. D. A storage gateway using cached volumes will cache frequently accessed data while storing the entire dataset on S3 in AWS.

122. C. A storage gateway using stored volumes will store all data locally while backing up the data to S3 in AWS as well.

123. C. A storage gateway using stored volumes will store all data locally, while all the other solutions store data in the cloud. Accessing local data will always be faster than accessing cloud data.

124. A. A storage gateway using stored volumes will store all data locally, providing low latency access to that data. Further, the entire dataset is backed up to S3 for disaster recovery. S3 is durable and available, but not as fast as accessing local data. A VTL provides a tape backup interface, but not necessarily fast data access.

125. B. The problem here is trying to tag individual folders. You can use IAM for permissions, but a particular folder cannot be tagged separately from other folders; only an entire bucket can be tagged.

126. D. A customer gateway with stored volumes provides the lowest latency for file access. A cached volume would not work because the majority of the files are the concern rather than just a small subset.

127. A. Configuring read replicas throughout all regions would provide the best response time on reads for customers spread across those same regions (A). While using multiple regions does provide some disaster recovery help, read replicas are really not a particularly effective disaster recovery approach. As for option C, read replicas do not increase network throughput; they just spread load out over the replicas, which may or may not desaturate the networks involved.

128. C. Read replicas are ultimately about providing faster read access to clients. If all your clients are in one region, then there is little advantage to adding read replicas to additional regions. Instead, providing replicas in the same region as the clients gives them the fastest access (C).

129. B. An argument could be made for option A here; customers will not be routed to a different region than the closest one if there are resources in a close region (so C is wrong) and D doesn't make much sense here. However, it is possible that if the primary region failed altogether, you could convert a replica in another region to a primary database, meaning that B has some merit.

130. A, D. Read replicas can be backed up manually, and of course read from. However, they effectively become read-only instances, so cannot be written to. You also cannot fail over to a read replica. You can convert it to a stand-alone instance, but that is a manual process that is not a failover. Therefore, A and D are correct.

131. A, D. This is a tough question because there is not much context other than knowing the database is not performing well, in a general sense. However, of the options given, switching to DynamoDB and adding Multi-AZ would do little to improve performance. (Note that switching to DynamoDB could help, as DynamoDB auto-scales to handle load, but this is still not the best of the available answers). Adding read replicas and looking at bigger instances are safer and better answers given this limited context.

132. C, D. Only C and D would have a guaranteed effect here. While it is possible that S3 would deliver the PDFs faster, you'd still have heavy network traffic over AWS, and there's no guarantee given the information here that S3 would be faster than RDS. B looks appealing, but note that the files are not accessed frequently. This means that caching is not going to help response time, as the files aren't accessed enough for caching to kick in and be effective. The best options are setting up read replicas and looking at beefing up the database instance.

133. B, C. There are typically a lot of "the database is being overwhelmed" questions on the exam, and this is one of those. The key here is understanding that data is accessed infrequently, meaning that caching solutions (A and D) likely won't help. Further, the staff is on-site, meaning that a customer gateway (C) could be a valid solution. Finally, it's almost always safe to at least consider upgrading the database instance.

134. B. Here, the key details are infrequent data access and a geographically distributed customer base. This means that read replicas spread out across the country are the best bet (B). Caching won't help, so A and D are out, and a storage gateway won't help customers that aren't accessing the data on-site.

135. D. This is a tough question, as several answers are valid. However, the key consideration here is that a single image is accessed several thousand times a day. Rather than adding instance power or read replicas (A and B), caching the images is the best approach, as it reduces overall database reads. In general, pulling an image from a cache (D) is far faster than performing a database read.

136. A, C. Route 53 offers a number of different routing policies: simple, failover, geolocation, geoproximity, latency-based, multivalue answer, and weighted.

137. A, B. Route 53 offers a number of different routing policies: simple, failover, geolocation, geoproximity, latency-based, multivalue answer, and weighted.

138. B, C. Route 53 offers a number of different routing policies: simple, failover, geolocation, geoproximity, latency-based, multivalue answer, and weighted.

139. C. Simple routing is ideal for sending all traffic to a single resource.

140. B. Failover routing is used to send traffic to a single resource but then to failover routing to a secondary resource if the first is unhealthy.

141. C. Geolocation routing uses the location of a user's DNS query to determine which route to use.

142. B. Latency-based routing uses the latency of regions to determine where routing should direct users.

143. C. Multivalue answer routing can direct requests to multiple resources and also performs health checks on those resources.

144. D. Weighted routing uses predefined weights to determine how traffic is routed across multiple resources.

145. A. When there is a single resource to which traffic should be directed, simple routing is the best option.

146. A, C. The two options here that are valid are geolocation and geoproximity routing, both of which consider the location of the user before routing that user to a resource. Geographical routing is not a valid routing policy for Route 53.

147. D. Weights are simply integers that can be summed to determine an overall weight and the fractional weights of each resource to which traffic is directed.

148. C. A weight of 0 removes the resource from service in a weighted routing policy.

149. A. In a weighted routing policy, the numerical weights are added up, and each resource's weight is divided by the sum of all the weights. In this case, the total weight is 400, so A is 25% of that (100/400), B is 25% (100/400), and C is 50% (200/400).

150. A, C. A simple routing policy allows single and multiple resources for both the primary and secondary resources, so A and C are true. Weighted policies do honor health checks (so B is false), and D is inaccurate as weight numbers do not affect health checks.

151. A, B. The issues here are geographical proximity from EU users and load on the database, which has high CPU utilization. Therefore, those problems must be addressed. ElastiCache (A) should reduce load on the RDS instance, and CloudFront (B) caches responses in a way that should serve EU users more quickly.

152. B, D. This is another memorization question. Valid instance types begin with T, M, C, R, X, Z, D, H, I, F, G, and P. Frankly, it's hard to memorize these; the questions like this aren't frequent, but they can sometimes appear. In this case, E and Q are not valid instance type prefixes.

153. B. IAM offers permissions for AWS resources as well as access rights for users of the AWS platform.

154. A, C. IAM controls permissions for resource-to-resource interaction as well as user access to the AWS console. It does not provide an authentication interface or single sign-on.

155. B. IAM stands for Identity and Access Management.

156. A, C. IAM only applies to permissions for users, roles, and groups and does not affect billing or cost or specific application feature accessibility.

157. B, C. IAM does handle user permissions for accessing AWS (A) and EC2-to-S3 access (D), so these are both true and therefore incorrect. It does not handle hosted application permissions (B) or relate to SNS, making B and C the correct answers.

158. B. IAM is not the managed service for handling MFA Delete setup on S3 buckets.

159. B. Anytime a single account in AWS is shared, you likely have a security risk.

160. C. The only requirement here is creating a sign-in link that is not the same as the root sign-in link. Turning on MFA for the root or all accounts is not required, and while it is common to create an IAM group at this stage, it is not required for access.

161. A, B. Users, groups, roles, permissions, and similar constructs are part of IAM. Organizations and organizational units are part of AWS Organizations, a different facility.

162. A, D. Users, groups, roles, permissions, and similar constructs are part of IAM.

163. A, C. In this case, you'd need to create a role that allows an EC2 instance to communicate with another AWS service, in this case S3. While a default role would probably cover this use case, you might also write a custom policy if you had particular needs for something other than the default role's allowances.

164. A, D. You can provide console access and programmatic access via IAM. Programmatic access incudes API and CLI access.

165. A, C. There are four types of policies in IAM: identity-based, resource-based, organization SCPs, and access control lists (ACLs).

166. B. IAM policies are written in JSON.

167. A, C. IAM policies can be attached to users, groups, and roles in the case of identity-based policies, and AWS services and components via resource-based policies.

168. B. MFA stands for Multi-Factor Authentication and can be enabled on a user account by IAM.

169. A, C. IAM aids in scalability primarily by consolidating and centralizing management of permissions, both to AWS users (A) and from instances to services (C).

170. C, D. IAM provides permissions, groups, users, and roles, and AWS Organizations provides logical groupings and account management. Both operate across all AWS resources.

171. C. Power user access is a predefined policy that allows access to all AWS services with the exception of group or user management within IAM.

172. D. Root users can perform all actions related to IAM.

173. A. Power users can work with managed services, but they cannot create (or otherwise manage) IAM users.

174. B. Although it might sound odd, AWS strongly recommends you delete your root user access keys and create IAM users for everyday use.

175. A, C. As a starting point, always consider that the root account is typically required for account-level operations, such as closing an account (A). It's also needed for very privileged access; in this case, that's creating a CloudFront key pair, which essentially provides signed access to applications and is a very trusted action. IAM does allow you to distribute user and policy management (B and D).

176. A, B. Affecting another account is generally something that requires root account level access. In this case, that's D, as well as restoration of user permissions (C). Both A and B are available to non-root users.

177. D. It is impossible to remove access for the AWS account's root user.

178. C. This is a bit of a "gimme" question but sometimes comes up. AWS firmly believes that root account access should be highly limited, but also not confined to a single user. C, having a very small group of engineers (ideally AWS certified) is the best approach to reducing root account level access as much as possible.

179. D. AWS defines and keeps updated a number of IAM policies for users, including Administrator, Billing, and Power User.

180. A, C. You will always need to provide non-root sign-in URLs for new users, so A is essential. The remaining answers are concerned with permissions, and of the choices (B, by the way, isn't an actual option), the Developer Power User policy is a much better fit than the View-Only User policy.

181. D. Unless your manager is both highly technical and working on actual development issues, D is the best option: It provides View-Only access to AWS without adding unneeded privileges for the manager.

182. D. The Data Scientist policy is designed for just this purpose: running queries used for data analytics and business intelligence

183. A. This is a System Administrator role. While Power User would give permissions to the same services, it is likely too permissive. Remember, the key with these questions is to find the role that allows the specified operations without going beyond those any more than is necessary.

184. B, C. It is impossible to remove a root user's access to EC2 instances (B). Further, IAM is concerned with the raw AWS resources, not access to running web applications (C).

185. D. IAM changes apply immediately to all users across the system; there is no lag, and no need to log out and back in (D).

186. A. New users have no access to AWS services. They are "bare" or "empty" or "naked" users, in that it is merely a login to the AWS console (if a URL is provided). They cannot make any changes to AWS services or even view services.

187. C, D. New users have no access to AWS services. They will need a URL to use for logging in (C) and permissions via a valid AWS group such as Administrators or power users. Options A and B refer to groups that are not predefined by AWS.

188. A, B. To access the console, users need a sign-in URL (A) and a username and password. This is not the access key ID and secret access key referenced in B. Therefore, A and B would effectively block a user from accessing the console. There is no Log In To Console box for users.

189. C. AWS usernames have to be unique across the AWS account in which that user exists.

190. B, D. Programmatic access requires an access key ID and a secret access key pair. Usernames and passwords are used for console access.

191. A, C. Console access requires a username and password. Access keys and pairs are used for programmatic access, not console access.

192. B. IAM policy documents are written in JSON.

193. A. Of these, SSO is single sign-on, IAM is more generally applied here, and JSON is the language used for policy documents. But SAML, the Security Assertion Markup Language, is used directly to implement single sign-on.

194. C. If you have an external Active Directory, you'd want to federate those users into AWS. This allows you to use the existing user base, not re-create each individual user.

195. D. A policy document is a collection of permissions in IAM.

196. D. IAM users are global to an AWS account and are not region-specific.

197. C. Like IAM users, policy documents are global. There are no changes or steps you need to take to make these work globally.

198. A, B. Auto Scaling is most focused on capacity management (B), ensuring that your applications can perform by keeping the capacity sufficient. Further, it performs a minimal amount of monitoring to effect this (A). It does not limit cost, although it does help in cost reduction, and it has nothing to do with permissions management.

199. A, C. Auto Scaling helps you to quickly set up scaling (C) and to then keep costs to a minimum (A). It does not affect network performance, and while there is a reduction of overhead, this is not related to maintaining individual VPCs (D).

200. A, C. Auto Scaling can be applied to both Aurora (and specifically read replicas) and DynamoDB.

201. A, D. EC2 instances as well as ECS containers can both be scaled up and down by Auto Scaling.

202. C. A collection of components, such as EC2 instances that will grow and shrink to handle load, is an Auto Scaling group.

203. B, D. When creating an Auto Scaling group, you can specify the minimum and maximum size as well as a desired capacity and scaling policy. You cannot specify how many instances to add at once, nor the desired cost.

204. A, B. When creating an Auto Scaling group, you can specify the minimum and maximum size as well as a desired capacity and scaling policy. While you can specify triggers that are used to grow or shrink the group, you can not specify a memory allocation or a minimum processing threshold (neither is an actual AWS term).

205. B, C. A launch configuration contains an AMI ID, key pair, instance type, security groups, and possibly a block device mapping.

206. B, C. A launch configuration contains an AMI ID, key pair, instance type, security groups, and possibly a block device mapping. Cluster size is not part of a launch configuration, although a maximum number of instances can be added to an Auto Scaling group. Maximum memory utilization also is not part of a launch configuration but can be a trigger for scaling.

207. A, C. There are a number of valid scaling policies for Auto Scaling: Maintain current instance levels, manual scaling, schedule-based scaling, and demand-based scaling.

208. A, D. There are a number of valid scaling policies for Auto Scaling: Maintain current instance levels, manual scaling, schedule-based scaling, and demand-based scaling. Resource-based scaling and instance-based scaling are not actual scaling policy options.

209. D. You can choose to maintain current instance levels at all times. This is essentially ensuring that no instances are added unless an instance fails its health checks and needs to be restarted or replaced.

210. A. Demand-based scaling allows you to specify parameters to control scaling. One of those parameters can be CPU utilization, so this is the policy you'd use for this use case.

211. B. This one should be pretty easy. Schedule-based scaling allows you to specify a particular time period during which resources should scale up or down.

212. C. Manual scaling allows you to specify a minimum and maximum number of instances as well as a desired capacity. The Auto Scaling policy then handles maintaining that capacity.

213. A. Manual scaling allows you to specify a minimum and maximum number of instances as well as a desired capacity. You would specify a time to scale up for a schedule-based policy and maximum CPU utilization as well as scaling conditions for a demand-based policy.

214. A, C. The most common approach is to use CloudWatch triggers—such as memory or CPU utilization—to notify AWS to scale a group up or down. However, you can also manually scale up or down with the AWS console.

215. C. While you can remove the instance altogether (B), you'd eventually want to put it back in the group, meaning you're incurring extra work. The best approach is to put the instance into Standby mode. This allows the group to scale up if needed, and then you can troubleshoot the instance and then put it back into the InService state when complete.

216. C, D. InService and Standby are valid states for an instance, while Deleted and ReadyForService are not.

217. B. You have to create a launch configuration first, then an Auto Scaling group, and then you can verify your configuration and group.

218. B. A launch configuration needs a single AMI ID to use for all instances it launches.

219. D. Security groups work for launch configurations just as they do with instances: You may use as many as you like.

220. D. All of these are valid options for creating an Auto Scaling group.

221. B, C. All of these are acceptable options, but the best options are to use the existing EC2 instance as a basis for a new Auto Scaling group and to set up demand-based scaling. Anytime you have an existing instance that is working, you can simply start from there, rather than using a launch configuration and duplicating the setup. Demand-based scaling will respond to changing conditions better than having to manually scale up and down or to set a desired capacity (which is unknown based on the question).

222. A, B. This is a case of having a recurring performance issue, which points to using schedule-based scaling. Further, you know that access is centered around the US East regions. C might help the issue, but without knowing more about the application, it's not possible to tell if caching content would significantly improve performance.

223. C. Here, the determining factor is the requirement of instant access. S3 One Zone-IA will give you that access, at a lower cost than S3 standard and S3-IA. According to AWS, all three classes have the same first byte latency (milliseconds).

224. D. Glacier takes 3–5 hours to deliver the first byte.

225. D. This is easy to miss, and often is. All three of these S3 storage classes share the same first-byte latency: milliseconds.

226. D. Spot instances offer you significant costs savings as long as you have flexibility and application processes can be stopped and started.

Domain 3: Specify Secure Applications and Architectures

1. B, D. Option A is false, but option B is true. Default security groups prevent all traffic in and allow all traffic out. Options C and D are about whether or not a security group is stateful: whether an incoming connection automatically can get back out. Security groups *are* stateful, so D is true. If the subject of the question was a NACL, then option C would be true, as NACLs are stateless.

2. B. D is not a good answer because relying on encryption outside of S3 does not best address the concerns around consistency. It is generally better to allow AWS to handle encryption in cases where you want to ensure all encryption is the same across a data store. SSE-C, SSE-KMS, and SSE-C all provide this. However, among those three, KMS is the best option for providing clear audit trails.

3. A, C. A bastion host is a publicly accessible host that allows traffic to connect to it. Then, an additional connection is made from the bastion host into a private subnet and the hosts within that subnet. Because the bastion must be accessed by public clients, it must be exposed to the Internet (A). If it is within a private subnet (B), it will not be accessible, making that answer incorrect. There also must be an explicit route from the bastion host into the private subnet (C); this is usually within a NACL. Finally, the security of the bastion *must* be different from the hosts in the private subnet. The bastion host should be hardened significantly as it is public, but also accessible; this is in many ways the *opposite* of the security requirements of hosts within a private subnet.

4. A, C. AWS sometimes asks questions like this to ensure that you understand that the root account is truly a root account and you cannot restrict that account's access. Anything that involves removing access for the root account is always invalid.

5. B. This is a "gimme question" that AWS will often ask on exams. You should never store your application keys on an instance, in an AMI, or anywhere else permanent on the cloud—meaning option B is true. Additionally, D makes no sense; application keys are for programmatic access, not console access.

6. A, C. Site-to-site VPN connections require a virtual private gateway (on the AWS side) and a customer gateway (on the local side). A private subnet is optional, but not required, as is a NAT instance.

7. B, D. There are two pairs of answers here, and you need to choose the correct pair in each case. For private subnet instances, you need a route out to a NAT gateway, and that NAT gateway must be in a public subnet—otherwise, it would not itself be able to provide outbound traffic access to the Internet. That means option D is correct, as is answer B: 0.0.0.0/0 means "traffic with a destination in the Internet at large," more or less.

8. A, B. The easiest way to handle this question is by thinking of a NAT gateway as essentially a managed service and a NAT instance as an instance (which you manage) for networking. That helps identify B as false (you never choose instance types and sizes for managed services) and C as true (AWS patches managed services). Further, since AWS manages NAT gateways, they are automatically highly available and do not need you to associate security groups. This means that A is false—NAT instances *can be* made highly available, but not without your manual intervention—and D is true.

9. A. Option A is true, and if you know that, this is an easy question. However, it doesn't seem obvious, as all custom NACLs *disallow* all inbound and outbound traffic. It is only a VPC's default NACL that has an "allow all" policy. As for B and C, these are both reversed: NACLs are stateless (allowing independent configuration of inbound and outbound traffic) and security groups are stateful. This also explains why D is false: NACLs are stateless.

10. A. Permission changes to a role now take place immediately and apply to all instances using that role.

11. C. If an allow-everything doesn't set off alarm bells, the reference to SSH should. Security groups, by default, don't allow any traffic in. They require you to explicitly allow inbound traffic (C); the other options are all false. And security groups are stateful—remember this, as it will come up in almost every single exam.

12. C. All outbound traffic is allowed to pass out of a VPC by default, although no inbound traffic is allowed.

13. C. EBS volumes can be encrypted when they are created. All other options typically affect snapshots of the volume, but not the volume itself.

14. A, D. Security groups only contain allow rules, not deny rules (and prevent rules are not an actual rule type). Then, you can create both inbound and outbound rules.

15. B, C. You specify allow rules for security groups, so A is false. B and C are true: Default security groups allow all outbound traffic, and you specify separate inbound and outbound rules. Finally, security groups are stateful, not stateless, so D is false.

16. A, D. A is false, as security groups don't provide for deny rules. B and C are both true (and therefore are not correct answers). D is false, because without specific outbound rules, nothing is allowed to flow out. (Note that by default, there is an allowance for all outgoing traffic in security groups, although that can be removed.)

17. B, C. A security group can actually have no inbound or outbound rules, so A and D are not required. A security group does require a name and description, though.

18. B. A security group can be attached to multiple constructs, like an EC2 instance, but is ultimately associated with a network interface, which in turn is attached to individual instances. This is a tough question and probably at the very edge of what the exam might ask.

19. A, C. The easiest way to work this is to recognize that default security groups never allow broad inbound traffic. That eliminates B and D and leaves rules that allow all outbound traffic for both IPv4 (A) and IPv6 (C).

20. A, D. Security group rules have a protocol and a description. They do not have a subnet, although they can have CIDR blocks or single IP addresses. Instances can associate with a security group, but a security group does not itself refer to a specific instance.

21. B, C. They key here is not the endpoint, but the actual protocol used to access the endpoint. In this case, HTTPS is secure, while HTTP is not, so the answers using HTTPS—B and C—are correct.

22. A. Client-side encryption involves the client (you, in this example) managing the entire encryption and decryption process. AWS only provides storage.

23. C. With server-side encryption, AWS handles all the object encryption and decryption.

24. B, C. For client-side encryption, you'll need a master key, which can either be a KMS-managed key (option B) or a client-side master key. You'll also need an SDK for encrypting the client-side data (C).

25. C. You'll probably simply need to memorize this one. SSE-S3, SSE-KMS, and SSE-C are all valid approaches to S3 encryption; SSE-E is made up.

26. B. The word *audit* should be a trigger for you: always choose KMS when you see a need for strong auditing. SSE-KMS provides a very good audit trail and security, perhaps the best of all these options for most use cases.

27. D. SSE-C allows the customer (the C in SSE-C) to manage keys, but S3 then handles the actual encryption of data.

28. C. Client-side encryption allows the customer to manage keys and encrypt data themselves, then store the data on S3 already encrypted. There's a lot of overhead with this approach, but it's ideal for the use case described.

29. A. In general, SSE-S3 is the "starter" option for encryption. It's by no means a simple or amateur approach to security, but it is low cost compared to KMS and has much less overhead than client-side or SSE-C encryption keys.

30. A, C. Here, you must recognize that EU West and EU Central are both EU regions and the other two options are not.

31. B, C. Option A isn't valid because US-West isn't an EU region. Options B and C are valid as they both provide EU regions, and S3 and S3-IA both can survive the loss of an availability zone; option D would *not* survive the loss of an AZ.

32. B. Multi-AZ RDS instances use synchronous replication to push changes.

33. B. MFA Delete is the most powerful anti-deletion protection you can provide without disabling delete via IAM roles. Option A doesn't affect your object storage—EBS is block storage. Options C and D both won't help; delete requests can't be blocked by Lambda, and there is no "DELETE endpoint" on the S3 API.

34. A, B. MFA Delete is the right option here (B), but A is a required step to enable MFA Delete. Option C doesn't actually make sense, and while option D would technically prevent all deletions, it isn't what the question is asking: You must prevent accidental deletions, not remove the ability to delete objects altogether.

35. D. You must enable versioning to enable MFA Delete. The region of the bucket doesn't have any effect here (B and C), and there is no way to disable the REST API (A), although you could remove programmatic access via IAM or removal of access keys.

36. D. AWS Trusted Advisor does all three of the above: improve performance, reduce cost, and improve security.

37. D. AWS Trusted Advisor provides advice on cost, fault tolerance, performance, and security but does not address account organization.

38. A, B. Here, it's not reasonable to memorize the seven core AWS Trusted Advisor checks. Instead, consider which of these are valid improvements that Trusted Advisor might make. A and B relate to security and permissions, while both C and D are pretty far afield of cost, security, or performance suggestions.

39. A, C. This is tricky. First, MFA on the root account is a standard recommendation, so you can select that. For the remaining three answers, the one that is most directly a "common security recommendation" would have to be S3 buckets with write access, and that is the correct answer.

40. B. The only one of these that's not possible with IAM is denying the root account access to EC2 instances. That's not possible—with IAM or any other mechanism.

41. B, C. A is true, and D is true; if you know this, choosing B and C is simple. Otherwise, you need to recognize that just supplying a client key to S3 is not enough; some form of client-side encryption or server-side encryption using client keys must be enabled. EBS volumes can be encrypted outside of S3 and stored regardless of how S3 is encrypting data.

42. A, B. There are four types of data encrypted when an EBS volume is encrypted: data at rest on the volume, data moving between the volume and the instance, any snapshots created from the volume, and any volumes created from those snapshots.

43. B, C. This is tricky, as both answers that involve unencrypted data have some tricky wording. First, B is not a case of encryption; if data never touches the encrypted volume, it is not automatically encrypted. Second, for C, data that is on the instance but never moves to the encrypted volume is also not automatically encrypted.

44. D. All of these are encrypted. Data moving to and from the volume as well as data at rest on the volume are all encrypted.

45. C. KMS is used as the encryption service, but this is not the S3-KMS that is specific to S3 encryption. You will also sometimes see this KMS referenced as AWS-KMS.

46. C. This is a case of pure memorization. The URL is always http://169.254.169.254 and the metadata, which is what you want, is at /latest/meta-data/.

47. A, D. Encryption of a volume affects snapshots of the volume and instances created from that snapshot, but nothing else.

48. A, D. The only steps required here are to copy the snapshot to the new region (usually via the console), and then create a new volume from it.

49. D. You cannot encrypt a running instance; you have to create the instance with encryption enabled.

50. D. You cannot encrypt a running RDS instance, so B is incorrect, and you have no access to the underlying instance for RDS, so C is also incorrect. Option A sounds possible, but it will not address any data created by the database itself (such as indices, references to other data in the database, etc.). The only way to encrypt an RDS instance is to encrypt it at creation of the instance.

51. C. The only option here is the manual one. You must set up encryption when creating a new instance from scratch (snapshots won't work) and then move data into it so that this data is encrypted as it moves into the new instance.

52. A. You cannot encrypt an existing volume "on the fly." You must create a snapshot and then encrypt that snapshot as you copy it to another, encrypted snapshot. You can then restore from that new snapshot.

53. D. None of these will work. The important thing to remember for a question like this is that you must make a *copy* of an unencrypted snapshot to apply encryption. There is no in-place encryption mechanism for volumes or snapshots.

54. B. The only way to encrypt an EBS volume is to encrypt it *at creation time*. Remembering this one detail will help on lots of questions in this vein.

55. C, D. You cannot encrypt an existing EBS volume, so A is incorrect. And you cannot encrypt a snapshot that is unencrypted, so B is incorrect. You *can* encrypt a copy of a snapshot and restore an encrypted snapshot to a volume that is encrypted (C and D).

56. B, C. Snapshots of encrypted volumes stay encrypted—whether you copy them (B and C) or create volumes from them (D). So A and D are true, while B and C are false.

57. B. You can copy snapshots across accounts, but the default permissions do not allow this. So you have to modify those permissions, and then the snapshot can be copied to any other AWS account, regardless of account owner.

58. B. You can only create volumes from snapshots in the same region. Since the instance is desired in US West 1, a copy of the snapshot must be made in that region first, so B is correct.

59. C. You can copy a snapshot to a different region without any special considerations.

60. A, C. Security groups control the inbound and outbound traffic allowed into and out of instances.

61. C. An instance must have a security group but can have more than that.

62. A. In addition to security groups, NACLs (network access control lists) can be used to further refine inbound and outbound routing into and out of a VPC. Security groups are attached to instances, and NACLs to VPCs, building a complete security picture of your VPC and its instances.

63. C. NACLs are virtual firewalls, and they operate at the subnet and VPC level rather than at an individual instance level. Also note the words *custom, user-created*. The default NACL does allow in and out all traffic; created NACLs do not.

64. D. IAM roles and permissions control access to NACLs.

65. B, C. Security groups support only allow rules (A is false). They do evaluate all rules (B is true) and operate at the instance level (C is true). D is false, as security groups aren't associated with a subnet.

66. A, D. Security groups are stateful and are associated with an instance (or instances), so A and D are true. They are not stateless, and they process all rules rather than processing rules in order.

67. B, C. NACLs are stateless; rules must be specified for traffic going both in and out (so A is false, and B is true). They also process rules in order (C is true). They're associated with subnets, not a particular instance (so D is false).

68. A, C. NACLs are associated with a subnet (A) and support both allow and deny rules (C). B is false; NACLs and security groups work together. D is false, as rules are processed in order.

69. B. NACLs are always evaluated first because they exist at the border of a subnet. As security groups are attached to instances, they are not processed until traffic passes through the NACL and into the instance's subnet.

70. A, B. Both security groups and NACLs can—and usually do—apply to multiple instances in a subnet. The NACL applies to all instances within the associate subnet, and a security group can be associated with multiple instances.

71. B. NACLs are associated with subnets.

72. A, B. The default NACL allows in and out all traffic, which is somewhat unintuitive. Keep in mind that the default *security group* disallows inbound traffic, but the default NACL allows that traffic in.

73. C, D. Unlike the default NACL that comes with the default VPC, custom NACLs disallow all inbound and outbound traffic by default.

74. A. Each rule in a NACL has a number, and those rules are evaluated using those numbers, moving from low to high.

75. B, D. A and C are true. B is false; NACLs are stateless. D is false, because a NACL can be associated with multiple subnets.

76. B. A NACL is associated with a subnet, not an instance or VPC. It can be associated with a single subnet or multiple subnets.

77. A. A subnet is associated with a NACL. However, a subnet can only be associated to a single NACL at a time.

78. D. A subnet is associated with a NACL but can only be associated to a single NACL at a time.

79. B, D. NACL rules have a rule number, a protocol, a choice of ALLOW or DENY, and a CIDR range and port or port range for inbound and outbound traffic.

80. A, B. NACL rules have a rule number, a protocol, a choice of ALLOW or DENY, and a CIDR range and port or port range for inbound and outbound traffic.

81. B. Almost none of this detail actually matters. The only key parameter is the rule number. NACLs evaluate lowest-numbered rules first, so Rule #100 would go first, option B.

82. D. SSH is not explicitly mentioned, so it is not allowed on a custom NACL. Every protocol must explicitly be mentioned.

83. A. SSH is not explicitly mentioned, but because the question asks about the *default* NACL on the *default* VPC, all traffic is allowed in unless explicitly denied.

84. B. SSH is allowed here, but only from a specific CIDR block.

85. D. While there is a rule allowing SSH from the CIDR block 192.0.2.0/24, that rule would be evaluated after the lower-numbered rule 110, which disallows any traffic not allowed in from lower-numbered rules (in this case, just rule #100).

86. D. Technically, B and C are correct; SSH is a type of TCP traffic. However, that is not the most specific answer, which is what the question asks. A is partially correct but does not call out the CIDR block limitation that D does. Therefore, D is the most accurate answer.

87. B. The *most accurate* answer here includes several components: the type of TCP traffic (HTTP), the allowed source CIDR block (the entire Internet), and IPv4. This rule does *not* explicitly allow IPv6 traffic. Further, this rule is only effective if there are no lower-numbered rules that short-circuit this rule.

88. B. 0.0.0.0/0 represents IPv4 addresses, and the entire Internet. However, a CIDR block does not represent any type of traffic, inbound or outbound.

89. C. ::/0 represents IPv6 addresses, and the entire Internet. However, a CIDR block does not represent any type of traffic, inbound or outbound.

90. B. ::/0 represents IPv6 addresses, so the answer must be either B or D. The route should go from all IPv6 addresses to the ID of the NAT gateway, which is nat-123456789. There is no intermediate -> NAT that should be inserted into the routes.

91. D. A VPC spans all the availability zones in a region.

92. B, C. You must always select a region to create a VPC, and you must always provide a CIDR block. VPCs span all the AZs in a region, so that is not required, and security groups are associated at the instance level rather than at the VPC level.

93. C. For a single VPC, you can add one or more subnets to each availability zone within that VPC.

94. B. A subnet cannot span availability zones. It can be added to a single AZ.

95. B. A subnet cannot span availability zones. It can be added to a single AZ and can only exist within that single AZ.

96. B. A VPC can have a single primary CIDR block assigned to it for IPv4 addresses and an optional IPv6 CIDR block. While you can add secondary IPv4 CIDR blocks, you *cannot* add additional CIDR blocks for IPv6 at this time.

97. C. A VPC can have a single primary CIDR block assigned to it for IPv4 addresses and an optional IPv6 CIDR block. However, you can add *additional* secondary CIDR blocks to a VPC (up to four).

98. D. Any subnet that routes traffic through an internet gateway is a public subnet by definition.

99. B. Instances in a public subnet are not automatically reachable. They must have either a public IPv4 or IPv6 address (B) or an elastic IP address.

100. D. A public subnet, as well as existing Internet-accessible instances, indicates a working internet gateway, so C is not correct. A is not an actual AWS option, and B—Auto Scaling—would not address public accessibility. This leaves D, which is correct: Instances in a public subnet that are intended to be Internet accessible need either a public IP address or an elastic IP address assigned to the instance.

101. A, C. When creating a VPC, you can specify an option name, a required IPv4 CIDR block, and an optional IPv6 CIDR block.

102. A, C. When creating a VPC, you can specify an option name, a required IPv4 CIDR block, and an optional IPv6 CIDR block. You cannot assign tags to a VPC at creation time.

103. B, D. A public subnet is one in which traffic is routed (via a routing table, B) to an internet gateway (D).

104. B, C. A VPN-only subnet routes traffic through a virtual private gateway rather than an internet gateway.

105. A, B. At a minimum, a VPC-only subnet must have a routing table routing traffic and a virtual private gateway to which traffic is routed. Neither elastic IP addresses nor internet gateways are required.

106. B. You can only create 5 VPCs per region by default. Creating more requires a request to AWS.

107. D. This is a high number, but accurate: You can create 200 subnets per VPC.

108. B. This is a very hard question, but it can come up, albeit rarely. This limit is your primary CIDR block and then, in addition, 4 secondary CIDR blocks.

109. B. You're allowed 5 elastic IP addresses per region, unless you have the default limits raised by AWS.

110. B, D. Subnets must have CIDR blocks (so D is false), and the block must be the same as or smaller than the CIDR block for the VPC within which it exists, so while A and C are true, B is false.

111. C. A VPC peering connection connects one VPC to another VPC via networking and routing.

112. C. A VPC VPN connection links your on-site network to a VPC within the AWS cloud.

113. A, C. A VPC VPN connection requires a customer gateway, a VPN connection, and a virtual private gateway.

114. B, D. Customer gateways (A) and virtual private gateways (C) are used in VPN connections. For security, a NACL (B) is used at the subnet level, and a security group (D) can be used at the instance level.

115. B. A NACL is best for dealing with all traffic at a subnet or VPC level, as it is associated at the subnet level.

116. D. Anytime you are protecting or limiting traffic to or from specific instances, a security group is your best choice. Security groups are associated with specific instances, so they can effectively limit traffic to some instances while allowing other instances—using different security groups—to still be accessible.

117. A, C. This takes a little careful reading. First, it is not considered a good practice to mix private and public instances within a subnet—although this is not a hard-and-fast rule. So C, moving the private database instances into a different subnet, is at least worth considering. D is not helpful in this case. If you have two subnets, one private and one public, then A is a good idea: NACLs can protect one subnet and keep another public. Finally, B is *not* valid, because of the word *single*. You cannot have a single security group that allows traffic to one instance but not to another. This leaves A and C as the best combined solution.

118. C. A security group denies all traffic unless explicitly allowed. This means it functions as a whitelist: Only specific rules allow in traffic, and all other traffic is denied.

119. C, D. A security group operates at the instance level, and a NACL operates at the subnet level.

120. A. A security group performs stateful filtering, meaning that traffic allowed in is automatically allowed back out, without the need for an explicit outbound rule.

121. D. Network ACLs are stateless. Inbound traffic is not automatically allowed back out; an explicit rule must be present for traffic to move from within a subnet back out of that subnet.

122. D. VPC peering allows a VPC to connect with any other VPC: in the same region, in a different region, or in a different account altogether.

123. B, D. VPC peering allows a VPC to connect with any other VPC, so the options that don't involve VPCs are incorrect: B and D.

124. B, D. As long as there is a gateway (internet or virtual private) on the source VPC, and routing through that gateway, an instance in a VPC can communicate with other instances. So in this case, you'd want B and D. There is no "cross-VPC communication" option, and security groups won't actually help this scenario.

125. A, D. This is a little difficult, but it comes down to accessibility: How can the target instance be reached? Of the answers available, a public IP would make the target available, as would a VPN connection.

126. D. VPCs are fundamental to AWS networking and are available in all AWS regions.

127. D. A VPC automatically spans all the availability zones within the region in which it exists.

128. B. When you launch an instance, you must specify an availability zone. This could be as simple as accepting the AWS default, but it is your choice.

129. B. EBS volumes can be encrypted, but it must be done at launch time (B).

130. D. A VPC endpoint is a connection to an AWS service and explicitly does *not* use internet gateways, VPN connections, or NAT devices.

131. B. A VPC endpoint is a virtual device, not a physical one.

132. C. A VPC endpoint is for attaching to AWS services and explicitly does *not* require an internet gateway (C).

133. C. By default, IAM users don't have permissions to work with endpoints. You may need to create an IAM role. You would *not* need a NAT device (A or B) or a security group (D) to use a VPC endpoint.

134. B. A private subnet is not accessible without a bastion host or other connection and routing from the public Internet to an accessible host and finally into private instances.

135. B. Bastion hosts should be in a public subnet so that they can be accessed via the public Internet. They can then route traffic into a private subnet.

136. C. Bastion hosts are also sometimes called jump servers, because they allow a connection to "jump" to the bastion and then into a private subnet.

137. D. Bastion hosts are intended to provide access to private instances in private subnets; in other words, instances inaccessible via the public Internet in any other way.

138. D. Bastion hosts are publicly accessible and have access to your private hosts. Therefore, they must be the *most* secure hosts on your network. Use a network ACL for the subnet in which it resides, a security group for the instance, and OS hardening to reduce access within the instance itself.

139. B. Shell access only requires SSH, and you should therefore only allow that protocol. Always allow *only what is absolutely required* for bastion hosts.

140. D. Internet gateways scale horizontally, not vertically. They are also redundant and highly available automatically.

141. C. Internet gateways attach to VPCs and serve multiple subnets (if needed).

142. B. The route 0.0.0.0/0 catches all IPv4 traffic intended for the public Internet. ::/0 is for IPv6, 0.0.0.0/24 limits traffic to a certain CIDR block, and D is an internal IP address.

143. C. The route ::/0 catches all IPv6 traffic intended for the public Internet. 0.0.0.0/0 is for IPv6, 0.0.0.0/24 limits traffic to a certain CIDR block, and D is an internal IP address.

144. D. An instance must have IPv6 communication from itself (with a public IP address) through a subnet with IPv6 addresses, in a VPC with IPv6 addresses, to reach the Internet via IPv6. A virtual private gateway is not connected with any of these.

145. A, B. For an instance to reach and be reached to and from the public Internet, the instance must have either a public IP address or an elastic IP address associated with it. IAM roles do not provide public access, and NACLs are attached to subnets, not instances.

146. A, C. A public subnet, by definition, is a subnet with an internet gateway attached. And the default VPC has an internet gateway automatically attached.

147. B. ALB stands for application load balancer.

148. B. Application load balancers operate at the Application layer, which is layer 7 of the OSI model. ELBs (classic load balancers) operate at the Transport layer, layer 4, as well as layer 7, and network load balancers operate at layer 4 as well.

149. A. Application load balancers operate at the Application layer, which is layer 7 of the OSI model. ELBs (classic load balancers) operate at the Transport layer, layer 4, as well as layer 7, and network load balancers operate at layer 4 as well.

150. C. Application load balancers operate at the Application layer, which is layer 7 of the OSI model. ELBs (classic load balancers) operate at the Transport layer, layer 4, as well as layer 7, and network load balancers operate at Level 4 as well.

151. D. Both network and classic load balancers operate at the Transport layer. Classic load balancers also operate at layer 7, the Application layer. Application load balancers operate at the Application layer, which is layer 7 of the OSI model.

152. D. Both classic and application load balancers operate at the Application layer. Classic load balancers also operate at layer 4, the Transport layer. Network load balancers operate at the Transport layer, which is layer 4 of the OSI model.

153. C. By default, subnets in the default VPC are public. The default VPC has an internet gateway attached and the default subnets are public as a result.

154. A. By default, subnets in custom VPCs are private. Other than the default VPC, custom VPCs don't have internet gateways attached by default, and created subnets don't have public access.

155. C. Instances launched into non-default subnets have a private IPv4 address, but not a public one, so C is correct. All instances have a security group created or associated, and instances can always talk to other instances in the subnet by default.

156. C, D. Instances launched into non-default subnets have a private IPv4 address, but not a public one, so they need an elastic IP address, as answer C indicates. (A public IP address would work as well.) You'd also need an internet gateway for the instance (D).

157. D. Instances launched into default subnets in the default VPC can automatically reach out to the public Internet, as that VPC has an internet gateway and instances get a public IPv4 address.

158. A. A NAT device—network address translation—provides routing for instances to an internet gateway but can prevent undesired inbound traffic.

159. D. A NAT device provides access to the Internet from private instances—they allow outgoing traffic rather than incoming traffic.

160. B, C. AWS offers two NAT devices: a NAT instance and a NAT gateway.

161. A, D. Instances always require an AMI. In this question, the two instances are EC2 instances (A) and NAT instances (D).

162. B. A NAT gateway is an entirely managed device from AWS. All the other options require maintenance by the user of OS-level patches and updates.

163. B. A NAT instance does not provide automatic scaling, whereas DynamoDB and NAT gateways are managed services and do. There is really no such thing as "scaling" of an SNS topic, although SNS as a service does do some scaling in the background to ensure that demand is met.

164. **A.** Of these options, only bastion hosts and NAT instances are unmanaged services, making them the only two possible answers. A bastion host typically has SSH routing and permissions to private instances, making it the most important to properly secure. While a NAT instance is usually available to private instances, traffic flows out from the NAT instance and not into the private instances.

165. **D.** A NAT instance is a candidate for a bastion server. The other options are all managed services.

166. **C, D.** A site-to-site VPN connection requires a virtual private gateway on the VPC side (C) and a customer gateway on the on-site side (D).

167. **A, C.** A site-to-site connection is going to require a private subnet on the AWS side (C), with private instances within it. Further, you'll need a NAT instance (A) or similar device to route traffic and receive traffic as a static IP holder.

168. **B.** An egress-only gateway is for use with IPv6 traffic only.

169. **C.** An egress-only gateway is for use with IPv6 traffic and only allows outbound traffic. A VPC endpoint connects to managed AWS services, and an internet gateway (that isn't egress only) allows both inbound and outbound traffic. A NAT gateway is for allowing outbound traffic from a private subnet rather than a public subnet.

170. **A, C.** A NAT instance must be in a public subnet so that it is accessible from the Internet. It also must have access to private instances in private subnets in your VPC.

171. **B, C.** Egress-only internet gateways are stateful and support IPv6 traffic. This is a matter of memorization, although you can somewhat reason that the gateway—absent a NACL— allows responses to come back to instances that use it to communicate with the public Internet.

172. **C.** The most important thing here is to remember that egress-only internet gateways only work with IPv6 addresses. This eliminates A and B. Then, only C addresses the entire public Internet in an IPv6 format.

173. **A, D.** IPv6 addresses are public by default (D) *because* they are globally unique. There is no need to have private IPv6 addresses because the range is so large.

174. **B, C.** An elastic network interface is virtual and can have multiple IPv4 and IPv6 addresses as well as security groups, a MAC address, and a source/destination check flag.

175. **D.** An elastic network interface is virtual and can have multiple IPv4 and IPv6 addresses as well as security groups, a MAC address, and a source/destination check flag. NACLs apply to subnets, though, not network interfaces on instances.

176. **C.** An instance has a primary network interface in all cases but can have additional network interfaces attached, so the answer is C, one or more.

177. **A.** Traffic follows the network interface rather than sticking to any particular instance. So in this case, traffic is redirected to the new instance but stays targeted at the elastic network interface (A).

178. C. An elastic network interface can only be attached to a single instance at one time but can be moved from one instance to another.

179. B. You actually can't increase network throughput with multiple interfaces, making B false. All three other options are legitimate reasons to attach multiple interfaces to an instance.

180. C. An instance's primary network interface cannot be detached (C), making that the correct answer. You can detach secondary interfaces (A), attach multiple interfaces (B), and move network interfaces (D).

181. D. Elastic network interfaces do not have routing tables, but they do have (or can have) IPv4 and IPv6 addresses and a source/destination check flag.

182. C. Elastic IP addresses are specifically for avoiding being tied to a specific instance, so A and B are not correct. Security groups are typically not associated with a specific IP address (D). This leaves C, a valid reason for an elastic IP address: It can move from one instance (if the instance fails) to another.

183. A. Elastic IP addresses are, by definition, an IP address that will not change, so A is correct—you cannot change the IP address while it is in use. You can move elastic IPs (B), including across VPCs (C), and you absolutely would associate it with a single instance (D).

184. B, C. An elastic IP can mask the failure of an instance (B) by moving traffic to another running instance transparently. It also allows all the network interface attributes to be moved at one time (C).

185. A, D. To use an elastic IP, you must first allocate it for use in a VPC and then associate it with an instance in that VPC (A and D). Route 53 is not involved at this stage, and you cannot detach the primary network interface on an instance.

186. D. There is not such thing as an "EBS management tool" separate from the AWS API, CLI, and console.

187. C. Although instances exist in a region and VPC, and can be part of an Auto Scaling group, they are provisioned into specific availability zones (C).

188. A. EBS snapshots are backed up to S3 incrementally.

189. A. Changes to IAM roles take place immediately.

190. A. You can only assign a single role to an instance.

191. B, D. You can only assign a single role to an instance (D), but you can also create a new role that combines the desired policies (B).

192. A, D. You always need to make the actual role changes (A). There are then no more actions required for these changes to take effect on the instances.

193. B, D. You'll first need to create an IAM role with the desired permissions (B). Then, you can attach the role to a running instance to avoid downtime completely (D). Note that this is relatively new; older versions of AWS required restarting the instance.

194. A. If a snapshot is the root device of a registered AMI, it cannot be deleted.

195. A. Encryption can only be applied to EBS volumes at creation time, so A is correct.

196. B. By default, root volumes do get deleted when the associated instance terminates. However, you can configure this to not be the case using the AWS console or CLI (B).

197. C. Using defaults is not part of the well-architected framework, and it often is not the most secure approach.

198. A, C. The well-architected framework recommends automating security best practices and responses to security events.

199. A, B. AWS is responsible for securing the cloud itself, and then you as a customer are responsible for securing your resources and data in the cloud.

200. A, D. AWS is responsible for securing the cloud itself, which means anything that is infrastructure, such as edge locations and availability zones.

201. D. AWS is responsible for networks, but not the actual traffic across those networks (D).

202. A. AWS manages DynamoDB as a managed service. All the other options are your responsibility as a customer of AWS.

203. C. The well-architected framework includes four areas for security in the cloud: data protection, infrastructure protection, privilege management, and defective controls.

204. C. The well-architected framework suggests encrypting everything where possible, whether it is at rest or in transit.

205. A, B. The well-architected framework suggests encrypting everything where possible, whether the data is at rest or in transit.

206. C. While you are ultimately responsible for the security of your data, AWS provides and accepts responsibility for tools to enable security.

207. B. S3 durability is 99.999999999%, which is often called "11 9s" (or sometimes "11 nines") of durability.

208. C. AWS will never initiate the movement of data between regions. Content in a region must be moved by the customer or moved in response to a customer action.

209. D. S3 data can be protected via MFA Delete and versioning, both of which provide a layer of protection against accidental deletes. Additionally, IAM roles can ensure that only those who *should* be able to delete data *can* delete data.

210. A, C. All of these options are valid, but only two should be done for all environments: enabling MFA on the root account and setting a password rotation policy. Enabling MFA Delete on S3 is a good idea but may not apply to all situations. Further, not all users may need an IAM role; some, for example, are fine with the default roles.

211. C. AWS infrastructure operates at the VPC layer and is almost entirely virtual.

212. A, C. CloudWatch and CloudTrail both provide monitoring and logging, both of which can identify security breaches. CloudFormation is a deployment mechanism, and Trusted Advisor can identify potential holes, but not actual breaches.

213. C. IAM provides access management through users, roles, and permissions, all of which are related to privileges.

214. D. MFA is Multi-Factor Authentication, which adds a layer of protection related to privilege management.

215. A. Trusted Advisor is AWS's service for looking at your system and finding standard "holes" in your infrastructure that might allow for security breaches and then to suggest remediation.

216. C. AWS's well-architected framework provides for five pillars: operational excellence, security, reliability, performance efficiency, and cost optimization. Organizational issues are considered outside of this framework (C).

217. B. AWS's well-architected framework provides for five pillars: operational excellence, security, reliability, performance efficiency, and cost optimization. Usability is not a key concern of the cloud (B), although it is important for applications hosted within the cloud.

218. C. C is a misstatement of the correct principle; apply security at *all* layers. Security should be present at all layers, not just at the highest layers.

219. D. While A and C are both good ideas, they are more specific than the well-architected framework's principles. B is a part of a principle, but data should be protected at rest and in transit. This leaves D, and people should be kept away from direct access to data. Instead, tools and APIs should provide a layer between users and data.

220. A, D. The five areas are Identity and Access Management (A), detective controls, infrastructure protection, data protection, and incident response (D).

221. A. AWS takes responsibility for physically securing cloud infrastructure.

222. A, C. The root account is the first account in every account (A), but it should only be used for creating other users and groups (C). It is *not* intended for everyday tasks (B), and once account setup is complete, you are encouraged by AWS to delete any access keys (D).

223. C, D. A good password policy has minimum length and complexity requirements.

224. C. Users with console access are more privileged users and should be required to use MFA (C). Password policies apply to all users, so A is incorrect. Further, passwords are the mechanism for logging into the console, so B is wrong in that access keys are not used for console login.

225. A, B. SAML 2.0 and web identities both provide a means of working with an existing organizational identity provider.

226. C. The principle of least privilege suggests that users only be allowed to do what they have to in order to perform their job functions.

227. B. AWS Organizations groups accounts into organizational units (OUs), allowing for groupings of permissions and roles.

228. A. An SCP in AWS Organizations is a service control policy and can be applied to an organizational unit (OU) to affect all users within that OU. It effectively applies permissions at an organizational level, much the way that a group applies them at a user level.

229. C. Service control policies (SCPs) are applied to OUs (organizational units) in AWS Organizations.

230. A. Service control policies (SCPs) provide for working across AWS accounts (A). Organizational units (OUs) are groupings of accounts, and IAM roles are applied to users and groups, not cross-account structures.

231. C. AWS Organizations offers a means of organizing and managing policies that span AWS accounts.

232. D. AWS provides all of the above options as a means of providing security of the AWS environment.

233. B. SSE-S3 offers encryption at rest while deferring key management to AWS. SSE-KMS does the same but has a higher cost and is more suitable for stringent auditing. The other two options involve work on the client side, which the question states is undesirable.

234. C. SSE-KMS is the best solution for any encryption problem that requires a strong audit trail.

235. C. New users should be given a new IAM user, and when permissions are the same across users, a group should be used instead of individually assigning permissions.

236. B. Most of these answers are overly complicated. S3 is highly available by default, so simply setting up a bucket in an EU region is sufficient.

237. D. All S3 storage classes provide SSL for data at transit as well as encryption of data at rest.

238. D. All S3 storage classes provide SSL for data at transit as well as encryption of data at rest.

239. A. The shared responsibility model defines the portions of the cloud that AWS secures, and the portions that you, the AWS customer, must secure.

240. B. This is pretty tough unless you've read the AWS shared responsibility white papers and FAQs. It's really a matter of memorization and knowing that while AWS uses the term *managed services* in lots of areas, that term is *not* used in the shared responsibility model as one of the core types of services.

241. C. AWS is responsible for the security of virtualization infrastructure. All other items in this list are your responsibility. As a hint on questions like this and related to the AWS shared responsibility model, AWS is typically responsible for anything with the word *infrastructure*, although there are some exclusions (for example, *application infrastructure*).

242. A. An IAM role is assumed by an EC2 instance when it needs to access other AWS services, and that role has permissions associated with it. While these permissions are formally defined in a policy (B), it is the role that is used by the instance for actual service access.

243. A, D. Just as is the case with a compute instance (EC2), a task in a container needs an IAM role with permissions to access S3 (A), which in turn requires a policy specifying a permission that lets ECS tasks access S3 (D). Both of these are required to ensure access. Security groups apply to network traffic and would not affect S3 access, and while a VPC endpoint could be used (C), it is not required.

244. C. By default, newly created S3 buckets are private. They can only be accessed by a user that has been granted explicit access.

Domain 4: Design Cost-Optimized Architectures

1. A, B. When instance cost is the issue, the answers are almost always to consider some form of lowered instance pricing. AWS provides reserved instances and spot instances and the spot market for this purpose. Further, paying for reserved instances all up front is the most cost-effective means of getting reserved instances. Therefore, A and B are correct. C is problematic, as running a smaller instance for longer is not necessarily any cheaper than running a large instance for shorter amounts of time. Option D has some validity, but AWS is almost certainly going to point you back to either reserved instances or the spot market (A and B).

2. C, D. Reserved instances can be paid for in no up-front, partial up-front, and all up-front models, where all up-front is the least expensive and no up-front is the most expensive.

3. D. Reserved instances are locked to the region in which they are created, so D is correct. You would need to create a new reserved instance in the new region.

4. C. This should be an easy correct answer: Spot instances via the spot market are the potentially least expensive option, given that your compute has flexible timing and needs.

5. B, C. Applications with spiky workloads are reasons to use on-demand, as on-demand can scale up and down quickly. Flexible start and end times is a criterion for choosing spot instances, and steady-state usage is ideal for reserved instances. Anytime you're testing a new application, on-demand is a good choice

6. B, D. Applications with spiky workloads are reasons to use on-demand, as on-demand can scale up and down quickly. Flexible start and end times is a criterion for choosing spot instances, and steady-state usage is ideal for reserved instances. Spot instances also make heavy compute affordable when it would not be on other instance types.

7. C, D. The first option is easy, as it actually has *reserved* in the wording. Steady-state usage is also a use case for reserved instances, to gain cost savings. Large and immediate additional capacity needs are best facilitated by spot instances, and on-demand instances are best for users with no initial payment ability.

8. A, B. S3 shares the durability of all S3 storage classes at 11 9s. It also provides the highest availability throughput of all S3 storage classes. Infrequent access is a use case for S3-IA, while the ability to re-create objects would suggest S3 One Zone-IA.

9. A, D. The problem here is that instances are scaling down too quickly. This results in them then being restarted, which incurs cost. The solutions here should be ones that cause instances to stay around a bit longer, which meets demand. Both A and D do this. Cool-down timers increase the time for the group to ensure that previous scaling actions were completed (A), and the CloudWatch alarm period for scaling down should also be increased (D).

10. D. This is a pretty "by the book" question, and in this case, is the exact use case for which S3-IA (Infrequent Access) was built. Instant access with less frequent requests is ideal for S3-IA.

11. A. S3-IA is less expensive than S3, regardless of use case. It is certainly possible that S3-IA is not *appropriate* for a certain use case, but it is less expensive on a "per byte retrieved" case.

12. C. CloudFront will allow you to cache files that are frequently accessed. In this case, that should actually reduce costs. While CloudFront does incur a new additional cost, it would likely be offset by reduced egress from the EFS as well as the compute of additional EC2 instances to handle requests.

13. D. All the description here suggests using Glacier. The documents are a large archive, and many will never be accessed. However, the requirement for quick retrieval points to a need for expedited retrieval. Glacier with expedited retrieval is still going to cost less than S3-IA for access that isn't that frequent.

14. B. First, EBS is a much better choice than EFS for a single-instance application. While a database would certainly benefit from IOPS, there's no need; peaks are small, and usage overall is low. A General Purpose SSD is sufficient here.

15. C. If you have a larger database workload, provisioned IOPS SSD is ideal.

16. D. A cold HDD is the least expensive EBS volume type.

17. A. This is a tough question. You can eliminate B and C because both involve additional services: CloudWatch, Lambda, and additional EC2 instances. Taking EBS snapshots is good, and by moving those snapshots into S3 (which is the default), you get durability automatically. Mirroring data is also a great option—providing fault tolerance—but this does not provide a durability component, something the question specifically requires. Therefore, A is the best answer.

18. B. There are two components to this question: which storage medium is appropriate, and how should older records be deleted. To get both immediate retrieval and lifecycle management, you'd need S3, as in option B. (Also, EBS does not offer lifecycle management, in option D.)

19. A, C. RDS read replicas would take some of the read load off of the database instance, as would ElastiCache. The first allows reads to go to other instances, and the second caches already accessed data.

20. B, D. Glacier is the easy choice, as it can handle the oldest data and still meet the 10-hour retrieval time. S3 RRS is deprecated and shouldn't be considered. This leaves S3 and S3-IA. S3-IA is always less expensive than S3, so it's the better option here.

21. B. Placement groups are typically in a single availability zone, but now spread placement groups can be placed across availability zones.

22. B. It is typical to think of a spread placement group as a group spread across availability zones, but that is a misnomer. The *spread* in spread placement group means that the instances are spread across distinct underlying hardware, and although they *can* be spread across availability zones, they don't have to be.

23. C. A spread placement group can have a maximum of seven running instances per AZ.

24. A, C. Spread placement groups primarily offer reduced network lag between instances (C). They also allow for cross-VPC spanning of instances (A).

25. C. The only false statement here is C: Spread placement groups cannot be set up across regions, and therefore this entire statement is untrue.

26. B, C. Egress always has a cost associated with it (B), while ingress is always free. Transferring data across regions is treated the same as transfers to the Internet. Only inter-AZ data transfer is guaranteed to be costless (D), making C the other correct answer.

27. C. The least cost is always going to be "free," so look for anything that might be ingress. In this cost, uploading to S3 is straight ingress and is therefore free and the cheapest option.

28. B. There are no ingress options here, so nothing is guaranteed to be free. In that case, you should then look for something that moves data within the same availability zone. That's always the least expensive (and usually free, depending on IP addresses), and in this case, that's option B: inter-AZ data transfer between instances.

29. A, B. First, CloudFront is always a good option. It's free to move data from EC2 to CloudFront, so that could reduce how far data must travel, and associated costs. Then, private IPs allow for communication that doesn't route out to the Internet, and generally AWS charges less for communication from private IP to private IP.

30. B. Although there is a free tier, it's a billing option and not an actual support level. That makes B the non-level in this answer set.

31. C. AWS reduces the need for large capital expenditures and provides a pay-as-you-go model instead.

32. B. AWS uses a pay-as-you-go model for all of its services.

33. D. D is incorrect; you actually pay even less as AWS grows, due to economies of scale.

34. C. "Migration only" is not a pricing model for instances. The only model not mentioned here is dedicated hosts.

35. B. AWS suggests using reserved instance pricing in TCO calculations, as it is closest to on-premises servers in an apples-to-apples comparison.

36. A. Standard reserved instances often provide up to a 75% discount as compared to on-demand instances.

37. C. There is no "half upfront" payment option. The valid options are no upfront, partial upfront, and all upfront.

38. C. Paying all upfront is the cheapest option of these three and provides the greatest savings over on-demand pricing.

39. B, D. Reserved instances can be purchased for either one- or three-year terms.

40. A, C. A spot instance (A) is a valid model, but spot market (B) is not; spot market is where you purchase spot instances. Dedicated hosts (C) is another valid model. All upfront is a payment option, but not an actual pricing model for instances.

41. A. Spot instances are recommended for applications with flexible start and end times, that need to run with low compute prices, or that may have urgent compute needs for large amounts of additional capacity.

42. B. On-demand instances are best when usage patterns swing severely and can't be predicted.

43. B. On-demand instances are ideal for any usage that swings wildly in unpredictable patterns, particularly if a job cannot be halted. If usage is predictable, a long-running job might benefit from a reserved instance, and if the job can be stopped, then spot instances would be better.

44. A, D. This is a little tricky, as dedicated hosts function a bit differently than the other instance types, in both purchasing and payment. In this case, it's important to note that the question is about purchasing, and *not* payment (which would drive you to answer "all upfront," "partial upfront," or "no upfront"). Dedicated hosts can be purchased as an on-demand instance or as a reservation for significant savings.

45. B, C. Reserved instances are the best option for steady-state applications and require at least a one-year commitment, which would point to options B and C.

46. D. Spot instances are not ideal for spikes in usage, as those instances may be terminated at any time.

47. B. In this scenario, you want to ensure that instances stay up (eliminating the spot market) and that there is no long-term commitment (eliminating reserved instances). Dedicated hosts don't make sense, so this leaves on-demand instances.

48. A, B. The spot market provides instances that can stop and start at any time. Now, applications on these instances can be stopped and restarted (A). Additionally, costs are significantly lower than on-demand pricing (B). However, the hardware can change often, and spikes in usage are *not* well suited for spot instances.

49. D. On a pure "storage per GB" comparison, Amazon Glacier is the least expensive storage class.

50. A. S3-SSE is an encryption solution. Standard IA is infrequent access, RRS is reduced redundancy (and is now deprecated), and of course Glacier is a valid S3 storage class.

51. C. Uploading data is the textbook definition of ingress, and ingress never has associated fees.

52. A. It is always free to move data into CloudFront. There may be a cost associated with egress from CloudFront, but the transfer to CloudFront is cost-free.

53. B. The AWS free tier is *just AWS* but without a cost. You can use up to several limits of services (data transfer, compute, storage, etc.) at no cost within the AWS free tier.

54. D. The AWS marketplace offers free and paid software products, many of which run on the AWS free tier. You can find AMIs and services as well as many trial offerings from third parties.

55. D. AWS free tier offers almost everything that paid AWS does, simply at lesser volumes.

56. D. The four AWS support plans are basic, developer, business, and enterprise.

57. C, D. This should be pretty intuitive: The higher and more business-oriented levels of support offer 24/7 support; in this case, business and enterprise.

58. B. AWS Trusted Advisor is an online resource that helps you reduce cost as well as increase performance and improve security. However, it does not provide logging (C) or affect Auto Scaling limits or configuration.

59. C. There are five core Trusted Adviser checks: cost optimization, security, fault tolerance, performance, and service limits. Note: In some places, AWS will say that there are seven checks, but in others, five. The most current documentation indicates the five checks noted here.

60. A, B. AWS Trusted Advisor provides advice that typically is useful in all environments, for all use cases. In this set of answers, the two that meet that criteria are turning on MFA for the root account and avoiding global Internet access to an S3 bucket. These recommendations will apply to almost all situations. The other two options—C and D—are use-case specific and therefore would not be suggested by Trusted Advisor.

61. D. AWS Trusted Advisor makes recommendations about S3 bucket usage, IAM usage, and snapshots (both EBS and RDS) but does not make recommendations regarding DNS, so D is correct.

62. B. AWS Trusted Advisor makes recommendations in five categories: cost optimization, performance, security, fault tolerance, and service limits.

63. A, D. AWS Trusted Advisor makes recommendations in five categories: cost optimization, performance, security, fault tolerance, and service limits.

64. A, C. First, C is an easy choice: MFA on the root account is one of the most common recommendations. Then, consider the areas in which Trusted Advisor can make absolute recommendations; underuse of DNS records doesn't make a lot of sense (how do you "underuse DNS?") and coming up with the "correct" S3 storage class involves understanding use cases, which Trusted Advisor can't do. This leaves A, idle load balancers.

65. A, B. AWS makes five standard recommendations: Right-size your services to meet capacity needs at the lowest cost, save money by reserving, use the spot market, monitor and track service usage, and use Cost Explorer to optimize savings.

66. C. AWS makes five standard recommendations: Right-size your services to meet capacity needs at the lowest cost, save money by reserving, use the spot market, monitor and track service usage, and use Cost Explorer to optimize savings. Using the spot market (C) falls into that last category. The other answers are all use-case driven and really don't fit into general cost-saving recommendations.

67. C. This should be pretty basic: AWS Cost Explorer provides reports via analysis for evaluating your overall AWS costs over time.

68. B. This is largely a matter of recognizing the valid AWS tools—AWS Trusted Advisor and AWS Cost Explorer—and then determining which deals with costs. In this case, that's AWS Cost Explorer.

69. B. Cost Explorer gives you reports on EC2 monthly cost and usage that can help analyze monthly spending on instances.

70. C. While AWS Cost Explorer can give you information about your monthly storage costs, AWS Budgets allows you to set alerts and then add custom programming to reduce or halt those costs.

71. D. This is an important question. None of the tools listed allow for actual "cutoffs" at cost thresholds. AWS Budgets allows you notifications when a threshold is met but does *not* allow you to cut off spending at a certain point on its own.

72. C. Elastic Transcoder allows you to produce media files that are optimized and well suited for various device types.

73. A. This question is as much about recognizing the various AWS service acronyms as anything. Here, RDS—the Relational Database Service—allows you to use Oracle on an AWS managed service.

74. A. Elastic Beanstalk can deploy your code and handle capacity provisioning, load balancing, and setting up Auto Scaling and health checks, all with very little oversight. Note that you'd still need personnel to keep an application like this running, but Elastic Beanstalk can reduce initial resources needed for application deployment.

75. B. CloudFormation allows you to automate provisioning and, in this case, to create standardized JSON scripts that can be lightly modified to stand up entire stacks for multiple applications that share a common structure.

76. D. Snowball is almost always the most cost-effective approach to data transfer when you approach 50 TB, and there are good reasons to consider it even at 10 TB or more.

77. A. Storage Gateway is a hybrid storage service and allows your on-premises data store to interact with S3.

78. C. Large data should always make you think, "Snowball." Snowball gives you a reliable, scalable, petabyte-scale data transfer solution.

79. D. Redshift is AWS's managed service for OLAP and business intelligence.

80. A. EMR, Elastic MapReduce, is a web service targeted at processing large amounts of data. It is optimized for this task and often provides cost savings over EC2 instances running similar processes.

81. A, D. QuickSight is a business analytics service, and Redshift is ideal for business intelligence and OLAP. While you could build high-performance applications using EC2 instances and provisioned IOPS EBS volumes, managed services like QuickSight and Redshift are almost always going to be more cost effective.

82. D. Both A and B are going to incur significant costs and custom code. C is not a bad option on the analytics side but will still likely require custom code to aggregate the data sources. QuickSight, however, is designed exactly for this task: combining data sources and then performing analytics and extracting insights.

83. C. Glacier is Amazon's long-term data archival solution.

84. A. CloudFormation is ideal for automating deployment without manual intervention, but it's actually Elastic Beanstalk that handles the *provisioning* of resources.

85. C. Kinesis is intended to handle streaming data sources. It collects and processes data from these streaming sources in real time and would be ideal to replace custom code that handles this same process, as the question asks.

86. A. Lambda allows you to "ignore" the underlying resources required for running code. You simply give Lambda the code to run, and Lambda will handle provisioning resources in a scalable and cost-effective manner.

87. D. CloudWatch provides monitoring of applications and is a low-cost solution for AWS monitoring.

88. A. CloudTrail is the AWS service for logging and is particularly helpful for auditing and compliance.

89. C. Almost all of these add unnecessary steps and involve multiple instances or either Oracle or PostgreSQL. The easiest, most cost-effective option is to migrate directly from Oracle to PostgreSQL using DMS, the Database Migration Service.

90. A. S3 is the AWS choice for durability and flat-file (non-relational data) storage.

91. A. IAM is the best option for handling users, groups, and permissions within AWS.

92. A, B. IAM is the best option for handling users, groups, and permissions within AWS. You can then add Cognito to offer single sign-on capabilities to your applications.

93. B. Trusted Advisor is a great start to find glaring holes or deficiencies in an AWS environment.

94. C. OpsWorks is a configuration management tool that actually can use Chef, so many of the existing modules would plug right in and existing expertise would translate directly over.

Domain 5: Define Operationally Excellent Architectures

1. B. AWS does guarantee that all SQS messages will be delivered *at least* once, but the message *may be* delivered more than once (making option A incorrect). This is not related to the number of requests to the queue or the applications using the queue; therefore, both C and D are incorrect. This leaves B, the correct answer.

2. B, C. This is a common question AWS often asks to ensure that you understand that managed services like RDS and DynamoDB are indeed completely *managed*: You cannot access the underlying operating system of the service. This leaves EC2 and EMR as the remaining, and correct, answers. While EMR does provide you with a lot of functionality "out of the box," it still allows root level access, as do EC2 instances.

3. C. SQS queues have a visibility timeout that controls how long a message in the queue is marked as "invisible" while being processed. This accounts for the message "disappearing." Then, if application processing fails—as in option C—the message is remarked as visible and is available for processing again. Option A correctly notes this timeout, but reducing the timeout would not cause the message to be processed correctly. It would just reduce the time that the message is "invisible." Option B is not how queues work; they cannot ask a sender to resend a message. Option D is incorrect as well, as the queue is operating as intended with regard to visibility of messages and timeouts.

4. D. Snapshots are accessible through the console via username/password and through AWS CLI and APIs via application key.

5. B. SNS is the Simple Notification Service and functions like a mailer, sending out notifications that can be subscribed to by other applications.

6. A. SNS sends out notifications to subscribed listeners, and SWF pushes out messages as they arrive. Only SQS holds messages until the queue is polled. Redshift is not a messaging service at all but rather a data warehousing solution.

7. B. SNS and SWF operate on a push approach. SQS holds messages until they are pulled out of the queue. S3 is not a message store.

8. D. Both SWF and SQS deliver a message at least once, but only SWF guarantees that a message will *only* be delivered a single time.

9. B. Messages in SWF are tasks; messages in SQS are messages; messages in SNS are notifications. S3 is a storage solution, not a messaging solution.

10. C. Messages in SWF are tasks; messages in SQS are messages; messages in SNS are notifications. S3 is not a messaging solution at all.

11. D. Messages in SWF are tasks; messages in SQS are messages; messages in SNS are notifications. S3 is not a message store. Since SQS is not an option, the answer is D, none of these.

12. C. SWF is more than a simple queue. It automates workflow, moving a task (what SWF calls its messages) from one application component to the next in a predetermined order.

13. B. SWF is not exactly a true acronym. It stands for Simple Workflow Service but is not represented by SWS. Instead, the *WF* refers to *workflow*.

14. A, D. Both EC2 and ECS provide environments on which your custom code can run, and both are compute services. S3 is a storage service, and Redshift is a data warehousing solution. While Redshift can be helpful in analysis of data, it is not suitable for running custom scripts.

15. B. Of the choices available, Amazon Lightsail is the easiest solution for getting simple applications running quickly. EC2 and ECS are both much more complex. While S3 website hosting is a web hosting solution, it does require quite a bit of AWS knowledge (security, permissions, etc.).

16. B, D. An EBS snapshot cannot be deleted if it is the root device of a registered AMI while that AMI is in use. You'll need to deregister the AMI first (B), and then you can delete the EBS volume and any snapshots and stop using the AMI.

17. A. EBS is considered a subset of EC2 functionality. Therefore, you use the `aws ec2` commands; for example, `aws ec2 delete-snapshot`.

18. C. A records are used to point a specific domain or subdomain to an IP address. CNAMEs point to a different URL, which in turn can be resolved further by DNS. In this case, you'd want to create a CNAME record for `applestoapples.com` and point that record to `applestoapples.net` and then let DNS resolve that domain. Using an A record means you'd have to lock the record to a specific IP rather than the domain name for `applestoapples.net`. That's a problem, though, as over time, the domain may be served by different resources with different IP addresses, making the A record dated and incorrect.

19. A. A records are used to point a specific domain or subdomain to an IP address. CNAMEs point to URLs or other domain names. In this case, since you're pointing at an ELB, you'd need to use a CNAME, as ELBs don't expose a public IP address.

20. A. This is a little trickier in terms of picking the *best* answer. It is possible to set a CNAME up and point that at the ALB's URL (B). However, AWS prefers that you use an A record and configure it as an alias record, allowing you to direct traffic to the ALB. This is different than a standard A record, which can only point at an IP address. Option C is incorrect because ALBs don't expose an IP address, and D doesn't even make sense in this context.

21. A. AWS supports zone apex records for all domains. A zone apex record is a DNS record at the root, or apex, of a DNS zone. So `amazon.com` is an apex record (sometimes called a naked domain record). Route 53 absolutely will support zone apex records and allows alias records (of A type) at this level as well.

22. A, D. First, A is false. A zone apex record is a DNS record at the root, or apex, of a DNS zone. So `amazon.com` is an apex record (sometimes called a naked domain record). Route 53 absolutely will support zone apex records and allows alias records (of A type) at this level as well. D is also false; Route 53 supports zone apex records for AWS and non-AWS domains and services.

23. A, D. Route 53 is scalable by design, so there are no steps required to make it highly available; this makes D true. Additionally, it supports all AWS services, including auto-scaling, so A is true.

24. D. By default, a single account can manage 50 domains using Route 53. However, this is a default, and AWS will raise it pretty willingly if you call and explain your need for management of additional domains.

25. D. RDS is a managed system by AWS and does not allow any access to its underlying operating system.

26. C, D. VPC peering is a networking connection between two VPCs but is not limited to a single region (so A is false) and is neither VPN nor gateway-based (so B is false). This leaves C and D, both of which are true: VPCs can be used to share data and can peer across regions.

27. B. AWS calls a connection between two VPCs via peering across regions an inter-region VPC peering connection.

28. C. When a VPC peering connection is set up, each VPC will need a route manually added to allow communication to the peered VPC.

29. D. Most of these statements are false: VPCs in different regions (A) and in different accounts (B) can be peered, and if both VPCs are in the same account, they can share a security group (C). However, two peered VPCs *cannot* have overlapping CIDR blocks (D).

30. B. A VPC can have multiple subnets, so a VPC peering relationship is a one-to-one relationship between two VPCs (B).

31. C. While it is true that transitive peering relationships are not allowed (A), you can still peer VPCs B and C to allow traffic to flow between the two VPCs.

32. B, C. VPCs with overlapping CIDR blocks cannot be removed as is (B), and therefore the overlap must be removed (C). Changing either VPC to IPv6 *might* be a working solution (D) but is not a requirement.

33. A. Regardless of subnet, NACL, or any other networking consideration, you can only create one VPC connection between two VPCs at a time.

34. B. A VPC can be a part of an unlimited number of VPC connections, as long as those connections are all with different VPCs and you stay within AWS's overall account limits. Only one peering connection between two specific VPCs is possible; for example, only one connection can exist between VPC A and VPC B. But VPC A can have as many peering connections—each with a different VPC—as there are VPCs with which you can connect.

35. C. Transitive VPC relationships are not allowed in AWS. Most of these answers are complete gibberish!

36. B, D. First, AWS does not support IPv6 inter-region communication. This means that for IPv6 communication to work, the two VPCs must be in the same region (D). Then, you must ensure that both VPCs have IPv6 addresses and that routing is set up to use those addresses (B).

37. A, C. EC2-Classic was a flat network that offered very little in the way of multiple options. With VPCs, you can assign multiple IP addresses as well as multiple network interfaces (A and C).

38. A, D. Default VPCs come with both an internet gateway and public subnets. If you think through this, these two go hand in hand: A public subnet would need an internet gateway to function as public.

39. A, D. The default VPC has public subnets within it. Further, it provides a default routing table that provides access to and from these instances and the public Internet (A). Additionally, an internet gateway is added to the VPC by default (D).

40. C. Non-default subnets and their instances are not public by default. Therefore, they are assigned a private IPv4 address (C) rather than a public one.

41. B, C. Non-default subnets are private by default. Therefore, you need an internet gateway on the containing VPC (C) as well as giving the instance a public IP address (B). While a NAT instance *might* work (D), it would need to be in a different, public subnet rather than in the same subnet as the instance trying to reach the Internet.

42. D. SAML, the Security Assertion Markup Language, allows you to provide federated single sign-on access to the AWS management console.

43. C. Remember that AWS provides a principle of least privilege and always wants to limit access to only what a user (or service) needs. Therefore, new IAM users do not have any access to AWS services and must be granted access to any service explicitly.

44. B. IAM stands for Identity and Access Management.

45. A, C. IAM users logging into the AWS console will need a username, password, and the sign-in URL. If the user needs access to AWS APIs or the SDK, then they will need their access key ID and secret access key. Keep in mind that these credential pairs are *not* interchangeable.

46. A. Of these groups, only the Administrator group provides write access to all AWS services. The Power User group provides access to developer-related services, but not *all* services (like IAM). The Support User group is for creating and viewing support cases.

47. D. New users will need a customized sign-in link for accessing the console (D). They will then use this link to sign in using their username and password.

48. B. There are two key parts to this question: the mobile client that must have an endpoint to which it can send data and the receiver for a huge amount of data, as the question indicates millions of users. Mobile SDK is a bit of a giveaway for the mobile component. This also helpfully narrows the answer choices down to A and B. Of the two options, Kinesis and EC2, only Kinesis is built to handle a massive data stream. While you could theoretically scale up enough EC2 instances to serve an API for that volume of requests, it really makes no sense. Kinesis is built for incoming data streams, so is the better option.

49. B. A new AWS account requires the company email (or account owner email) for the root account holder, or a generic email for the company as a whole.

50. A, D. Both the Administrators and the Power Users default policies provide read and write access to most AWS services. Power Users limits access to IAM, but that would not affect access to S3 or EC2.

51. C. A policy is AWS's document type for describing a set of permissions.

52. B. ECS is the Elastic Container Service, AWS's service for running applications in containers and managing the starting, stopping, and scaling of those containers.

53. C, D. Containers allow you to reduce startup times, as they are launched into already-running instances in most cases (C). This also touches on AWS's facility to manage and provision the instances on which the containers run (D), another advantage. While you can scale applications in containers (A), you can just as easily scale applications on EC2 instances. Finally, option B is simply false.

54. A. The first thing here is to know these various acronyms. ECR is the Elastic Container Registry, ECS is the Elastic Container Service, EC2 is Elastic Compute Cloud, EMR is Elastic MapReduce, and of course S3 is Simple Storage Service. Given that, only A has all the needed components: the registry (ECR), the management service (ECS), and instances on which to run containers (EC2). Note that even though you might not use EC2 explicitly for your containers, it or Fargate will be required to manage instances at some level, even if only by AWS for you.

55. C. You'll need to know these various acronyms. ECR is the Elastic Container Registry, ECS is the Elastic Container Service, EMR is Elastic MapReduce, and S3 is Simple Storage Service. ECC isn't an AWS acronym, so it is immediately out. Of those left, ECR, the Elastic Container Registry, is most closely associated with ECS.

56. B, C. Containers allow you to co-locate applications on instances and more effectively use your available instances without a lot of overhead, so B is true. C is in a similar vein: Containers reduce the management overhead of instances. A is not true, as containers don't significantly change your cost structure, and D is false, as containers and instances can both scale up and down to meet demand.

57. A, D. Containers are applications (D) that scale based on application load (A). Lambda, in contrast, runs isolated pieces of code and not entire application tiers. Additionally, Lambda launches based on events rather than load. (Note that you could actually set up load monitors in CloudWatch and trigger Lambda based on load, although that is not automatic as it is in containers.)

Practice Test

1. A, C. First, a larger instance with the fastest possible volume type—provisioned IOPS—is generally going to improve overall performance, so A is a good idea. Second, ElastiCache will provide faster responses and reduce database reads over time. A and C are both valid approaches. A Multi-AZ setup is for disaster recovery, and sharding is high overhead and could potentially increase response time, rather than reduce it, in this use case.

2. B. redis and memcached are engines available for use by ElastiCache. reddit is an online information site, and Redshift is a data warehousing and OLAP service.

3. B, C. AWS allows a number of options for encrypting data at rest. In the supplied solutions, AWS Key Management Service (KMS) is an AWS-managed solution for data encryption, and customer-provided keys are allowed as well. In the latter case, customers provide the keys and AWS handles encryption of data using those keys. ElastiCache for memcached does not support encryption and, further, is not a solution for encrypting data but instead a caching service. AWS Encryptic is not an actual AWS service.

4. A, D. AWS Organizations allows the management of multiple accounts in one place and allows tracking of those individual accounts (D). Additionally, in many cases, AWS will allow discounts based on total services used rather than treating each account individually (A).

5. B, C. The biggest issue here is that all the users are using the root account, meaning there's a shared password and that users have far more permissions than they should. These can both be addressed by creating new IAM users for each user (B) and putting those users in predefined groups according to their job function (C). Developers don't need access to IAM in general, so D is incorrect, and while changing the root password is a good idea, A is also incorrect because a financial manager (and possibly support engineers) may not need the AWS CLI as their access mechanism.

6. D. The best choice for I/O intensive applications and databases is provisioned IOPS (D). The only other potentially confusing option is B, throughput optimized HDD. These are not SSD volumes, and they are better for data warehousing rather than intensive I/O.

7. B, C. There are two potential problems here: network throughput and failed transmissions not being retried. Solution B addresses throughput by increasing the ability of the NAT instance to handle large amounts of data from multiple instances. Solution C addresses failed transmissions by treating them as a problem that should be retried by instances.

8. A, B. You cannot encrypt an existing EBS volume (A). Additionally, once a snapshot is encrypted, you cannot create an unencrypted copy of that snapshot (B). You can attach encrypted volumes to instances (C), and you can create an encrypted volume from an unencrypted snapshot (D).

9. C. First, realize that when you see a question asking about writing to S3, you want a URL that is not set up for static website hosting. This means that the bucket name follows the trailing slash and is not part of the domain itself. This means that B and C are the only valid options. Then, remember that the service (s3) and the region (in this case, eu-west-2) are *not* separated by a dot delimiter, but instead a dash. This leaves C as the correct answer.

10. C. CloudWatch is the AWS preferred solution for monitoring events. While data from flow logs could be handled by RDS and analyzed by Redshift, neither of these are as targeted a solution for monitoring as CloudWatch.

11. C. Lambda is best for writing custom code without the overhead of provisioning EC2 instances, so both A and C are potentially correct answers. While SQS does offer queuing of code, SWF (the Simple Workflow Service) offers you prebuilt tracking of application-level events and tasks. Attach Lambda to this and you have a ready-to-use event-driven service.

12. B, D. Non-default VPCs do not have an internet gateway attached, so B provides that remedy. Attaching an internet gateway to the VPC will provide public instances with a path out to the Internet. Solution D is also correct; NACLs on non-default VPCs will not allow HTTP or HTTPS traffic in (nor will security groups, for that matter) and need to explicitly allow in HTTP/S traffic.

13. D. Most of these answers will not help the problem. The NAT instance should be in a public subnet, so A is not useful. The EBS volume of the NAT can be an issue, but not in providing Internet access for connecting instances (B). The subnet containing the EC2 instances using the NAT instance should be private, so C is both incorrect and a bad design decision. This leaves D: NAT instances must have Source/Destination Check disabled to function properly.

14. D. All S3 storage classes share the same durability: 11 9s (99.999999999%). That's often unintuitive, so it's best to recall that all S3 classes have durability in common and decrease in availability from S3 to S3-IA to S3 One Zone-IA.

15. C. The keys here are that cost is a driver and that the image processing code is fast and inexpensive. That effectively means that if images were lost after processing, they could be reprocessed without affecting the overall system cost. As a result, it's possible to pick an S3 class where images post-processing might be lost, *if* that results in a lower overall cost. This allows for S3 One Zone-IA, the cheapest of the provided S3 classes aside from Glacier, which has load times much longer than would be acceptable. S3 One Zone-IA might lose your processed images, but since they can easily be re-created, this isn't a deterrent.

16. C. EFS, the Elastic File System, is effectively a NAS in the cloud and can provide storage accessible to multiple EC2 instances at one time.

17. C, D. Non-default VPCs do not have an internet gateway attached and will need one to host any public subnets, so C is required. Then, with the internet gateway attached, instances within the subnet will need a route through this gateway for Internet traffic (D).

18. A, B. AWS defines several custom request headers, and all begin with x-amz rather than x-aws. This will help you eliminate incorrect answers; in this case, it means that A is valid and C is not. Then, you'll simply have to memorize the other request headers; Content-Length (C) is valid, while Content-Size (D) is not.

19. A, C. There are four AWS support levels: basic, developer, business, and enterprise. Neither professional nor corporate is a valid support level.

20. B, D. RDS supports a number of database options: MariaDB, Aurora, PostgreSQL, MySQL, Oracle, and SQL Server. DynamoDB is not a relational database, and DB2 is not supported.

21. B. Scaling in is the process by which an Auto Scaling group removes instances. You can think of scaling in as "moving *in* the boundaries of the group" and scaling out as "moving *out* the boundaries of the group." Of the available choices, only B—5 instances—represents a reduction of instances.

22. B, D. CloudFormation templates can be written in JSON and YAML.

23. C. Only geolocation routing will ensure that the location of the user is the primary factor. While latency-based routing would seem to translate to location-based, it is conceivable that network traffic to a nearby region could cause latency to be lower for a user in (for example) Australia to be routed to US regions. Therefore, only geolocation routing would ensure that the closest region geographically is used by the major user bases.

24. C. A CNAME record allows you to direct traffic to a DNS name, and in this case, that DNS name would be the ELB. ELBs do not provide an IP address, so an A record would not work. An MX record is for email, and an AAAA record is for IPv6 addresses.

25. A, C. The key here is that you are not creating new users (and B is therefore incorrect); instead, you need to use an existing Active Directory setup. That requires an identity provider (A). Then, you can issue temporary tokens (C) to get users started, and they can update credentials from there.

26. D. This is a question with a relatively easy answer, but lots of red herring answers as well. When you have a specific recurring traffic period, scheduled scaling is an easy solution (D). All the other options are much more complex and may not work at all.

27. D. DynamoDB is a prototypical example of an AWS managed service. It handles its resources and does not provide controls for these to the user (answer D). In the case of proactivity, DynamoDB and AWS will handle scaling up. Additionally, DynamoDB already uses SSDs and multiple instances, without user intervention.

28. B. The default settings for CloudWatch specify a 5-minute interval at which metrics are collected.

29. B, C. The issue here is CPU, which you can essentially convert in your head to "too many things are being asked of the database at one time." The easiest way to reduce CPU on any database is to decrease requests and reads, and both an ElastiCache instance and read replicas do just that: reduce load on the primary database instance.

30. A. The Simple Workflow Service is ideal for tasks that need to execute based on steps within an application. Additionally, SWF has hooks built into applications that you get automatically without custom infrastructure code.

31. B. SQS queues in standard configuration are FIFO, but ordering is not guaranteed. If ordering must be preserved, the queue should be set as a FIFO (first-in, first-out) queue (B). With a LIFO queue (D), ordering is reversed and wouldn't meet the requirements of the question.

32. C. Route 53 has a number of valid routing policies: simple, failover, geolocation, geoproximity, latency-based, multivalue answer, and weighted. Of the provided answers, only load-balancing is not valid.

33. D. The only potentially useful answers here are B and D: you need more processing power to handle requests, and you need to deal with nonresponsive instances at peak times. The spot market will do nothing to help here, and pre-warming the load balancer will still not handle traffic when that traffic is sudden and produces a large spike. Of B and D, only D addresses nonresponsiveness. By having requests go to a queue, you should not have users experience a nonresponsive application at all; the SQS queue will scale as needed, and then instances can handle requests as they become available in the queue.

34. A, B. Processes suitable for the spot market must be able to run at any time (B) because the spot market makes instances available unpredictably, and the process must be able to stop and start and continue work (A) because spot instances can stop at any time.

35. D. All of the S3 storage classes offer 11 9s of durability (99.999999999%).

36. A, C. EBS uses block-level storage, while S3 uses object-based storage (A). Additionally, EBS volumes by default are deleted when the attached instance is stopped. While this can be changed, it does result in EBS volumes being ephemeral by default, as compared with S3, which does not disappear by default.

37. B. The key here is the requirement to manage costs. Option C is not cost-effective, as it requires expensive Oracle licenses. Option D is going to require larger instances, which will also incur new costs. Option A might be effective, but running a custom database installation will likely cost more than RDS and also incur significant overhead costs. Only option C provides an "in-place" cost option. Aurora typically outperforms MySQL in an apples-to-apples comparison, although there will be some overhead in migrating from MySQL to Aurora.

38. C, D. Both ELBs (elastic load balancers) and DynamoDB provide fault tolerance, and ELBs provide load balancing. Further, both services are automatically redundant without user intervention. Lightsail and AWS Organizations are services used for deployment and management of AWS rather than for providing redundancy and high availability.

39. A, D. EC2 instances are not automatically redundant; you would need to do additional work as the architect to ensure that applications on EC2 instances are redundant across AZs. While RDS as a service is fault tolerant, it is not automatically highly available. A Multi-AZ setup would address that need, for example. On the contrary, both S3 (B) and SQS (C) are automatically highly available across availability zones.

40. D. AWS does not allow vulnerability scans to be run without advance notice. There are some preapproved scans using AWS-approved tools, but in general, you'll need to contact your AWS account manager or support team in advance of running vulnerability scans.

41. A, D. Although cost is an important factor, the solutions here would remain the same even if it were not explicitly mentioned. First, an SQS queue is ideal for capturing what needs to be accomplished, independent of running queries. That queue will need to be accessible from EC2 instances that will run those queries. Additionally, spot instances are ideal for long-running queries that can be interrupted and restarted. Even better, the spot market also addresses the cost concerns mentioned in the question.

42. D. Spot instances terminate when the maximum set bid price is reached. Increasing the bid price will effectively raise the threshold for termination, causing them to run longer. This will cost more but, overall, keeps the application design intact.

43. B. A cached volume gateway stores your data in S3 while caching frequently accessed data. While a stored volume gateway would keep all data locally, it would not address the on-site storage costs mentioned in the question.

44. C. Network access control lists (NACLs) and security groups are the primary mechanisms within AWS that replace traditional firewalls.

45. A, C. By default, AWS creates a VPC with a public subnet, and that subnet by definition must have an internet gateway. NAT devices (instances and gateways) and virtual private gateways must explicitly be set up and are not created by AWS by default.

46. B. Auto Scaling groups scale in using a very specific set of criteria. Highest priority is the availability zone with the most instances, then the age of the launch configuration of instances, and finally, the nearness of instances to the next billing hour.

47. B. This is a tough question, and right on the edges of what might be asked on the exam. Hardware virtualization is fully virtualized (compared to "para" virtualization, partly virtualized) and therefore works with all instance types (making C false) and all hardware extensions (making B true). Since B is advantageous for hardware virtualization, it is the correct answer.

48. A. Provisioned IOPS is the fastest class of drive for high performance. It is built upon SSD (solid-state drives) and provides mission-critical low-latency workloads.

49. A. Changes to security groups take place immediately, regardless of whether the updates affect instances, ELBs, or any other AWS constructs.

50. C. A read replica would provide an additional database instance to service the queries (C). A Multi-AZ setup handles failover (B), and the secondary instance would not be in service normally. Adding memory would not address the CPU issue (A). The implicit assumption here is that the data requested and processed each night is new data, so an ElastiCache instance (D) would have little to cache and therefore affect little.

51. C. Only the bucket owner of an S3 bucket can completely delete a file once versioning has been enabled.

52. B. While in many cases SSE-S3 is perfectly adequate (C), the additional auditing and compliance requirements indicate that SSE-KMS is a better option (B). Anytime you see a need for audit trails, you should think KMS. This is a common exam question, so memorize the association between auditing and KMS and you'll probably get a free correct answer out of it!

53. B. Read replicas are updated asynchronously (B), and this is not configurable (so C is not an option). While network latency could be an issue (D), you still won't be able to avoid the occasional lag in updating due to asynchronous replication.

54. C. You can create 100 buckets in a single AWS account before you need to contact AWS support and ask for a limit increase.

55. B. There is no requirement to use an elastic IP in creating a public subnet. It is just as possible to create public IP addresses for instances in the subnet without using elastic IPs. However, you do need an internet gateway and routes to that gateway for Internet traffic.

56. C. The SSD volumes types, as well as optimized HDD and cold HDD, can all be as large as 16TiB.

57. A. Only A is false: You cannot attach multiple EC2 instances to a single EBS volume at one time.

58. D. This one should be pretty simple: RDS is a Relational Database Service and does not use key-value pairs.

59. A, B. The HDD options for EBS are generally less expensive than SSD options, so anytime lowering cost is a priority, HDD options are ideal; this makes A a valid answer. Data throughput for a throughput optimized HDD is actually greater than that of a general-purpose SSD (HDDs can go up to 500 MiB/s versus only 160 MiB/s on General Purpose SSDs), so B is another valid answer. Performance-critical workloads (answer C) are best served by provisioned IOPS SSDs, and the environment is not a factor in this case (answer D).

60. D. Of these options, only InnoDB is not supported by RDS.

61. A, C. AWS automatically creates a public subnet with new accounts. This public subnet will have instances that are public by default (A) via public IP addresses, but those IPs are *not* elastic IPs (so B is false). The instances will all access the Internet through an internet gateway (C), but the containing VPC will not have a virtual private gateway attached (so D is false).

62. A, D. Classic load balancers do support HTTP and HTTPS, but they do not support SSH or any flavor of FTP that does not use HTTP (or HTTPS) as an underlying protocol.

63. C. RRS, or reduced redundancy storage, is the predecessor to One Zone-IA but is less durable and currently deprecated. However, it can still show up on exams at odd times. Both its durability and availability are 99.99%. Another way to recall this is to note that all current S3 classes of storage have 11 9s durability, leaving only S3-RRS as a possibility here.

64. B, C. Delete protection is best accomplished through versioning and MFA Delete. Also note this is a rare time when the word *audit* does *not* pair with KMS as encryption is never discussed in the question.

65. B. If you know that you will use instances over a long period, reserved instances are always going to be cheaper than on-demand instances. Spot instances, however, will start and stop often and are not candidates for steady usage.

Index

Comprehensive Online Learning Environment

Register to gain one year of FREE access to the comprehensive online interactive learning environment and test bank to help you study for your AWS Certified Solutions Architect - Associate (SAA-C01) exam.

The online test bank includes:

- **Practice Test Questions** to reinforce what you learned
- **Bonus Practice Exams** to test your knowledge of the material

Go to http://www.wiley.com/go/sybextestprep to register and gain access to this comprehensive study tool package.

Register and Access the Online Test Bank

To register your book and get access to the online test bank, follow these steps:

1. Go to bit.ly/SybexTest.
2. Select your book from the list.
3. Complete the required registration information including answering the security verification proving book ownership. You will be emailed a pin code.
4. Go to http://www.wiley.com/go/sybextestprep and find your book on that page and click the "Register or Login" link under your book.
5. If you already have an account at testbanks.wiley.com, login and then click the "Redeem Access Code" button to add your new book with the pin code you received. If you don't have an account already, create a new account and use the PIN code you received.